Children, Culture

D0537579

Childhood is increasingly saturated by technology: from television to the internet, video games to 'video nasties', camcorders to personal computers. Many companies now engage in the development of specifically child-orientated technologies such as computer software packages. Children engage with and exercise competence in a whole range of technologies in the home, at school and in the public social world.

Children, Technology and Culture looks at the interplay of children and technology which poses critical questions for how we understand the nature of childhood in late modern society. This collection brings together researchers from a range of disciplines to further our understanding of the theoretical implications and methodological consequences of exploring the relationships between children and technology. The book addresses four aspects of this relationship:

- children's access to technologies and the implications for social relationships;
- the structural contexts of children's engagement with technologies with a focus on gender and the family;
- the situatedness of children's interactions with technological objects;
- the constitution of children and childhood through the mediations of technology.

Childhood studies is an area of increasing interest in various disciplines from sociology to social work, education to anthropology. This valuable new book will be of interest to students studying in these areas, as well as practitioners in the social, child and youth services and NGOs who focus on children.

Ian Hutchby is Senior Lecturer in Communication and Sociology at Brunel University. **Jo Moran-Ellis** is Lecturer in Sociology at the University of Surrey.

Future of Childhood series
Series editor: Alan Prout

Children, Technology and Culture

The impacts of technologies in children's everyday lives

Edited by Ian Hutchby and Jo Moran-Ellis

London and New York

First published 2001 by RoutledgeFalmer
11 New Fetter Lane, London EC4P 4EE

Simultaneously published in the USA and Canada
by RoutledgeFalmer
29 West 35th Street, New York, NY 10001

RoutledgeFalmer is an imprint of the Taylor & Francis Group

© 2001 Ian Hutchby and Jo Moran-Ellis

Typeset in Bembo by The Midlands Book Typesetting Co. Loughborough
Printed and bound in Great Britain by University Press, Cambridge

British Library Cataloguing in Publication Data
A catalogue record for this book is available from the British Library

Library of Congress Cataloging in Publication Data
A catalogue record for this book has been requested

ISBN 0-415-23634-7 (hbk)
ISBN 0-415-23635-5 (pbk)

Contents

Tables and figures

Tables

Figures

Contributors

Ferran Casas. Senior Lecturer in the Faculty of Educational Sciences, and Director of the Research Institute on Quality of Life Studies, University of Girona, Catalonia Spain.

Karen M. Clarke. Researcher in the Computing Department, Lancaster University, United Kingdom.

Amber Delahooke. Associate Researcher in the Centre for the Study of Health, Brunel University, United Kingdom.

Keri Facer. Lecturer in the Graduate School of Education, University of Bristol, United Kingdom.

Dave Francis. Senior Lecturer in the Department of Sociology, Manchester Metropolitan University, United Kingdom.

John Furlong. Professor of Education in the School of Social Sciences, Cardiff University, United Kingdom.

Ruth Furlong. Senior Lecturer in the Department of Media and Visual Culture, University of Wales College, Newport, United Kingdom.

Carmelo Garitaonandia. Professor of Journalism, University of the Basque Country in Bilbao, Spain.

Terry A. Hemmings. Senior Research Associate in the Institute of Communications Studies, University of Leeds, United Kingdom.

Sarah Holloway. Lecturer in the Department of Geography, Loughborough University, United Kingdom.

Ian Hutchby. Senior Lecturer in the Department of Human Sciences, Brunel University, United Kingdom.

Ann Jones. Senior Lecturer in the Institute of Educational Technology, the Open University, United Kingdom.

Paxti Juaristi. Researcher and Lecturer in the Faculty of Social Sciences and Communication, University of the Basque Country in Bilbao, Spain.

Riitta Koikkalainen. Research Assistant in the Research Unit for Contemporary Culture, University of Jyväskylä, Finland.

Nick Lee. Lecturer in the School of Social Relations, and Deputy Director of the Centre for Social Theory and Technology, Keele University, United Kingdom.

Liz Marr. Lecturer in the Department of Sociology, Manchester Metropolitan University, United Kingdom.

Jo Moran-Ellis. Lecturer in the Department of Sociology, University of Surrey, United Kingdom.

Jose A. Oleaga. Researcher and Lecturer in the Department of Sociology, University of the Basque Country in Bilbao, Spain.

David Oswell. Lecturer in the Department of Sociology, Goldsmiths College, United Kingdom.

Alan Prout. Series Editor. Professor of Sociology at Stirling University, United Kingdom, and Director of the ESRC Children 5–16 Programme.

Emma Price. Previously a Research Assistant in the Institute of Educational Technology, the Open University, United Kingdom, and now works as a psychologist at Parkhurst Prison.

Dave Randall. Lecturer in the Department of Sociology, Manchester Metropolitan University, United Kingdom.

Ian Robinson. Reader in the Department of Human Sciences, and Director of the Centre for the Study of Health, Brunel University, United Kingdom.

Annikka Suoninen. Researcher in the Research Unit for Contemporary Culture, University of Jyväskylä, Finland.

Daniel Süss. Senior Researcher in the Institute of Communication, University of Zurich, Switzerland.

Rosamund Sutherland. Professor of Education in the Graduate School of Education, University of Bristol, United Kingdom.

Gill Valentine. Professor of Geography, University of Sheffield, United Kingdom.

Preface

The conjunction of the terms 'children' and 'technology' has a powerful but ambiguous contemporary resonance. On the one hand it can, especially when focused on information technology, provoke utopian visions of a childhood radically unlike anything known before: at ease with arcane knowledge, empowered, connected and freed from the constraints of locality. At the same time these very visions promote fears about the despoilation of childhood and the transformation, for the bad, of relationships between the generations. Much – generally debunking – research effort has gone into investigating these different claims, as successive waves of technological development have occurred: cinema, radio, TV, video and, currently, the internet.

The new social studies of childhood have made an important contribution to the field by directing attention to the active role of children in social relations, including their use of technologies. In principle this can be applied to many types of technology, not only those in the field of communications. However, media studies have been at the forefront of showing how children actively appropriate, read and interpret messages rather than being simply their passive recipients and 'cultural dopes'. This was an important corrective to the tendency to see children as blank slates on which the media could inscribe any message. Nevertheless, this feature can be overplayed, to the point at which children's active role is redrawn as a celebration of media consumerism. This neglects important ethical and political questions about the power of a global communications industry that is dominated by corporate commercial interests.

What this underlines is the need to see the relationship between children and technology as two-way and mutually constitutive: contemporary discourses and forms of childhood partially shape technology, and technology partially shapes them, in networks and circuits that operate to link them. This point underlay a framework for investigating the role of medical technology in the everyday lives of children developed by Pia Christensen and me in the mid-1990s. We suggested that it was important to examine both the production of everyday medical artefacts (such as spectacles, inhalers and mobility aids) and the context of their use by children in their family, school and peer relationships. These spheres, we suggested, could be seen as separate but connected through complex pathways that feed back from one to the other.

On the basis of preliminary ethnographic observation in school, however, it appeared that children creatively deployed artefacts such as spectacles or inhalers in the everyday construction of their social relationships with others, both children and adults. We speculated that such devices could act as what Nick Lee, in this volume, refers to as 'extensions of childhood', playing an important part in the construction of agency, identity and autonomy.

Our particular concern was medical technology but it was also clear that these themes might also have some purchase on other arenas of the technology–childhood nexus. Of course, they represent only a part of the possibilities explored in this volume but it is especially interesting for me to see how they have been arrived at, or taken up, across research projects concerned with a range of different technologies and different contexts of use. Collectively the chapters of this book explore the childhood–technology connection showing how an artefact can both impact on its context of use and be modified by the complex layers of practice encountered there. Given the rapid pace of contemporary technological change and its involvement in social change, this volume makes an important contribution to interrogating the central theme of the series to which it belongs: *The Future of Childhood*.

Alan Prout
Series Editor

Introduction

Relating children, technology and culture

Ian Hutchby and Jo Moran-Ellis

Childhood, it seems, is increasingly saturated by technology. From television to the internet, video games to personal computers, camcorders to mobile phones, children engage with and exercise competence in a whole range of technologies in the home, at school, and in the wider social world. The increasing interplay between children and technologies poses critical questions for how we understand the nature of childhood in late modern society. What kinds of changes might such technological availability be bringing to children's social worlds?

In most sociological studies of technology, little account has been taken of children in analyses of major technological changes and their impact on everyday social and economic life. Yet since the advent of television and its widespread domestic adoption, there have been adult anxieties about what children might see and know through this new medium. The same focus of attention and the same anxieties have coalesced around children's relationships with new electronic technologies. In particular, children's engagement with the internet and with computer games have generated considerable lay concern and mass media commentary. All too often, however, in such commentaries both 'childhood' and 'technology' come to be accorded an unproblematic status, each treated as having a stable and self-evident existence in which there is a straightforward impact of one upon the other. This narrow perspective has been shown to be far from adequate for understanding both childhood (James *et al.* 1998) and technology (Grint and Woolgar 1997).

In addressing the nature of childhood recent studies have demonstrated, in the light of findings from a wide range of contexts, that the status of this category is inevitable neither from a biological basis nor a social one (James and Prout 1990; Mayall 1994; Hutchby and Moran-Ellis 1998; James *et al.* 1998; Corsaro 1997). Thus across different cultures children are looked after in periods of dependency in a variety of social arrangements, are cultural participants in varying degrees of inter- and intragenerational segregation and integration, and occupy the status of 'child' for varying lengths of time. Furthermore, within cultures, multiple childhoods emerge influenced by personal biographies, structural factors, and subcultural meanings and ideologies. Coming from a range of disciplinary backgrounds (social anthropology, sociology, social psychology, and others), these findings converged in a social constructionist perspective which Prout and James (1990) defined as a 'new paradigm in social studies of childhood'. The constructionist framework represented a necessary corrective to more traditional, developmental theories which often tended to focus on 'the child' as a universal category. But the shift of focus effected here towards 'childhood' as a socially constructed status, while crucially important, tended to downplay the need for close empirical analyses of the embodied practices of children themselves, as they actively occupied what we in an earlier volume (Hutchby and Moran-Ellis 1998) referred to as the 'arenas of action' in which children's social competence is exercised.

Thus, while early work in the sociology of childhood tended to privilege a discursive and constructive angle, the material embodiments of actual, empirical childhoods are equally important, and analyses of the social orderings and social worlds of children and their childhoods need to integrate these aspects (Prout 2000). To talk of *children* and technology one must be prepared to explore the range of interfaces between material presence and the mutable social statuses of childhood. For example, if childhood is a status produced and sustained through interaction and everyday practice, what are the significances of electronic technologies for the status of being a child? How do children utilize the material presence of technologies in their everyday lives as 'arenas of action' in which to manifest and organize displays of social competence? And if children and technologies can be said to have both material and ideological presences within cultures, what might be the significance of cultural contexts in mediating the relationship between the two?

We need to engage with equally complex contingencies in speaking of children and *technology*, where technology itself is not a given. In the sociology of technology, the view has developed that, in a whole range of ways, social processes and the 'properties' of technological artefacts are interrelated and intertwined (Mackenzie and Wajcman 1985; Bijker and Law 1992). This position is counterposed to an earlier, technological determinist stance in which the inherent characteristics of new technologies were posited as having inevitable transformative effects on social structures. The social constructionist position, by contrast, begins from the viewpoint that precisely what the characteristics of any given technology are, as well as their relationship with social structures, are both socially constructed: the outcome of a whole range of social factors and processes. Such an anti-determinist move is taken to its logical conclusion by Grint and Woolgar (1997), who argue that the question is one not of anti-determinism but of anti-essentialism: the view that technological artefacts cannot be said to have any inherent properties at all outside the interpretive work in which humans engage to establish what those artefacts 'are'. In a move reminiscent of some of the more radical perspectives in the social construction of childhood, Grint and Woolgar argue that what counts as a 'technology' is just as much the outcome of interpretive accounts, some more persuasive than others, as the technology's uses, effects, or even material presence in social settings.

Again, while this constructionist move is an important one, and opens up a range of ways to view technologies as both culturally and historically contingent phenomena, it has, like the earlier work in the sociology of childhood, led to a tendency to focus on representations of technological artefacts within discursive contexts at the expense of a more focused empirical concern with the materiality of artefacts in contexts of social interaction. The issue of how representations of technologies are constructed deflects attention from the ordinary embodied practices in the context of which such artefacts take on their significance for human actors (Hutchby 2001).

In these empirical terms, the significance of technology lies not in what an artefact 'is', nor in what it specifically does, but in what it enables or affords as it mediates the relationship between its user and other individuals. Thus, the important question is not 'what is the impact of technology use on childhood?' (a frequently posed adult concern, to which the answer is often couched in wholly negative terms), but rather, what are the shapes and the outcomes of specific, situated encounters between children and technologies: how do children interact with, and in light of, the affordances that technologies have; how do those affordances constrain such interactions; and how is the complex of relations brought about here consequential for our understanding both of children themselves and of technological forms?

Through a variety of approaches the following chapters explore such questions and raise others. This volume emerged out of a conference on children, technology and culture that we organized at Brunel University in 1998. In that conference we were keen to bring together some of the empirical work around children and new technologies that was in progress at the time, and set it within the context of wider questions about the relationships between children's social worlds, childhood as a cultural phenomenon, and technologies in the broadest sense. The same goal holds for this book: not only to reflect the range of empirical engagements with forms of technology available to children but also to explore fundamental sociological issues of context and contingency, social transformation and reconfiguration, agency and interaction.

Given the rapidity of technological development in recent decades, it is perhaps inevitable that when the topic of technology is brought into sociological view there is a tendency to focus on electronic technologies, often at the expense of wider considerations of the fundamental part played in culture by other technologies. This book, however, sets out to incorporate that wider agenda through a collection of chapters which both explore children's use of and interaction with various types of high level electronic technologies (computer and video) and analyse the more mundane, small-scale technologies within social encounters and the centrality of technology as a mediating factor in the cultural presences of childhood. This breadth of interest is reflected in the volume's overall thematic organization. Part One focuses on empirical work on children and new electronic technologies, encompassing cross-national studies, new technologies in the home, and new technologies in the classroom. Part Two focuses on the contingencies of a variety of mundane medical, educational and research technologies and their interactive configurations. Part Three develops the theoretical dimensions of technology as mediation, examining its relevancies as an extension of self, and finally arguing that many of the sociological stances taken on the question of childhood themselves constitute ethical technologies for situating children within given cultural contexts.

NEW TECHNOLOGIES, NEW CHILDHOODS?

As we move beyond the opening of the twenty-first century the persistence, in common-sense and mass media accounts, of a techno-determinism coupled with a utopian vision of a techno-future is striking. The rhetoric of the 'information age' is persuasive, promising as it does a new democracy where participation is enabled through technologies which simply require the modern citizen to be computer literate and connected to the internet (see for example the UK Government's policy statement on linking all schools to the internet and integrating information and communication technology (ICT) into education, as laid out in *Connecting the Learning Society* (DfEE 1998). The fundamental flaw in such claims derives from the decontextualizing and uncoupling of ICT from cultural and social relationships. As Moran-Ellis and Cooper (2000) argue, this asocial vision of technology brings with it a naive approach to its presence in educational settings. Such a perspective is strongly challenged through the findings that emerge in the empirical work in Part One. In these chapters the contextual dimensions of the relationships between children and new technologies is explored through an examination of the materiality of ICT and its impact on the spatial and temporal organization of the domestic sphere (Facer *et al.*); an analysis of cross-cultural variations in children's and young people's use of, and relationship with, electronic technologies (Süss *et al.*); the location of video-gaming in peer subcultures as well as family dynamics in Spain (Casas); and resistance to engagements with ICT by young people, especially girls (Valentine and Holloway). Taken together these chapters raise fundamental questions for the assumptions that often underpin commentaries on the impact of new technologies on children and childhood.

Children's use of ICT and video games takes place within the cultural shapes and spaces of their daily lives. At a macro-level, the contributions from Süss *et al.* and Casas clearly illustrate the need for explorations of children's and young people's interactions with new technologies to be firmly located in wider settings of cultural and social processes: the institutional organization of childhood, schooling, family and the different uses of private and public space. The main cultural differences at a national level emerge not so much in who plays what and with whom, but rather the influence on these activities of socially-organized levels of regulation of children and childhood. Thus, the greatest contrast in ICT use and electronic game playing emerges between the two countries with the greatest difference in the amount of 'adult-free' time that children had: Spain and Finland. Finnish children, with higher levels of non-organized, non-adult supervised time, have higher levels of co-use of ICT, whereas Spanish children have less adult-free time and tend to be solitary users, although they make more use of arcade games. Casas's research into video gaming in Spain also demonstrates the role of video games in children's peer (sub)cultures, and describes in detail their place in children's everyday lives.

Inverting the question of how the social organization of everyday life affects ICT/video game use, Facer *et al.* demonstrate in their chapter the material impact of new technologies on the domestic space. They present a strong case for bringing to the fore the embodied everyday lives of young people, as well as the material dimensions of new technologies. Facer *et al.* locate readings of children's online engagements within the conditions of existence in which young people operate. They note that access to ICT in the home entails negotiation between family members, a literal reconfiguring of domestic space in creating a place for 'the computer', and struggles over fixing the meta-meaning of the multi-purpose computer in negotiations between homework, leisure, business and social uses. They trace both temporal and physical appropriations of computer hardware and software: contestation around the computer screen layouts, screensavers, backgrounds, as well as the physical location of the personal computer in the home. We thus see how cultural context has both a macro and a micro presence in children's use of computers and electronic games.

Valentine and Holloway take another approach to ICT use through a study of young people's interactions with one another and computers in a classroom setting. Their study illustrates the ways in which subcultural identities can relate to individual relationships with ICT. Focusing on a group of young people who present an image of being 'techno-phobic', they demonstrate ethnographically how this reluctance to engage electronically is at least in part a resistance to acquiring what is construed in this teenage setting as an undesirable identity – that of nerd or geek. The undesirability of such an identity is played out against the backdrop of the struggle for an individual yet peer-conforming status which often characterizes the social processes of adolescence, lived in the here and now. Like Casas, Valentine and Holloway also examine parental anxieties about technologies and find a major divergence between children and adults in this respect. Adults in their study displayed an orientation to the 'inevitability' of a computer-centred future, and their anxieties are fundamentally about their children's life chances in this technologically-driven economy, whilst children and young people are engaging in a framework of the here and now with very different pressing needs and desires from those of adults.

The simplistic notion that new technologies are going to radically reconfigure childhood (coupled as it usually is with a moral stance on this as either a very good or very bad thing) is undermined in this first section.

The sheer complexity of the dynamic relationship that emerges out of the encounters children and young people have with electronic technologies belies the possibility of such straightforward 'impacts'. The relationships charted empirically in this section flow in both directions between subject and object, and are located in layers of cultural contexts with greater and lesser degrees of permanence. Furthermore, other relationships which appear to be completely outside the scope of ICT and video game use can be seen to be key to those phenomena. Both children and new technologies have material and discursive presences in many different spheres, none of which can be eliminated *a priori* from the actual interactions that take place.

TECHNOLOGIES IN/AS INTERACTION

The indeterminancy and contingency of technologies and the role of interaction in the configuration of technologies is taken further in Part Two. Here, not only are the layers of cultural context present, but the materiality of a range of physical technologies is itself shown to be a shifting, interactionally-produced feature.

Robinson and Delahooke destabilize notions of a technological object having a fixed nature through a demonstration of the interactional ascription of other meanings to a medical technology (an asthma pump) within the school subculture of classroom friendships. This analysis of the subject–object–subject relationship is located within an anthropological approach to the social worlds and self-labour of childhood, where 'who I am' is a dynamic arena of interaction, of mutual constitution and/or challenge. The asthma pump remains an object of mediation in the everyday mundane practices of social relationships but is not present as a medical technology mediating therapeutic interventions from the absent health professional to the unhealthy child. Instead it is reconfigured as a status and exchange object stripped of its technological function and invested with identity work.

The amorphous nature of technology's physical presence is further sustained in the chapter by Hemmings *et al.* Taking an interactional, analytical approach, their analysis of children's encounters with an educational technology in a public museum demonstrates the centrality of interactional accomplishment to the task of technologically-mediated learning. Through detailed analysis of video-recorded encounters between groups of children and a 'hands-on' railway museum educational exhibit, the highly non-deterministic nature of educational technology is clearly revealed. Despite the technology being explicitly designed for the purpose of teaching children about railway technologies, and the setting being marked out as educational through signs and instructions (both written and oral), Hemmings *et al.* show that considerable intervention by 'educators' is required for the technology's desired educational status to be achieved.

As the authors observe, children encountering the technology may organize themselves to 'bring off' the educational task in an *ad hoc* way. While the lesson embedded in the configuration of material objects is meant to be that of discovering why different sorts of railway wheels roll down a curved track, rather than 'discovering' that lesson the children engage in finding what the technology enables, for instance by rolling the different sets of wheels until they come up with the 'correct' set that do not fall off. The conclusion that various material technologies of education (including, we should say, ICT) can only offer affordances is vitally important in any analysis of the relations and interaction between humans and technological objects (Hutchby 2001), and its exemplification within the realm of children's interaction should not be seen as any different from the realms of adult interactions. What may differ, however, or may at least have more primacy in some social settings compared to others, is the framework of social relations within which engagement with affordances occurs.

The final two chapters in Part Two focus more centrally on the role of technologies in interactions between children and adults in the context of therapeutic and welfare interventions. Hutchby looks at children in counselling following parental separation or divorce, while Jones and Price concentrate on therapy for children with emotional and behavioural difficulties. Both chapters, in very different ways, seek to demonstrate the positive role that can be played by the mediating presence of a technology (a recording device in the first case; a computer program in the second) in accomplishing the setting's therapeutic work. This represents a different perspective from that usually taken in respect of technologies in child–adult relations in institutional contexts, where the work of the adults is partially that of rendering the technology's presence as unobtrusive as possible. One place where this is seen is in the array of technologies that play a part in child protection. Initial interviews with children during child abuse protection are often videotaped to be viewed again at later points of the investigation, and for submission as evidence in court should a prosecution be taken forward. The concerns associated with the use of this technology have tended to focus on issues of safe storage of the videotapes, getting the right sort of talk captured on video so that it can stand up to court scrutiny as evidence, and getting good enough recording quality. If a child abuse prosecution does go forward to court, the child may then give his or her evidence via a live video link, and in addition photographs and the video-recording of the initial interview with the child may be presented at the trial. As Lee (2000) has argued, in the British legal system at least, it is the very presence and use of the video medium in these situations that enables the child to be a speaking subject in court. The technology allows for the child's voice and memory to be testable, or available for legal disputation. However, the ideal is for the process of technological mediation itself to be invisible. This is reflected in practice when the use of video recording is represented to children as being of little actual significance from their point of view. They are simply 'recorded' and reference to the technology in any of the interviews is something to be avoided.

Electronic recording technologies (oral and visual) also occupy a specific place in the culture of social scientific research itself. Again, the presence of such technological objects is generally considered intrusive, with a corresponding need to minimize and control any resultant distortion to the data collected. By contrast, Hutchby's chapter considers how the technology is made interactionally present and consequential by the participants, through an analysis of the talk between a child and counsellor in the context of therapy following parental separation or divorce. His findings undermine the current claims and assumptions that are made about disturbances to the 'natural setting' in methodological debates about capturing data. Instead he confronts the material presence of the tape recorder as it is observably oriented to by both child and counsellor, and demonstrates that the technology comes to have different forms of presence, both physical and moral, over the course of the counselling session. From this, Hutchby contends that rather than assuming that data is inevitably distorted by the presence of recording technology, its interactional presence and configuration should themselves become objects of analysis.

In a reflection of the therapeutic harnessing of the presence of recording technology that Hutchby explores, the chapter by Jones and Price shows the explicit configuration of technology and humans, this time through a different kind of therapeutic framework. Jones and Price analyse the use of technology in a welfare intervention, where it is used directly with children with emotional and behavioural difficulties to explore their experiences and feelings about social encounters that may lead to aggressive or otherwise socially problematic reactions. Here, technological innovation is harnessed to enable children to speak and play out different ideas about themselves and their interactants in a virtual encounter. Like Hutchby, Jones and Price show how the software used, *Bubble Dialogue*, enables a bridging of the public and private worlds of the child in specific encounters and furnishes insights that can be picked up in therapeutic interventions.

TECHNOLOGIES AND CULTURES OF CHILDHOOD

Culture as a wider issue is explored in Part Three, where theoretical chapters by Lee and Oswell engage not only with the ontology of technology but also the social processes of culture and the role of technologies in the very constitution of the category 'child'. Oswell challenges us to rethink childhood as revealed in modernity through the 'compass of cultural technologies including discursive technologies', whilst Lee draws on notions from McLuhan (1987) and Strathern (1992) to propose the vital contribution of technologies as extensions of self to the mixed economy of childhood dependence and independence at this juncture in our cultural history. Reflection on the debates on the history of childhood reveals the central role often proposed for technologies in the emergence of particular forms of childhood. For example, in an account that has generated some controversy, Postman (1983) makes claims for the invention of childhood in the late Middle Ages and rests those claims on the changes wrought in society by the technology of the printing press. Luke (1989) also links the emergence of a different form of childhood from the late Middle Ages onwards to the social changes made possible by the printing press, but, taking a Foucaultian view, locates the constitution of modern childhood in the discursive technologies of Lutheran reforms in sixteenth century Germany. In his chapter, Oswell draws our attention to technologies such as paintings and diaries that mediate presence. Here, the place of technologies in constituting social relations is made central. Stepping outside the confines of material notions of technology, the notions of both technology as mediation and mediation as a technology are richly demonstrated in these last two chapters.

This volume does not present a specific methodological stance on the social study of children and technology. Rather, the variety of methodological approaches represented in these chapters reflects the complexity of the questions that arise when considering the social relationships between children, technology and culture. Theoretical questions about the nature of technology are central. Currently there is an unreflexive equivalence granted to technology and ICT which has three main effects. First, it grants ICT a special place in society which obscures continuities with other forms of technology. Second, it leaves unexplored what it is that is at the heart of a technology from a social–relational point of view, thus unnecessarily ruling out other technologies, especially discursive technologies. And third, it fails to account for the contingent nature of technology, fixing it in the material object and rendering it effectively asocial and deterministic. This volume challenges each of these notions and does so through a variety of approaches. Lee and Oswell consider the ontology and epistemology of children and technology from within different concerns, drawing on contemporary social theory to do so. Understanding technology as a device of mediation frames a theoretical orientation to some central issues in the analysis of any relationship of children and technology. Süss *et al.* and Casas make use of quantitative analyses to look at the material presence of ICT and electronic technologies in children's lives in a variety of settings and cultural contexts. Facer *et al.* and Valentine and Holloway combine quantitative and qualitative data to explore the complexities of ICT use in the home and at school. Robinson and Delahooke also take a school setting and use a qualitative ethnographic approach to examine the symbolic positioning of one form of technology in children's everyday practices of friendship, whilst Hemmings *et al.* expose the tensions between affordances, intentions designed into technology and the uses of technology through conversation and video analysis. Hutchby also uses conversation analysis to effect a reflexive move which demonstrates the configured nature of social relationships with the technology of recording devices.

In conclusion, this volume sets out a wide agenda in considering social aspects of the relationships and encounters between children and technologies in cultural contexts. The necessity of considering the ontology of technology, its contingency and indeterminancy, as well as the embodied status of children themselves, are strongly demonstrated through a combination of theoretical and empirical work.

REFERENCES

Bijker, W. E. and Law, J. (eds) (1992) *Shaping Technology/Building Society*, Massachusetts: MIT Press.

Corsaro, W. (1997) *The Sociology of Childhood*, London: Sage.

DfEE (1998) *Connecting the Learning Society: National Grid for Learning. The Government's Consultation Paper*, London: The Stationery Office.

Grint, K. and Woolgar, S. (1997) *The Machine at Work: Technology, Work and Organisation*, Cambridge: Polity Press.

Hutchby, I. (2001) *Conversation and Technology: From the Telephone to the Internet*, Cambridge: Polity Press.

Hutchby, I. and Moran-Ellis, J. (eds) (1998) *Children and Social Competence: Arenas of Action*, London: Falmer Press.

James, A., Jenks, C. and Prout, A. (1998) *Theorising Childhood*, Cambridge: Polity Press.

James, A. and Prout, A. (eds) (1990) *Constructing and Reconstructing Childhood*, London: Falmer Press.

Lee, N. (2000) 'Faith in the body? Childhood, subjecthood and sociological inquiry', in Prout, A. (ed.), *The Body, Childhood and Society*, London: Macmillan.

Luke, C. (1989) *Pedagogy, Printing and Protestantism: The Discourse on Childhood*, New York: SUNY Press.

Mackenzie, D. and Wajcman, J. (eds) (1985) *The Social Shaping of Technology*, Milton Keynes: Open University Press.

McLuhan, M. (1987) *Understanding Media*, Massachusetts: MIT Press.

Mayall, B. (1994) *Children's Childhoods: Observed and experienced*, London: Falmer Press.

Moran-Ellis, J. and Cooper, G. (2000) 'Making connections: Children, technology and the National Grid for Learning', *Sociological Research Online* 5:3.

Postman, N. (1983) *The Disappearance of Childhood*, London: W.H. Allen.

Prout, A. (ed.) (2000) *The Body, Childhood and Society*, London: Macmillan.

Prout, A. and James, A. (1990) 'A new paradigm for the sociology of childhood? Provenance, promise and problems', in James, A. and Prout, A. (eds), *Constructing and Reconstructing Childhood*, London: Falmer Press.

Strathern, M. (1992) *Partial Connections*, Maryland: Rowman and Littlefield.

Part I

New technologies, new childhoods?

1 Home is where the hardware is

Young people, the domestic environment and 'access' to new technologies

Keri Facer, John Furlong and Ruth Furlong, and Rosamund Sutherland

The imminent convergence of telephony with computers to create the Information and Communications Technology (ICT) networks of the near future … is removing the sense of place from discourse, as physical location becomes not only transparent but immaterial.

(Abbott 1998:102)

The understandable optimism that surrounds the development of information and communications technology, specifically with reference to the world wide web, has led to a resurrection of faith in McLuhan's 'global village' in which the constraints of physical location – body, family, city and society – might be transcended by international communications networks (McLuhan 1964). Young people, it is suggested, are spearheading this revolution, developing online communities in which the local and personal significance of age, ethnicity, gender or class are rendered irrelevant by the medium of international communications technology. While we are now beginning to understand some of the forms, structures and reasons why new forms of multimedia digital communication and interaction gain significance within these online communities, what is less apparent in much research into children's use of digital technologies (Abbot 1998) are the ways in which the 'embodied' everyday lives of young people may both provide the impetus for cybercommunication and constrain the ways in which young people might inhabit these new 'virtual' spaces.

One result of this neo-Cartesian mind/body dualism in 'cybertheorist' research is that much analysis of young people's digital products declares the author dead even before he or she is discovered. This research into the ways in which young people inscribe themselves into the world wide web (through websites, chat rooms, hacking, etc.) or into the field of digital production (through DTP, word-processing, games design, etc.) has overemphasized an analysis of the text alone at the expense of an understanding of the producer and conditions of production of the text. Yet, as Abbott (1998) and Downes

(1998) have argued, the processes of digital production in word-processing, DTP, chat room and hacking environments function in such a way as to conflate 'conversation' or 'writing' with 'publication'. Young people's acts of writing and self-inscription could therefore be analysed as acts of production and – just as with other media products such as television, books and films – the conditions of the means of production, rather than being immaterial, may be central to the characteristics of these products (Hall 1997). How is 'freedom' from geographical and physical constraints, for example, identified and experienced in this new medium without the preliminary experience of these very constraints? We would therefore argue that young people's digital productions or contributions to the shape and form of online communities should be read against a fuller understanding of the conditions of production within which young people are operating. As Benedikt argues:

> Digital spaces are undoubtedly created through the imaginative interpretation of software by a human being. But the process of meaning-making is embedded in corporeal interaction between human bodies and computer hardware and software. Attending only to digital spaces ignores the physicality of technological production and consumption in everyday processes of interaction, and the negotiation of meaning that occurs during such encounters.
>
> (Benedikt 1991:45)

A separation of 'virtual' from 'real' space in existing research agendas has implications not only for the ways in which we might begin to analyse young people's digital productions, but also for policy initiatives intended to encourage participation in the 'information society'. Current government initiatives in the UK, for example, are premised on the assumption (or aspiration?) that once access to cyberspace is granted to young people then the inequalities that exist in the material world will be transcended in the virtual world of the internet. As the MP Nigel Jones implied in a House of Commons debate on the 'information society', the variations in the context of use, the body, the locality and the community are assumed to be overcome when 'the right of every citizen, wherever he or she might happen to live, to access the new services' is achieved (Jones 1997). The possibility that these very constraints might shape and alter the ways in which cyberspace is explored and valued, however, is an idea absent from political debate in the drive to achieve 'universal access'.

This chapter, therefore, will begin to explore some of the 'conditions of production' under which young people operate in their use of ICTs. Further, we will address the problematic aspiration to universal access to new technologies and assess its appropriateness as the benchmark of equal participation and production in the 'information age'. Specifically, we will ask what it means to 'get into cyberspace' from the home and argue that the significance of young people's digital productions can be better understood through a rich understanding of the social, physical and cultural environments within which young people are operating.

METHODOLOGY

The following argument draws on research funded by the Economic and Social Research Council (ESRC), involving a detailed questionnaire to 855 children in years five and eight of eight schools (four primary and four secondary) in the South West of England and Wales. The school communities can be characterized as 'leafy dormitory suburb', 'ex-mining town', 'multicultural city centre' and 'rural market town'. The sample is made up of 52 per cent boys, 48 per cent girls; 21 per cent aged ten to eleven years and the rest thirteen to fourteen years, 13 per cent were from low income families, and 66 per cent middle income, while 21 per cent would be considered high income. The questionnaire explored all aspects of ICT ownership and use outside school, and detailed case studies were made of sixteen families selected from the questionnaire sample. The children were selected on the basis of computer ownership and medium–high computer use, and represented equal numbers of girls and boys, children from each of the selected school communities and from a variety of different family backgrounds in terms of parental profession, family make-up, family ICT expertise and socio-economic status. Eight of the sixteen families have internet access in the home. The families were visited on four occasions over a year, with extensive interviews with all members of the family and in groups at school with the children and selected friends. The children's ICT use was observed and they also completed week-long diaries of ICT use on a monthly basis.

PROBLEMATIZING THE 'ACCESS = HARDWARE' EQUATION

Current definitions of 'access' to new technologies in the UK tend to equate access with home ownership of computer hardware. Given that the purchase of even a basic computer can extend into many hundreds of pounds, with internet access at present an additional and ongoing charge, this issue should not be underestimated, howevever we will argue that it should be rendered significantly more complex. Further, with 14 per cent of our respondents using computers in the home of a second parent, the elision between home ownership and young people's access to computers becomes even more problematic. There is, unfortunately, insufficient space here to explore the implications of changing family patterns for access to ICT by young people. We can, however, give a summary of the results of our questionnaire to provide a wider context for the discussions of ICT use in domestic environments that, drawing on our sixteen family case studies, will form the bulk of this chapter.

Of the children in this sample, almost 70 per cent had a computer in their homes with 20 per cent having a computer to which they had exclusive access. Differences in ownership between boys and girls and between children living in rural and urban locations, although present, were not statistically significant. The central factor in terms of ownership was, unsurprisingly, based on the socio-economic background of the children, with over a quarter more children from high income families (80.4 per cent) having access to computers in the home than those in families with low incomes (53.9 per cent). This factor alone should be taken into account in research into online communities, particularly considering that these figures do not highlight differences in the age and technical capacities of the computers with which children from different socio-economic backgrounds might be working.

Importantly, however, when the children were asked if they used a computer outside school 83.3 per cent responded in the affirmative, which was 13.4 per cent more than had a computer in the home. This finding immediately problematizes the easy elision between 'access' and ownership of hardware that is currently employed; as Livingstone and Bovill (1999) have pointed out, 'those without home access to IT do indeed seek it out elsewhere'. This tendency to use computers in sites other than the home was, however, found to reproduce rather than mitigate inequalities in computer ownership in the children's own homes, with young people who had access to a computer in the home significantly (χ^2 =36.540, df=2, p<0.0005) more likely also to use a computer at friends' houses.

From the questionnaire, however, it was apparent that although friends' houses are popular for game-playing, the home remains the primary site for the use of a computer for homework purposes. That children without computers are using them at friends' houses or other locations should not, then, be read as an argument that they have equal access to all areas of computing. Rather, the question of access to computers at a time of increased ownership of multimedia technology might have to be reframed and refined as a question about access to particular software.

Before commencing an analysis of the material environment within which the young people in our case studies are operating when they use the computer, two final results from the questionnaire survey seem pertinent. First, far from being the sole preserve of young people in the home, the computers were frequently located in spaces which suggest that the computer functions as a shared resource. Fifty-three per cent of home computers were located in family spaces (such as dining rooms, hallways, computer rooms, etc.) and only 43 per cent in bedrooms – bedrooms which may also, since the introduction of the computer into these spaces, function less as the private retreat of an individual child and more as a site to which several members of the family have access. Second, only 6 per cent of the children responded that 'no one' was likely to be using the computer when they wanted to use it. These two results suggest that computer use in the home is likely to be a contested activity, in which the demands for computer access must be balanced between several members of the family, demands which may suggest that computer use – far from being a purely mental and imaginative activity – is firmly grounded in the material and physical economy of the household.

HOME IS WHERE THE HARDWARE IS

It has been argued that the home is currently being constructed by families in the UK as an alternative leisure space for young people, in which parents increasingly invest substantial sums to provide their children with entertainment media in response to a perceived increase in threats to children's welfare outside the front door (Ward 1994; Buckingham 1999; Livingstone and Bovill 1999). This attitude is discernible amongst most of the families in our case studies, an attitude that at times was explicitly cited as the reason for the introduction of computer technology into the home:

Interviewer: What was the reason mostly you thought to buy it? [the computer]
Mr A: I thought that the reason is to get them occupied rather than get occupied in something else.
Interviewer: You thought it was a good thing to …
Mr A: I thought it was a good thing, you know, they'd enjoy it. Rather than they go into an arcade or something, going out, messing about, money involved. I don't like these kind of stuff.
Interviewer: So it seemed like a good thing to be doing in the home.
Mr A: Yeah, it's always the best thing in the home.

Although home computers have been available in the UK for almost twenty years now, the home PC, in its current form with large screen, perhaps printer, scanner and other peripherals, is still a relatively recent arrival to the domestic scene. The introduction of first radio and then television into British homes in the early part of this century saw these new audio-visual technologies replacing the fireplace as a focal point around which the family would gather as a group (Frith 1983). Similarly, in our case studies, a reconfiguring of domestic space can be seen in the arrangements that are made within families to incorporate these newer technologies, arrangements that both alter and draw upon the existing geography of the family space and indicate the functions constructed for this technology within the family system (Silverstone *et al.*, 1992).

Unlike the introduction of television and radio where the technology was incorporated into already existing family and communal leisure space, spare or 'dead' space is often co-opted to house the computer, with landings, understairs cupboards, the 'spare' bedroom, the dining room, and the loft conversion all functioning as newly reinvigorated spaces of frequent habitation. This location of the computer in 'out of the way', although easily accessible, areas suggests that this technology is frequently intended to be used by a single individual – the single chair that sits in front of the screen in many of these households (14 in 16 in our sample) further underlines this point and highlights the computer's infiltration of the home from the workplace (Haddon 1992).

Mrs H: Well because it's the other side of the house at the back so you don't have to hear it. So if you were in here watching television and we've got company then they're out the way.

Interviewer: Why did it go in the spare room? What was the reason? What was the thinking?

Mr D: Because it was a spare room.

Mrs D: Because it's nobody's room in there and just let everybody else use it. It's a sort of spare room cum office.

Steven, 13: It's not as private as your bedroom.

The introduction of computers into 'out of the way' areas sees these previously infrequently occupied spaces being invaded by the peripherals that are seen to support preferred uses of the computer: bookshelves with reference books, storage space for pens and pencils, games manuals, litter bins for draft prints of documents. While this introduction of the computer into the home sees a reconfiguration of the domestic landscape, so, reciprocally, do the material constraints of the existing home 'layout' impact on the ways in which the computer can be used.

Heather, 13: I don't like getting on the internet really, it's a bit too complicated for me. It takes up the phone lines and you have to get out the extension lead and I can't really be bothered. ·... you've got to get out the extension lead, plug it in, ask mum and dad ...

The physical and material 'make-up' of the home – whether the computer is located out of sight of the rest of the family in a custom-made space or in an under-stairs cupboard leading onto the sitting room within sight of both television and passing family traffic – constitutes specifically different environments in which young people are using computer technology, environments that may, as we indicate later in the chapter, impact on the ways in which young people negotiate the relationship between their physical and 'virtual' existences.

STAKING A CLAIM TO THE HARDWARE

As we indicated earlier, the purchase of a home computer for many families is a serious financial commitment, sometimes taking up a significant percentage of their income. Consequently, it is unsurprising to find that for many of our case study families (14 of 16), the computer is required to function as a shared resource. The implications of this shared 'ownership' are manifested in the ways in which access is negotiated to the computer, a negotiation that is frequently managed around the temporal organization (Jordan 1992) of the family:

Mum: Steven normally gets in first you see, so he would always get the opportunity of going to the computer first. So we said 'that's not fair'. So Mondays and Thursdays Helen has first choice. She can decide whether she wants to go on the computer or watch television and on the other … I mean it tends to be just the Tuesday and Wednesday because Friday you're quite often not here or doing other things … But we try and stick to only two hours on the computer each in any one day … Generally speaking that's probably about enough. In terms of playing games. If they want to then go on and do some homework, then that's fine …

This type of 'linear' organization of time, with activities clearly separated from each other, for example games distinguished from homework, is an example of the ways in which certain families attempt to contain the meaning of the 'multipurpose' computer, organizing the potentially fluid identity of this work and leisure tool to comply with existing family patterns of temporal organization. Despite the suggestion that young people are capable of 'multitasking' – using several different computing environments at once (Hepple 1995) – this socialization of the technology within the already-existing microsystem of the family indicates the ways in which the local context of usage may constrain and shape the ways in which young people exploit the potential of the computer environment.

Interviewer: What about … if either of you wants to go on it … do you do that together or do you do that on your own?
Nick, 10:   Well we do it on our own but if we're doing it at the same time we race each other up to the computer. Whoever gets there first
               …
Interviewer: Is that right?
Nick: Then we have fifteen minutes, each of us has fifteen minutes and then …
[…]
Nick: It was either, I think it was either half an hour or fifteen minutes and we decided on, because of our time restriction on the computer, fifteen minutes.

While Nick and his twin brother James negotiate access to the computer through a mix of physical ('whoever gets there first') and diplomatic ('we decided on, because of our time restriction on the computer') processes, other means of negotiating access are more 'subversive' of the temporal organization of the family. Another teenage boy, Steven, frequently disguises his game-playing or online activities as homework, and takes the opportunity of a visit by a researcher to the home to access internet games under the guise of 'research'. This 'opportunism' is a response to the high level of competition for access to the computer in this family, in which occupation of the digital landscape is only ever temporary and transient:

Helen, 10:   And I was having a go at that and I couldn't get past this particular bit and I called Steven ...

Steven, 13:   I did it in thirty seconds.

Helen: He did it in thirty seconds.

Interviewer: Right. So if Steven shows you something ...

Steven: He normally does it.

Interviewer: He normally does it and then you carry on.

Helen: And then I carry on. Or he normally does it. He pushes me off and he goes the rest of the game. He does that a lot of the time.

In this family Steven is acting, in de Certeau's (1984) terms, 'tactically' in relation to the computer, grasping an opportunity to access it as and when it presents itself, a means of acquiring access to a computer that may be particularly significant amongst young people, many of whom may not be able to claim 'ownership' of the technology but who, nevertheless, want to assert their right to use it in competition with others. This 'tactical' appropriation of the computer provides young people, in situations of competition for access, with a means of claiming ownership of the technology, if only ever for a finite period of time.

> The place of a tactic belongs to the other. A tactic insinuates itself into the other's place fragmentarily, without taking it over in its entirety, without being able to keep it at a distance ... Because it does not have a place, a tactic depends on time – it is always on the watch for opportunities that must be seized 'on the wing'. Whatever it wins it does not keep.
>
> (de Certeau, 1984: 23)

This temporal appropriation of the computer can also be seen in a second tactic through which individuals claim ownership of the computer: in these cases the screen functions as territory onto which family members can inscribe their identities and ownership by leaving traces of themselves and eradicating traces of others' occupation. An activity in which many of the children in our case studies participate, for example, is the process of changing the settings of the computer – the desktop layout is changed to lurid greens and purples, menu bars and icons are altered and relocated or the screen saver is changed to read 'kids' computer, keep out' or to represent images of favourite places, pets or pop stars. There is frequently a rapid turnover in screen savers and settings as different children eradicate the traces that signify previous habitation of the computer space and impose their own images and settings in their place.

This process can also be identified in the management of the computer's hard drive. In many families, for example, one person (often, but not always, an adult) takes responsibility for the setup of file management systems, installing shortcuts, de-installing software and freeing up memory for authorized or 'preferred' practices. The installation of games by young people onto family computers often intended for collective use for 'work' purposes has in several cases caused tensions around the description of the computer as entertainment or educational environment. These tensions are managed by whoever has sufficient knowledge or authority to take a 'meta-level' view of the computer; in other words, he (or she) who controls the system controls the duration and possibility of activities within that system in the processes of installation and de-installation of games and other 'unauthorized' software. Those within the family who do not have this access to the computer as an organizational system (either through lack of knowledge, inclination or more explicit prohibition) therefore occupy the computer only tactically, as the files, documents, shortcuts or bookmarks they have installed may be removed at any time by other members of the family.

Interviewer: So what package do you normally work in? Is it Word?
Heather, 13: Normally yeah, but I can't seem to find it. Because my mum works on the computer at home now …
Interviewer: So what's changed since your mum started working on it?
Heather: They put that bar up at the top where normally they would have it in the documents. And you go into File Office.
Interviewer: So you know your way in normally and now they've changed it?
Heather: Mm.

The installation of the game, creation of a shortcut, establishment of files or folders has its impermanence inscribed within it; in this digital landscape the alteration of desktop settings to greens and purples, or the installing of a screen saver can all be theorized as sorties into contested terrain, a transient victory of time over space in which, like graffiti on city walls, the inevitability of eradication provides the justification and necessity for the action. This poaching of the computer space, a temporal appropriation of technology, derives from the communal ownership that is explicitly referenced by the families and can also be seen as a negotiation to fix the meaning and, subsequently, function of a technology which has the potential for multiple purposes.

GETTING INTO CYBERSPACE

Given the media representation of a new generation hiding in their bedrooms with their technology (see, for example, Williams and Buncombe 1999), it is surprising that the child alone in the darkened bedroom with a computer (although not a Playstation) is notably absent from the majority of our case studies (14 out of 16). As we have already argued, it was apparent within the families who made up our case studies that the computer was frequently located within easy reach of all members of the family. This was either for the purpose of shared use of an expensive resource, or (equally significantly when considering the impact of the home environment on the ways in which young people access and negotiate cyberspace) for reasons of surveillance within the home.

Despite the investment in digital technology as compensatory leisure activity for young people, in which digital freedom is intended to compensate for physical freedom (Ward 1994; Livingstone and Bovill 1999), many parents in our case studies have expressly stated that they would not want computers in children's bedrooms because they would be unable either to access the technology for their own purposes, or, significantly, to monitor the activities that children are engaging with on the computer. This surveillance of children's use of digital technologies was made more explicit in relation to the use of the internet. A central concern among many families, for example, was the cost of the telephone bill generated by internet use. The socio-economic status of the individual family, to whom call costs may be more or less significant, and the present organization of internet access in the UK around charges for local telephone calls indicate the ways in which the geographical location and socio-economic status of the young person using the computer impacts – via time constraints – on access to digital spaces. Other concerns were, however, voiced by parents in relation to a need to monitor children's internet use:

Mrs R: … It's moved several times here. It's been into Henry's room and out.
Interviewer: Why did it come out?
Mrs R: Basically because …
Henry, 13:   So mum could use it as well.
Mrs R: Yes, it was difficult for me to do the scouting stuff and bits and pieces. I also felt I wanted to be able to see what he was doing as well. At least if he's in here …
Henry: One, to learn, and the other one's so she goes 'He's not doing that behind my back is he?'
Mrs R: No, otherwise he's in his room and I don't see him.
Henry: Because she might think that I'm telling lies and she doesn't need a modem and I'm bringing up all this internet access and stuff and she's like …

As this quotation highlights, the networking of computers, specifically the introduction of the internet into the home space, has begun to problematize the solution of protecting children from the threats of the outside world by keeping them indoors. As Lupton (1995: 10) has argued:

The main anxiety here is in the insidious nature of contact with others through the internet. The home is now no longer a place of safety and refuge for children, the computer no longer simply an educational tool or source of entertainment but is the possible site of children's corruption. 'Outside' danger is brought 'inside', into the very heart of the home, via the internet.

As the permeable boundaries of domestic space are made apparent in the introduction of the internet (and television before it) into the home, the space of the networked home computer becomes a site of surveillance in which children's activities are monitored in ways not dissimilar to those employed in the space outside the front door. This practice can be seen to extend to educational contexts as well. In Britain, for example, the Virtual Teacher's centre web resource is being constructed as, effectively, a playground of authorized and sanctioned websites in which teachers can allow children to play and explore, metaphorically similar to the after school club. The construction of the child as technologically literate, however, and capable of following 'hot links' away from these authorized spaces is akin to the moment when a child is able to walk away from the playground and, potentially, into the arms of strangers.

> The world is worried about children first and foremost, as is evidenced by the recent comments made by President Clinton. He said last week: 'With the right technology and rating systems, we can help ensure that our children don't end up in the red-light districts of cyberspace.'
>
> (Bruce 1997)

The internet, like the geographical space outside, is therefore a site of anxiety for parents and is constructed, in many homes and at policy level, as a site which must be policed. Unsurprisingly, then, access to this space is limited in a variety of ways by the families with which we have been working. In families in which parents are uncertain about the means to monitor children's use of the internet, several have either decided not to go 'online' or have told their children that there is no internet access in the home. In others, passwords are required to access the internet, passwords which the children are not privy to. In many of the families with younger children where the internet is present in the home, parents allow their children to access the net only with parental supervision and several families were considering a digital equivalent to parental supervision: the 'nannying' or filtering systems that are becoming widely available. At present, however, due to a lack of confidence in the ability of these programs to filter content effectively or a lack of understanding of the ways in which these work, none of the families was using one. At times the physical layout of the home is also such that access to the net can only occur when parents are aware of it – as children are required to link up cables and unplug the telephone. In one family, the disciplines of the workplace are ironically introduced into the home with a sign on the spare bedroom door (the gateway to the computer room) reading 'authorized personnel only'.

The increasing technological literacy of some young people, however, places pressure on rudimentary means of policing access to the internet, such as setting passwords; in response to this pressure unsupervised access is often granted on an understanding achieved between parents and children which relies on an internalized moral code, or on more subtle forms of surveillance, for its effectiveness.

Mrs C: Yeah I do trust him but then everybody trusts their kids don't they? I mean if when we were out one night I came back and Heather said 'Oh Scott's been on the internet looking at this, that and the other' I would be most shocked and disappointed in him, wouldn't you?

Mr C: Yeah.

Mrs C: And very, very surprised, cos he's very sensible.

Interviewer: So did you explain all that to him before you got him on there or did you just … I mean you know your son, so …

Mrs C: Scott has got a conscience which is to the extreme really. I mean he can't do anything that he shouldn't without having to come and confess.

Interviewer: Really?

Mrs C: Yeah. And if it's anything bad he'll get really upset about it. So if he's got the choice to make to do something bad or not do it he will always choose to not do it because of the knock-on effects it would have with us, isn't it?

Toby, 14:   Well I do chat, but not very much. Because you get people on there with rather explicit language and alternative methods of …

Interviewer: Who polices that? You or your mum, or both?

Toby: Well I know when people are getting silly. So I stop it. But if mum comes in and sees you …

Interviewer: She sees you on the screen (LAUGHTER)

Toby: She'll stop it too.

The reference to 'knock-on effects' in the first mother's statement and the location of the computer within a 'public' space in the home in the second, indicates that the location of the computer within the family home, far from being immaterial, may impact on the ways in which cyberspace is explored and experienced by young people and the extent to which cyberspace is considered a genuinely 'free' space by young people given the prohibitions that exist on certain types of usage. In studies of online communities, therefore, these negotiations required to gain access to the internet and the internalized practices of 'self-censorship' that may be operating, practices that rely heavily on culturally-specific constructions of appropriate youth activities, should be recognized as partially constitutive of the online experience.

The digital landscape, then, rather than being a circumscribed free space 'for children' as compensation for the lack of freedom in public spaces, is also subject to practices of surveillance and discipline. Access to and occupation of the much-celebrated disembodied cyberspace in which age, gender, religion and geography are insignificant can be achieved by young people, in many cases, only through a process of complex negotiation based on age, sex, family income, perceived maturity and culture.

CONCLUDING REMARKS

We have outlined some of the ways in which the computer in the home environment cannot be seen merely as a gateway to cyberspace, like the wardrobe providing access to Narnia, but rather that the materiality of this technology, as a shared and expensive family resource, is central to shaping the ways in which young people are able to access new technologies in the home. First, we have underlined the ways in which access to hardware is patterned along socio-economic lines with families on low incomes significantly less likely to purchase a computer. Second, we have argued that the location of the computer within the home impacts the spatial organization of the family, and that the ways in which the domestic space is arranged prior to the introduction of computer technology also reciprocally impact the ways in which the computer may be used. Rather than being a purely 'cerebral' activity, internet use in the home may, therefore, be taking place amongst the detritus of everyday living, cramped into a cupboard under the stairs with Mum's work files and the laundry basket, within earshot of parents and under the watchful eyes of a sibling who wants to 'get on' to finish some homework.

Centrally, then, we have wished to underline that ownership of computer hardware does not equate with easy access to 'cyberspace' but that, as with other goods in the home and with the space outside the front door, young people are required first to negotiate access and second to demonstrate certain types of 'trustworthy' behaviour before they are allowed free access to both the computer and the virtual world beyond the screen. This process of gaining access can be seen to be patterned along lines in which the social construction of appropriate behaviour for young people is seen to have continued validity. Specifically with reference to young people's use of the internet the combination of the domestic landscape (with computers frequently within easy view of other members of the family) and the restrictions that may be placed on types and duration of usage will, we argue, impact on the ways in which young people are able to claim the internet as a site of their 'own'.

Although we would not wish to develop an analysis of young people's digital media products using an essentialist model in which the product is considered to be determined solely by the young person's physical and geographical identity, neither would we wish to see a continued analysis of young people's online activities which fails to recognize the constraints within which young people may be operating. If, as Massey (1998) has argued, 'the control of spatiality is part of the process of defining the social category of "youth" itself', it would be naive to assume that access to and use of the world wide web is experienced and exploited by young people as a site without constraints.

What remains to be developed are the methodologies by which it is possible to explore these significant sites (such as web discussion rooms, news-groups and 'communities') by engaging both with the new opportunities that these may present for young people and with the constraints within which as young, gendered, socially constituted people they must operate in homes, schools and libraries around the UK. In the meantime, a continued uncritical reproduction of the mind/body distinction may serve simply to reinforce the inequalities that exist in young people's use of new technologies and support a technodeterminist political agenda that conceives the achievement of universal 'access' to computers as a panacea for the world's inequalities.

REFERENCES

Abbott, C. (1998) 'Making connections: Young people and the internet' in Julian Sefton-Green (ed.) *Digital Diversions: Youth Culture in the Age of Multi-Media*, London: UCL.

Benedikt, M. (1991) *Cyberspace: First Steps*, Cambridge MA: MIT.

Bruce, N. (1997) reported in Hansard, Information Society Debate, 22/7/97.

Buckingham, D., Davies, H., Jones, K., Kelley, P. (1999) *Children's television in Britain*, London: BFI.

de Certeau, M. (1984) *The Practice of Everyday Life*, London: University of California Press.

DfEE (1998) *Connecting the Learning Society: National Grid for Learning, The Government's Consultation Paper*, London: The Stationery Office.

Downes, T. (1998) 'Children's use of computers in their homes', unpublished D.Phil thesis.

Education and Training Group for Wales (ETAG) (1998) *An Education and Training Plan for Wales: a draft for consultation* (Cardiff: Manweb).

Frith, S. (1983) 'The pleasures of the hearth', in J. Donald (ed.) *Formations of Pleasure*, London: Routledge.

Haddon, L. (1992) 'Explaining ICT consumption: the case of the home computer' in R. Silverstone and E. Hirsch (eds) *Consuming Technologies: Media and Information in Domestic Spaces*, London: Routledge.

Hall, S. (1997) 'Encoding and decoding in television practice', CCCS Stencilled paper, No7.

Hepple (1995) *National Survey of Emergent Capability: Preliminary observations from the pilot study*. http://www.ultralab.anglia.ac.uk/pages/ULTRALAB/Team/Stephen/Projects_survey.

Jones, N. (1997) *The Information Society Debate* in Hansard, 11 July 1997.

Jordan, A. (1992) 'Social class, temporal orientation, and mass media use within the family system' in *Critical Studies in Mass Communications* 9.

Livingstone, S. and Bovill, M. (1999) *Young People, New Media*, London: LSE/ICT.

Lupton, D. (1995) 'The embodied computer user' in M. Featherstone and R. Burrows (eds) *Cyberspace, Cyberbodies, Cyberpunk: Cultures of Technological Embodiment*, London: Sage.

Massey, D. (1998) 'The spatial construction of youth cultures' in T. Skelton and G. Valentine (eds) *Cool Places: Geographies of Youth Cultures*, London: Routledge.

McLuhan, M. (1964) *Understanding Media*, New York: Mentor.

Sefton-Green, J. (ed.) (1998) *Digital Diversions: Youth Culture in the Age of Multi-Media*, London: UCL.

Silverstone, R., Hirsch, E., Morley, D. (1992) 'Information and communication technologies in the moral economy of the household' in R. Silverstone and E. Hirsch (eds) *Consuming Technologies: Media and Information in Domestic Spaces*, London: Routledge.

Ward, C. (1994) 'Opportunities for childhoods in late 20th century Britain', in B. Mayall (ed.) *Children's childhoods: observed and experienced*, London: Falmer Press.

Williams, R., and Buncombe, A. 'Our generation of couch potato kids stuck in their rooms and glued to TV', *The Independent*, 19 March 1999.

2 Media childhood in three European countries[1]

Daniel Süss, Annikka Suoninen, Carmelo Garitaonandia, Paxti Juaristi, Riitta Koikkalainen and Jose A. Oleaga

In this chapter we focus on two important factors in the everyday life of contemporary children: media and peer group. In western information societies, the media play a central role in everyday life and their importance is still increasing. Children acquire a significant part of their knowledge of the world through the media. Different kinds of communicative competencies are becoming more and more important in this information age. Frones (1989) has claimed that in complex societies peer relations play a fundamental role in the socialization process as communicative competencies can basically only be acquired 'by doing', by means of participation in different types of social environments and situations.

Our research is aimed at four age groups: six to seven, nine to ten, twelve to thirteen and fifteen to sixteen years. Drawing on the theories of Erikson (1977), Keupp (1988) and Ziehe (1992, 1995), we are interested both in similarities and in differences between cultures. What is the role of the peer group in the use of different media forms and in reception of media contents? What kinds of cross-cultural similarities and differences can be found in how media use is related to children's and teenagers' relationships with their peers? The chapter is based mainly on qualitative interviews with children and teenagers conducted in Finland, Switzerland and Spain in 1997 as part of the New Himmelweit study (see Livingstone and Bovill 2001). Interviews were conducted either as group discussions (each group comprising participants from one of the four age groups) or as individual in-depth interviews. In Spain and Switzerland, parents and teachers were also interviewed separately.[2]

The Finnish qualitative interviews consisted of seventy-nine group interviews with Finnish-speaking (93 per cent of the population) children and teenagers between six and sixteen years of age. The interviews were conducted in fifty schools in different parts of the country, in both urban and rural areas. The Spanish interviews included five group discussions between 9–16 year olds and five individual interviews with 6–7 year olds. The interviews were conducted in five Spanish cities and the children and teenagers were mainly from a middle-class background. In Switzerland, eighty-seven German-speaking (72 per cent of the total population) children between six and sixteen years of age were interviewed. Observations and focused interviews were carried out in kindergarten classes, in a computer camp and in families from different regions of the German-speaking part of the country. From Switzerland and Finland some survey data from autumn 1997 is also used. The Swiss survey (n=1131) included a representative sample of 6–16 year olds from all three language zones of Switzerland. The Finnish sample (n=754) comprised Finnish-speaking children and teenagers from different parts of the country. Both samples included urban and rural areas and different socio-economic groups.

CULTURAL DIFFERENCES IN MEDIA USE

The three countries compared in this chapter provide us with a combination of quite different social contexts in terms of media ownership and use and gender relations. We begin by briefly outlining these.

Finland (five million inhabitants) is a country with a progressive system of equal rights for men and women and a good support system for working parents, including a full-cover daycare system organized by the state and free school lunches offered to all pupils. A high percentage of mothers work outside the home, and young women's educational level is higher than that of men. Children have a lot of freedom and time of their own, especially during the afternoon. Attitudes towards media and new technology are quite liberal and children are encouraged to use media of all kinds at a very early age. Computers are available in some daycare centres and are widely used in schools at all levels. Two-thirds of comprehensive schools and four-fifths of public libraries, as well as an increasing number of private homes, are connected to the internet, and the number of internet connections per capita is the highest in the world.

In Switzerland (seven million inhabitants) the relationship between men and women is more conservative, especially in the rural areas. The work system forces a traditional model upon parents, in which the father works outside the home while the mother looks after the children with few possibilities of part-time work. With reference to the media, there is a discrepancy between the way parents view its influence and the way teachers view it. Many teachers do not want to have electronic media at school or to include media in the curriculum. Middle- and upper-class parents are keen for their children to follow certain rules when using the media. The possibility of access to electronic media is high in private locations, but comparatively low in public locations like schools or libraries.

In Spain (forty million inhabitants) the relationship between men and women is progressive in urban areas and conservative in rural areas. The family has an important role, with both parents and grandparents spending a great deal of their time with their children and grandchildren. The attitude towards media use in general is permissive and a very enthusiastic attitude towards computers has been adopted, especially by middle-class parents. Children may use media at home and in public freely, and also visit amusement arcades. The quantity of media equipment found in families and schools is as great as in Finland or in Switzerland in terms of television sets and video recorders, but not when it comes to computers and, above all, internet access; although the number of internet links is increasing rapidly (see Table 2.1).

Table 2.1 Media equipment in Finnish, Spanish and Swiss households (percentages)

Media	Finland		Spain		Switzerland	
	all households	households with children	all households	households with children	all households	households with children
Television	98	98	99	100	95	95
Video recorder	63	91	69	87	63	66
Computer	23	44	19	29	44	58
Games console	14	37	17	36	7	38
Internet access	9	16	2	3	9	15

Sources: Statistics Finland (1997); EGM Spain (1997); SRG Switzerland (1997).

THE ROLE OF MEDIA IN PEER GROUP RELATIONSHIPS

The use of media content and media technology should be seen in relation to other aspects of everyday life. Media use is an integral part of other daily activities, personal relationships within the domestic environment, the peer group and other contexts. To an extent, the use of media may only be properly understood if it is seen within the framework of interpersonal communication (Lull 1990; Morley and Silverstone 1992). Lull (1980) defined six different types of social uses for television:

- television may act as an environmental resource;
- television can be used for regulating daily activities;
- television may also facilitate communication by offering common topics for talk;
- television watching can be used to seek or avoid contact with other people;
- television programmes may be a means of social learning; and,
- television may be used for demonstrating competence or dominance.

Lull's typology was based on ethnographic observations in family situations, but these social uses can be found in other types of social environments too. Even though media use most often takes place at home, it can also influence relationships outside the home. For example, media content provides common topics for talk in the workplace and some popular television programmes or media happenings may regulate the life of a whole nation. In the case of children and teenagers, media and media contents have many social uses, especially in peer group situations.

In the next sections we look at some of the most important aspects of how media and media content affect peer group relationships of children and teenagers in three countries. First, we look at how the media are used with peers; second, how media offer common topics in interaction with peers; and third, how media are used in strengthening group identity and in building up an individual identity.

Using media together with peers

Media play an important role in children's everyday lives, but they can in no way be seen to replace peer relationships or play with friends. While there are friends around, younger children usually prefer play to media use, and certainly prefer the company of friends to the company of media. Older children and teenagers usually prefer to spend time with friends outside the home and not to use media together. But if the child is alone or feels lonely, the media can act as a friend; media offer social contacts in the form of para–social interaction; and using media is a symbolic activity that can also be played alone. As one seven year old Spanish boy put it: 'The thing I like best is to play a football match with friends and next best I like watching television or playing with computer games.'

The most important medium for children and teenagers in all three countries is television: practically every child has access to television and it is used – almost always – daily. Even though television is used mostly at home, either alone or in the company of parents or siblings, it is also important in children's and teenagers' relationships with their peers. But social uses in the peer group context mostly take place only after the use, not in the actual viewing situation.

Using media can itself be a social happening when shared with friends, siblings or parents. This is particularly the case with console and computer games; while children may prefer to watch television alone, they often think that playing games is more fun with friends around. Playing computer and console games can be an extremely sociable activity, especially for boys, when others gather around someone who is playing and give advice, take it in turns to play, and learn about the games and computers together. Older children and teenagers may also play games on the internet and in Finland it is also quite common to play games with friends through modem connections, where two or more players may take part in the same game.

> It is fun to play with a friend. We have NHL 98 (National Hockey League computer game) and we can play two at the same time as we have the keyboard and then the joystick, so two can play at the same time. I usually play with a friend.
>
> (Finnish boy, seven years)

It depends on the game whether I like to play alone or with a friend. If it is a game that only one person can play at a time, then I prefer to play alone. But of course if there is someone to give advice – like in the case of some strategy-game – it is better to have two brains working on together, to think about it.

(Finnish boy, fifteen years)

Not all children or teenagers have access to a games machine or computer at home but practically every child is familiar with these games as they may be used in friends' or relatives' houses or in public places. Finnish children play both computer (PC) and console games from a very early age, while in Spain and in Switzerland younger children are more familiar with television-linked games machines (console games) and they start using computers only when they are a little older. In Spain console and computer games are also strongly associated with different age groups, but in Finland and in Switzerland this is not the case to the same extent. In Spain, console games are preferred by the younger children, whereas computer games are preferred by the older ones:

The video console is already old-fashioned. We've got one at home, but we don't use it much. Now we play with computer games. Video consoles are for younger children up to about twelve years, because after that age you get bored to death with video games.

(Spanish boy, fifteen years)

When it comes to computer skills, there seems to be a clear difference between countries. Most Finnish six and seven year olds already use computers, while in Spain nine and ten year olds still need help to load the games from their parents or older siblings. This is probably due to different practices in these countries. In Finland (and also in Switzerland, especially in the higher social classes) children are allowed, and encouraged, to use computers alone from a very early age, while in Spain they are thought to need help, whether from parents or teachers, and are therefore not allowed to use them without the company of adults.

Watching videos with friends is fairly common in all three countries. Unlike television programmes, videos seem to lend themselves better to use in the company of friends as they can be used when it is most convenient. During the evenings the children may not have any free time to be with their friends, and if they do, they do not want to spend these rare moments watching television. But during the weekends when they have more time with friends, a couple of hours may be used for watching a film recorded from the television, rented from a video shop, swapped with friends, received as a present or bought.

I like to play Super Nintendo with my friends. And we watch video together. A friend of mine has Teleclub at home. He always registers movies from this channel, and then we meet at his house and watch these movies for two hours in the afternoon.

(Swiss boy, twelve years)

Video films can also be the centre of a deviant youth culture, as is the case, for example, of teenagers who watch horror films, splatter films or other films based on violence. These films, watched in a friend's house where the parents are either not at home or do not mind, can be used to impress other members of the group, especially when the 'hardest' film of the genre is shown.

There seem to be significant cultural differences in the way media are used in the company of peers. This is mainly due to the differences in the organization of everyday life. In Spain, children and teenagers have many organized after-school activities (sports clubs, foreign language classes etc.), and therefore their school days are long and they have very little unorganized leisure time during the week. In Finland, on the other hand, school days are shorter and organized activities take place later in the evening. And as most mothers are working outside the home, children and teenagers usually spend their afternoons with their friends, and using media together may be an important activity – but certainly not the only one – during these hours as both homes and media equipment are available to the children. In Switzerland, youngsters have more unorganized leisure time than in Spain, but spend less time without adult supervision than in Finland, and therefore they spend less time using media together with their peers.

Usually I watch television with friends in the afternoon after school. In the evening there are all the hobbies and everything. You don't have time in the evenings.

(Finnish girl, ten years)

Different media can also be used together with peers outside the home. Amusement arcades with computer games seem to be important, especially to Spanish teenage boys. They go to amusement arcades during the evenings and weekends, simply to go out somewhere and to play and chat with their friends. They realize that they cannot spend much money on the machines because they do not have much, but they go to the arcades anyway. Occasionally, a girl or a group of girls may be there, but this is quite unusual. In Switzerland, youngsters under eighteen years are not allowed to enter the arcades and therefore these are not a part of youth culture. In Finland, these arcades can be found only in the largest towns, so they do not play a big role for youth in general. In Finland children – and especially teenagers – can use media together with their friends in many different kinds of public places: they play computer games or use the internet in public libraries, and in some schools computer equipment can also be used during the evenings. In Switzerland and Spain, school computer equipment is only available to the pupils during lessons and under the supervision of teachers.

We use the internet and play computer games in the library. You can make a reservation for the computer but I don't usually know beforehand when I'm going. You can just go in if the machine is free, but then someone can come and say that they have a reservation. Usually the machines are busy, so if you don't have a reservation you can't get to the internet or anything. At least on the children's section, there are always little kids playing with the computer.

(Finnish girl, thirteen years)

Media as a source for common topics in play and talk

Even though youngsters may not use media in the company of their friends, media and media content enter their interaction with peers. For example, popular television programmes can be among the most discussed topics in peer groups. Older children and teenagers usually talk about the media content but for the younger children the most important form of communication is play. Young children often develop media-related role plays with one another. The characters and themes of play are often taken from popular media, especially from cartoons and other television programmes but sometimes also from computer games. Media and media content can in fact be seen as a very important part of the new 'kidslore': children's own cultural tradition. Swedish psychologist Rönnberg (1987) has said that media have taken the place of older children as 'bearers of tradition' and sources of models for play.

We play Spiderman. It's cool to pretend being able to walk on the walls. It would be fun to be like Spiderman. We also play with the Turtles. I have Donatello and Michelangelo. And then I have Rockstead. He is so stupid that he always loses. And Michelangelo is the best.

(Finnish boy, six years)

The form that children's media play takes, and where this play takes place, sometimes depends, however, on parents, teachers and other adults. The gap between children's own media culture and media use at home and the media preferred by teachers is especially clear in Switzerland, where electronic media and media-related toys are in some ways taboo in many kindergartens. Children are not allowed to bring any media-related toys to the kindergarten and teachers do not like them to play media-related games; instead, teachers try to encourage children to read picture books and play games that are connected with the stories in them.

Of course, it is very difficult to separate electronic media and picture books from each other, as the most popular books are those with a lot of merchandising products and these same stories and characters are often available in both book and audiovisual form. Kinder (1991) uses the term 'supersystem' when referring to the marketing worlds that surround one particular media character; often it is impossible for consumers and analysts to say which medium (television series, film, computer game, book, toy or other commercial product) is the original as they are all so closely connected to one another and their intertextuality is so strong.

> My favourite book is *Lion King*. We have a lot of Lion Kings, three of them at least, one is the board game *Lion King*, then the television, no, video *Lion King*, then a music cassette *Lion King*, then I have a *Lion King* magazine, and then a computer game *Lion King*. And the book *Lion King*.
>
> (Finnish girl, seven years)

As they get older, children no longer play media-related role plays as often as the younger children. Instead they may have endless discussions about television, videos and games with their friends; in effect, using words instead of plastic figures in their play-acting and their symbolic media play. Television programmes and videos are talked about at school and in other places where children and young people meet. A popular television programme may even be so important in the peer group situation that children 'must' see it every time it is on television; in order to be able to take part in discussions during school breaks they need to have seen the previous night's episode. Some programmes are very important only locally, but others like *Beverly Hills 90210* or *The X-Files* may even be common topics for talk and interest internationally.

> Sometimes [we talk about the paranormal things]. It depends on who you are with. Sometimes it then turns into very deep discussions, about would it be really possible? Well, it is really like making the whole world over again. I mean that we really talk about those things.
>
> (Finnish girls, fifteen years)

Boys talk a lot about computer and console games and exchange hints about the games with one another. This is one of the few noticeable differences between genders: girls also play games but they do not talk about them with their friends as much as boys, or at least not with the same level of enthusiasm.

Children and teenagers also read books, but they do not appear to have the same social significance in the peer group as the audiovisual media. One noticeable difference is that books seem to be less important in Spain, whereas Swiss and Finnish children own many books from an early age onwards. Swiss youngsters who prefer to stay alone in their leisure time tend to read books more often. In Finland reading cannot, however, be said to be an activity for 'loners', as reading books plays an important role in different kinds of subcultures, for example for those who like horses or are interested in science fiction.

The telephone is an important device for older children and teenagers to communicate with their friends, not only to arrange dates, but as a kind of private meeting place. On the phone they can share the advantages of being in their own room in privacy, away from adult control, especially if they have a cordless phone. Girls especially can have long discussions with their friends on the phone, even if they see each one another daily at school. In Finland a considerable number of teenagers also have their own mobile phones, which they carry with them everywhere.

> Every evening I go to a public telephone cabin to call my friends with my Calling Card ... Here I'm not disturbed by my parents. They complain if I use the telephone too long, and I don't want them to listen to me when I talk to my friends about problems I have with my boyfriend.
>
> (Swiss girl, fifteen years)

Electronic mail and chat groups on the internet are used for the same kind of interpersonal communication. And these are the parts of computer culture that girls are as interested in as the boys; in fact in Finland teenage girls use both e-mail and chat rooms more than boys.

> It is so easy to start to talk to people. When I've sometimes tried to talk with a guy something more deeply, then, well, it's quite difficult when you are face to face with each other. But in IRC (Internet Relay Chat) it is really easy.
>
> (Finnish girl, fifteen years)

Media, subcultures and identity

When children start to have more independence from their parents and family, they often want to stress belonging to a certain peer group or youth subculture. They want to dress and behave like their friends and their style is quite often taken from some idol or popular culture product (see also Baacke 1993; Vogelgesang 1997). Through their appearance young people want to make it clear to others to which group they belong.

Youth culture is becoming more and more related to consumerism, due to the youth marketing strategies of an increasing number of companies. Idols, pop groups, sports article brands and merchandising products for films and serials are produced in order to tie young people to certain shopping habits and brands. In this context, media products (like games, CD-ROMs, music tapes and CDs, magazines, videos) can be the centre of exchange networks. It is usually very important for children to be members of such networks as they are the easiest and cheapest way to gain access to new media. In the case of games, the exchange can also be of non-material nature as knowledge about games, hints, passwords, etc. are shared with friends (and often only with friends).

> We swap video games. We buy some and we swap others.
>
> (Spanish girls, twelve years)

We copy the computer games we use. We don't buy or rent them … They are very easy to copy.

(Spanish boys, fifteen years)

Young teenagers are quite often fans of something or someone, whether it be a music group, film star or a sports hero, and their condition of being a fan is usually shared with friends and peers. Nevertheless, in respect of youth idols, a gender difference appears following a more or less traditional stereotype, with girls mostly admiring good-looking male or female pop or film stars, and boys mostly being the fans of sporting heroes:

When I am older I want to be like the Spice Girls.

(Spanish girl, ten years)

My idols are the football stars Stephan Chapuisat and Lars Ricken. I have posters from both of them and from their football teams in my room. And I have their football strips too. I wear them sometimes, when I go playing football with friends. I watch *Bravo Sport* [television channel] because usually there is something new about my idols.

(Swiss boy, thirteen years)

Even when subcultural groups are not necessarily based on media products or media consumption (as in the case of some sports), this can direct the media choices of those belonging to a group, for it is seen as important to use the same media and know the same media content as the other members of the group, and of course the media chosen often has to do with the original theme of interest. Youth cultures can, however, also be born around media. This is the case in more or less loose groupings of people that are interested in using the same kind of media. Ravers are interested in techno music; science fiction fans or computer 'nerds' can be found everywhere. These special fields of interest are not usually bound to one type of media only, but young people seek first and foremost a specific media content and use all the media where they can find material on this theme, whether it be television, books, magazines, movies, computer games or the internet. In some cases the preferred media content can be so specific that there is no one else in the near environment that is interested in the same theme (for example in the case of a boy from a small town being interested in the Japanese *Manga*), so the reference group can also be a virtual one and the 'peers' found worldwide from discussion groups on the internet.

As in the case of any hobby, these media-related interests can play a different role in the lives of young people: for one person it may be the most important thing in the world but for someone else it is just one hobby among others. Usually this has to do with age; for older teenagers the bond with, for example, a certain music style or subculture is no longer exclusive, as it was earlier in their lives when fan cultures were more important and had strict frontiers. Someone who likes techno music does not necessarily identify only with 'ravers' but can have other hobbies, too. And a computer 'nerd' may also be interested in sports.

> I'm a Homeboy. I wear these extra large clothes ... And I'm a Raver, because I like the techno music. And I'm a sportsman. I don't have any idol. I'm not home often, mainly I'm out with my friend.
>
> (Swiss boy, fifteen years)

Older teenagers are still searching for their identity but they are more sceptical towards mass movements and commercial trends. Now a 'patchwork-identity' and more individualized tastes lead to combinations of different styles that depend on different moods or occasions. Television programmes or public relations events aimed especially at this age group often have little effect. The youngsters use popular culture as a source from which they can obtain symbols and combine them to create new forms.

> My idol is a singer, Claudia Jung ... actually, I'm not the age any more to have an idol ... but I just like her songs. She sings ballads, love songs ... I don't have posters of her in my room. I just like the way she sings.
>
> (Swiss girl, fifteen years)

> I like to watch the television serial 'Passionate Doctor' (*Ärztin aus Leidenschaft*), if possible every day. In between I like to watch violent films, but they don't have to be all too violent. Otherwise I don't watch them. And if I feel sad, I watch love stories. If I have troubles with my father for example, then I usually watch love stories, then I feel better again.
>
> (Swiss girl, fifteen years)

In interviews young Swiss people said that they completely rejected the media if it was supposed to reflect what they considered to be the 'real' youth culture. Finnish teenagers stressed in the interviews that young people choose their styles and patterns of media use according to their own interest, not according to what is 'supposed to be done' in any specific subculture.

DISCUSSION

The use of media technology does not appear to cause problems in youngsters' relationships with their friends. The use of media does not substitute for communication and interaction with real people in any of the age groups studied. Media use is integrated in social settings with friends in a variety of different ways.

Children and teenagers use media in the company of friends. Media usage is just one part of everyday life and interaction with other people takes place during it. Television viewing mainly takes place in family situations, whereas console or computer games are often played with friends as well. It was found that younger children frequently join in with the play activities (console and computer games) of older brothers and sisters and their friends; this is in fact a very effective way of learning computer skills. Media is also used together with peers outside the home: in friends' houses, schools, libraries and in open public places like games arcades.

Media also provide themes of conversation for youngsters. For the youngest children media content is an important source of role plays with their peers. Media-related toys are part of children's cultural environment. When children grow older, media-related play is substituted by discussions about media content. Even though children and teenagers tend not to watch television in the company of their friends, they very often comment upon and speak to one another about the television programmes and films they have seen. Among teenagers, music is widely discussed, as are console and computer games – both the electronic device itself and the different games.

Media use and media content can be used in strengthening peer relationships and a sense of group identity. The cost of media products and the limited financial resources of many youngsters create the need to swap tapes, CDs, videos and games with one another or to copy one another's records or games; belonging to an exchange network like this is the best way to get access to a greater variety of media products. Different subcultural groups express their group identity by similarities in media use. The identity of fan cultures is fed by films, serials, music, magazines and so on. Media can also be used as a means of expressing one's own personal identity: providing a variety of choices for more individualized tastes.

Most children are family-oriented when they are young. The older they get, the more they become peer-oriented, the more media are accessible to them and the more places are open to them. Therefore, the media which are mostly used at home become less important and media which can be used in public places, or 'mobile media', are more popular. Family-oriented youngsters use more media at home or in their bedrooms, whereas peer-oriented youngsters use more media outside their home.

During puberty, group identities become very attractive. Young teenagers want to be 'part of the gang', use the same media products and dress the same way as others; in short they imitate a style. Older teenagers become more sceptical towards mass phenomena or commercialized media offers. They use media content as a source of raw material for their personal construction of their own pattern of youth culture. For this, media provide an endless variety of lifestyles, values and speech and behaviour models. Therefore, the way in which the media are used becomes more important than the media content itself.

In this article we tried to look both for similarities and differences between cultures. Our data suggest that there are certain features that might be seen to support a general 'developmental' pattern, yet there are findings that show there to be important cultural differences that cannot be ignored. As this is a report from a project still in progress, the results should be seen as preliminary findings and provide guidelines for further analysis.

We suggest that there are differences both in individual as well as cultural timing. For example, belonging to groups and fan cultures seems to be of special importance for twelve to thirteen year olds in Switzerland, while in Finland this pertains more to the culture of nine to ten year olds and in Spain to fifteen to sixteen year olds. These differences in cultural timing might be seen to be connected with the level of independence of children and the role of the family in their lives. This kind of very strong commitment to a certain youth group belongs to the stage when children are gaining more independence from their parents and are moving towards youth cultures and building up an individual identity. The earlier step towards individual identity and individual media tastes in Finland could be explained by the amount of freedom that even young children have. Children are seen as independent and they organize their leisure time from an early age without adult supervision. In Spain and in Switzerland a less liberal and more protective style of parenting is widespread. Furthermore, boundaries within families are still narrow in Spain and the separation from parents and identification with the peer culture starts later than in the other two countries studied.

From a very early age, there seem to be gender differences in media use. Girls and boys prefer different media or different media genres and they have different media-related conversations. Both boys and girls spend their time watching television or playing computer games or console games, but boys and girls prefer different television programmes and games, and in general, boys play more computer games, are more interested in computers and talk more about them than girls do. The differences in adults' gender relations in the three countries are mirrored in the way in which girls and boys relate to media and integrate media content into their activities with friends. This is especially obvious in the use of new electronic media, where we found the broadest gender difference in Switzerland and the smallest gender difference in Finland.

NOTES

1   This is a slightly edited version of an article originally published in the *European Journal of Communication, Special Issue: Young People and the Changing Media Environment in Europe*, volume 13 (4) 1998: 521–538 under the title 'Media use and the relationships of children and teenagers with their peer groups: A Study of Finnish, Spanish and Swiss Cases'. Copyright Sage Publications 1998. Reprinted by permission.
2   The Finnish study was conducted by the Research Unit for Contemporary Culture at the University of Jyväskylä and the Department of Communication at the University of Tampere. The study was funded by the Academy of Finland, The National Children's Fund for Research and Development (ITLA) and the Finnish Public Broadcasting Company (YLE).

The Spanish research team was supported by a Basque Country University grant (UPV–EHU) in 1997 and 1998.
Research groups at the IPMZ–Institute of Communication at the University of Zurich, at the Secondary Teacher Training Department SLA of the University of Berne and at the Institute of Communication ISSCOM at the University of Lugano worked with Daniel Süss on the Swiss study. Special thanks to Research Assistant Giordano Giordani and to the TA–Media AG Zurich, Euro-Beratung Zurich and Intermundo Berne, for contributions to the funding.

REFERENCES

Baacke, D. (1993) *Jugend und Jugendkulturen. Darstellung und Deutung.* Weinheim: Juventa.

Erikson, E. H. (1977) *Identität und Lebenszyklus.* Frankfurt am Main: Rowohlt.

Frones, I. (1989) *On the Meaning of Peers.* University of Oslo, Department of Sociology, Working Paper 1.

Keupp, H. (1988) *Riskante Chancen. Das Subjekt zwischen Psychokultur und Selbstorgani-sation. Sozialpsychologische Studien.* Heidelberg: Roland Assanger.

Kinder, M. (1991) *Playing with Power in Movies, Television and Video Games*, Berkeley: University of California Press.

Livingstone, S. and Bovill, M. F. (eds) (2001) *Children and their Changing Media Environment: A European Comparative Study*, Mahwah, New Jersey: Lawrence Erlbaum.

Lull, J. (1980) 'The social uses of television', *Human Communication Research* 6: 197–209.

Lull, J. (1990) *Inside Family Viewing. Ethnographic Research on Television's Audiences*, London: Routledge.

Morley, D. and Silverstone, R. (1992) 'Domestic communication: technologies and meanings', in Morley, D. (ed.) *Television, Audiences and Cultural Studies*, London: Routledge.

Rönnberg, M. (1987) *En lek för ögat*, Uppsala: Filmförlaget.

Vogelgesang, W. (1997) 'Jugendliches Medienhandeln: Szenen, Stile, Kompetenzen', *Televizion* 10(1): 27–39.

Ziehe, T. (1992) 'Cultural modernity and individualization. Changed symbolic contexts for young people', in Fornäs, J. and Bolin, G. (eds) *Moves in Modernity.* Stockholm: Enqvist & Wiksell International.

Ziehe, T. (1995) 'Good enough strangeness in education', in Aittola, T., Koikkalainen, R. and Sironen, E. (eds) *Confronting strangeness. Towards a Reflexive Modernization of the School.* Jyväskylä University, Department of Education, publication No. 5.

3 Video games

Between parents and children

Ferran Casas

VIDEO GAME CULTURE

Video games were the first computer technology to be truly accessible by the masses. They have since taken on great significance in the broader entertainment industry. However, it has been underlined that what was really important about their emergence was that, as a result of combining television and computer technologies, it was possible for the first time to control what was happening on the screen. Video games are among the major precursors of the age of interactive multimedia (Levis 1997).

In 1992, video games and video consoles comprised around ten per cent of the overall worldwide audio-visual market. The two largest Japanese video console producers were on the list of the top ten audio-visual companies in the world. Video games became a new culture in a very short period of time – albeit that they indeed adapt many elements from the cinema and from the arcades tradition (Levis 1997). Playing video games, both with video consoles and with computers, has become a mass phenomenon among children during the last two decades. Indeed, video consoles are often considered to be only children's affairs – or even more specifically boys' affairs (although there is evidence of a growing interest among young girls). But the research community responded slowly to the emergence of the video games phenomenon, and for the most part the research that appeared was mainly focused on the hypothetically negative influences of video games on children. Given that video games have become a kids' culture, it is important to ask: how do adults understand that culture? How do children themselves understand it? Are there similarities and differences in the conceptions that adults and children have of the activity of video-gaming?

This chapter presents findings from quantitative research into video gaming that emerged from such questions about aspects of the new video game culture. The following specific issues are addressed:

- How do children's and parents' ideas about video games differ?
- Do parents of children who are enthusiastic about video games ever really discuss the subject with their children?

- What kind of personal communication do adults establish with children about video game-playing?
- Are parents really well-informed about video games?
- What kind of 'mediation role' might video games play in the communication among children and adults?

By means of a quantitative survey of uses and attitudes of video games and gamers, we sought to test the hypothesis that the different attitudes of parents and other adults towards video games and other technological equipment may have consequences for their communication and relationship with children, and for children's satisfaction with their communication with adults.

PRELIMINARY OBSERVATIONS

The research was carried out with a sample of children and parents from five different schools in Barcelona. The schools were middle class (both higher and lower), from different areas in the city. A questionnaire was designed to enable us to ask the same questions to children and to their parents separately. We chose children from sixth, seventh and eighth grades of the Spanish elementary school system; that is, children aged from eleven to sixteen years, which we considered very interesting from the point of view of the communication between parents and children. Students from only one classroom from each school were selected as our sample. The questionnaire to parents was very specific, asking questions only in relation to the actual child to whom we had administered the questionnaire at school. We got answers from almost 60 per cent of parents. A total of 183 pairs of valid questionnaires were obtained, and their results are presented below.

The sample contained slightly more boys than girls (52.5 per cent, 47.5 per cent). It was up to the parents which of them answered the questionnaire; the father did so in 28.4 per cent of the cases, the mother in 48.6 per cent and the two of them together for the remainder. No significant difference was found between the gender or the age of the child and which of the parents chose to answer the parents' questionnaire (see Table 3.1).

PARENTS' RESPONSES

In the questionnaire we explored the personal and practical knowledge that parents in our sample had of video games, with the following results:

- 35.2 per cent of parents had absolutely never tried to play;
- 36.3 per cent had 'just tested' on some occasion;
- 24.7 per cent played seldom;
- 2.7 per cent played often;
- 1.1 per cent played very often.

Table 3.1 Adult respondent to parental questionnaire, by gender of child respondent

			Gender		Total
			Boy	Girl	
Respondent completing parental questionnaire	Father only	N	29	23	52
		% of total	15.8%	12.6%	28.4%
		Standard residuals	0.3	−0.3	—
	Mother only	N	45	44	89
		% of total	24.6%	24.0%	48.6%
		Standard residuals	−0.2	0.3	—
	Father and Mother together	N	22	20	42
		% of total	12.0%	10.9%	23.0%
		Standard residuals	0.0	0.0	—
Total		N	96	87	183
		% of total	52.5%	47.5%	100.0%

Those that never tried to play are more often mothers than fathers (22 per cent of the total sample versus 5.5 per cent), but there is a slightly different picture among those who say they play often or very often, where mothers accounted for a greater percentage than fathers (2.2 per cent versus 1.6 per cent – although in our sample, that means only four mothers and three fathers).

According to these results we should expect that a high percentage of parents never play video games with their children. The answers to our second question (Do you ever play video games with your child?) revealed that over 60 per cent of parents (more often mothers than fathers; $p = 0.001$) never play any video games with their child; while just over one third play seldom and 6 per cent 'often' (see Table 3.2). Age and gender of the child had little effect on their parents' answers.

Table 3.2 Parents' reported frequency of playing video games with their child

			Respondent			Total
			Father	Mother	Both parents together	
Parents' reported frequency of playing video games with their child	Never	N	21	65	24	110
		% of total	11.5%	35.7%	13.2%	60.4%
		Standard residuals	−1.9	1.6	−0.3	—
	Seldom	N	24	21	16	61
		% of total	13.2%	11.5%	8.8%	33.5%
		Standard residuals	1.6	−1.6	0.5	—
	Often	N	8	2	2	11
		% of total	3.8%	1.1%	1.1%	6.0%
		Standard residuals	2.2	−1.4	−0.3%	—
Total		N	52	88	42	182
		% of total	28.6%	48.4%	23.1%	100.0%

More than half the parents in our sample say that they never chat with their child about the video games he or she is playing (35.8 per cent speak 'seldom' and 10.2 per cent 'often'). There is no significant difference discernable by the gender of the respondent, except that the answer 'often' is more frequent among fathers. However, when the answer is 'often' there is a clear tendency to refer to boys more than to girls. There is a clear tendency among the parents that never played video games also never to chat with their child about such games (altogether 27.3 per cent of the parents). Only twelve parents (6.9 per cent) that never played said that they talked now and then or often about video games with their children (as shown in Table 3.3). Almost half of parents in our sample (44.3 per cent) neither play nor chat with their child about the video games he or she plays. More surprising, perhaps, two fathers mentioned 'often' playing with their child (one boy and one girl), but at the same time claimed never to talk with him or her about video games.

There is an important difference between those parents that never play at all – a total of sixty-four, those that never play with their child – one hundred and ten and those that never chat with him or her – ninety-six. There are at least forty-six parents in our sample that do have some experience of playing video games, but never play with their child. Only five parents have the opinion that their child (four boys and one girl, aged thirteen years or over) plays video games too much; while 22.7 per cent consider the child plays too much 'only sometimes' (more frequently boys than girls, and aged fourteen to sixteen years), and 74.6 per cent felt that their child is not playing too much.

Table 3.3 Relationship between parent–child video game playing and parent–child video game talk, as reported by parents

			Parental report of talking with their child about the video-games he/she plays			
			Never	Seldom	Often	Total
Parental report of frequency of playing video games with their child	Never	N	48	11	1	60
		% of total	27.3%	6.3%	0.6%	34.1%
		Standard residuals	2.7	–2.3	–2.1	—
	Only tried	N	29	29	7	65
		% of total	16.5%	16.5%	4.0%	36.9%
		Standard residuals	–1.0	1.2	0.1	—
	Seldom	N	15	23	7	45
		% of total	8.5%	13.1%	4.0%	25.6%
		Standard residuals	–1.9	1.7	1.1	
	Often	N	3	0	3	6
		% of total	1.7%	0%	1.7%	3.4%
		Standard residuals	–0.1	–1.5	3.0	—
Total		N	95	63	18	176
		% of total	54.0%	35.8%	10.2%	100.0%

Summarizing the results from this part of our survey:

- 30.1 per cent of parents play and chat about video games with their child;
- 15.9 per cent do not play, but do chat;
- 9.6 per cent play, but do not chat;
- 44.3 per cent neither play nor chat.

The question 'Do you help your child to exercise self-control when playing too much?' received some intriguing answers. Parents of eleven and twelve years olds more frequently answer 'yes'; those of thirteen year olds more frequently 'no'; and of older children more frequently 'I try' (p = 0.009). A fifth agree that they use video games as a reward for good behaviour on the part of the child: more frequently for boys than for girls (p = 0.024). Some parents also attempt to regulate video game playing, placing conditions on the child's access (17 per cent answered 'sometimes' and 9.9 per cent 'often'), again more frequently with boys than girls (p = 0.011), with no age difference. Consequentially, 73.1 per cent of parents do not consider that they regulate the conditions of playing.

Almost half of the parents tended not to offer alternative activities to video games (44.8 per cent), while 28.5 per cent do offer an alternative regularly, and the rest offer alternatives on occasion. Alternatives are offered more frequently to boys than to girls, and more frequently by fathers than mothers, but the differences here are not statistically significant.

Finally, parents were asked some Likert-scale questions (scale from 1: strongly disagree, to 5: strongly agree) concerning their attributions to the child of emotion, preference, self-control, fantasy-related thoughts, and social relationships around video game playing; we also explored parents' opinions about the utility of video games for the child. Parents do not attribute strong emotions to their child in relation to playing video games. They attribute moderate enjoyment (mean = 3.55; s.d. = 1.28); yet boys are thought to enjoy such activities significantly more than girls (p = 0.002). Parents tend not to agree that their child is over-insistent about playing (mean = 1.7); often becomes angry when they cannot play (mean = 1.65); is more aggressive after playing video games (mean = 1.6); or tries to forget problems by playing (mean = 1.83). No significant difference is observed about parents' attributions of such emotions between boys and girls. When we compare answers given by fathers to those of mothers, we find the following differences: mothers seem slightly more likely than fathers to attribute aggressive behaviour to their children after playing some video games (non-significant); and are more likely to feel the child is playing to forget problems (p = 0.018).

Parents tend to assert that their child exhibits good self-control while playing video games. They do not think the child plays too much (mean = 1.66) or is sometimes unable to stop playing (mean = 1.73), or that game playing gets in the way of school homework (mean = 1.69). However, they do not express a very clear opinion on whether the child minds very much whether they lose or win (mean = 3.18). Boys are thought significantly more frequently than girls to play video games too often and to be sometimes unable to stop playing. Once again, if we compare answers given by fathers with those by mothers, we find an interesting difference: mothers more often feel that their children play video games too often and that sometimes they do not complete school homework because of video games (p = 0.002).

Boys are believed by their parents to have more fantasy-related thoughts than girls when playing video games, even if such thoughts are always perceived to be of low intensity. Parents disagree that the child treats the video console like a friend (mean = 1.75); tries to imitate characters (mean = 1.42); talks to the video console when playing (mean = 2.03); or would like to be like a video game hero (mean = 1.7). Of these, only the first showed no significant difference between the sexes; otherwise boys seemed the more susceptible. Mothers more often than fathers say that the child talks to the video console (p = 0.003) or would like to be like a video game hero (p = 0.003).

We also explored parents' thoughts on the child's preferences in relation to video games. Most parents think that if the child had something better to do, he/she would stop playing video games (mean = 3.67); and this significantly more often for girls than for boys (p = 0.038). Parents slightly disagree with the following two statements: 'My child likes video games better than most other games' mean = 2.33); 'My child prefers video games to watching TV' (mean = 2.25). And they more emphatically disagree with the statement 'My child prefers video games that are aggressive' (mean = 1.81). On each of these questions, disagreement is significantly more emphatic if the child is a girl, with no significant difference between father and mother; although the third question almost reaches significance (p = 0.053), fathers disagreeing more emphatically than mothers.

Next, we explored parents' attributions in relation to the child's social relationships. Parents in general only slightly disagree with the proposals that the child plays video games either because he/she can play alone (mean = 2.55) or is able to chat about video games with peers (mean = 2.45). They more clearly disagree that he/she plays to be able to play with other children (mean = 1.88), and energetically disagree about the fact that he/she meets peers less frequently because of video game-playing (mean = 1.32). Significantly fewer girls than boys are thought to play in order to be able to chat with peers.

We asked about perceptions of the utility of playing video games for the child. In general parents slightly agree that such activity is time wasting (mean = 3.3). They slightly disagree that video games develop the child's reflexes (mean = 2.67) and more clearly disagree that video games are useful for learning (mean = 1.99) or that they teach children to compete (mean = 1.83). No significant difference is observed between boys or girls, but in all cases there are significant differences depending on whether the father or the mother answers. Mothers disagree more emphatically than fathers about the notion that video games are useful for learning (p = 0.012) and develop reflexes (p = 0.019), and agree more emphatically with the statement 'playing video games is time wasting' (p = 0.002). On the other hand, fathers disagree more clearly than mothers do about the idea that video games teach children to compete (p > 0.41).

Whether playing video games is time wasting or not seems to dramatically divide parents: in fact, almost one third totally agree with the statement, twice the number of those who totally disagree. The more extreme cases are mainly those parents who never play video games with their child. In a very similar way, just over one-third of parents totally disagree that playing video games may stimulate reflexes (significantly more mothers than fathers), while slightly less than half this number totally agree with this statement and a handful more slightly agree. Curiously, perhaps, most of those in total disagreement say they never play video games with their child (almost one-quarter of the total sample).

CHILDREN'S RESPONSES

On average, children in our sample say they play video games less than two days a week (mean, s.d = 1.96), and a little more than one hour a day (mean, s.d. = 1.13) (see Tables 3.4 and 3.5). In contrast they watch television six and a half days and three and a half hours a day on average (s.d. 1.16 and 2.03 respectively). The only children claiming to watch television three days a week or less are girls (N = 7). Girls in general watch TV significantly fewer days a week than do boys (p = 0.003), but there is little observable difference in how many days a week they play video games, nor in the number of hours a day they watch TV (p = 0.423). However, girls say they play video games significantly fewer hours per day than boys (p = 0.003). These results suggest that, while the distribution of time spent in front of screens differs according to gender, the overall time used may not be significantly different. There is no significant difference between age groups in the number of hours watching TV every day, except among children watching TV six hours a day or more – most likely in the eleven to twelve age group, and less so in the over fourteens. Only eleven children from all age groups (eight boys and three girls) claim to both play video games and watch TV for six or seven days a week (see Table 3.5). And only two children (one boy of thirteen and one girl of twelve) claimed to both play video games more than four hours a day and watch TV more than six hours a day (see Table 3.4).

One interesting finding is that the twelve children who watch TV and play video games every day tend to believe that their performance at school is 'good': only three of the boys do not think this (one saying he has a 'medium' and two a 'bad' performance). The boy and girl who claim to spend most hours in front of the screen both rated their school performance as 'medium'.

The perception children have of how much of their leisure time they invest playing video games is usually not high. Almost one third (30.3 per cent) say the time they invest is 'nothing' in proportion to their overall leisure time

Table 3.4 Relationship between gender and time spent per day playing video games, as reported by children

			Gender of respondent		
			Boy	Girl	Total
Children's reports of the number of hours they spend per day playing video games	One or less	N	69	78	147
		% of total	38.3%	43.3%	81.7%
		Standard residuals	−1.0	1.0	—
	2 or 3	N	22	5	27
		% of total	12.2%	2.8%	15.0%
		Standard residuals	2.1	−2.2	—
	4 or more	N	4	2	6
		% of total	2.2%	1.1%	3.3%
		Standard residuals	0.5	−0.5	—
Total		N	95	85	180
		% of total	52.8%	47.2%	100.0%

Table 3.5 Relationship between children's reports of the number of days per week they play video games and age of the child

			Respondent's age			
			11 and 12 years	13 years	14 to 16 years	Total
Number days a week that the respondent plays video games	3 or less	N	59	47	47	153
		% of total	32.8%	26.1%	26.1%	85.0%
		Standard residuals	0.7	0.3	−1.0	—
	4 or 5	N	1	2	10	13
		% of total	0.6%	1.1%	5.6%	7.2%
		Standard residuals	−1.7	−0.9	2.5	—
	6 or 7	N	3	4	7	14
		% of total	1.7%	2.2%	3.9%	7.8%
		Standard residuals	−0.9	−0.1	0.9	—
Total		N	63	53	64	180
		% of total	35.0%	29.4%	35.6%	100.0%

available; while 55.1 per cent consider they invest less than half of their leisure time; and 14.6 per cent half or more. No relation is observed between that perception and self-attributed performance at school.

Almost one-quarter of the children said they usually do not play video games alone but rather with friends, at friends' homes and in other places. One-third say they play video games for two players 'often'; while just under half answer 'seldom' and the rest 'never'. In contrast, almost half of the sample never play with friends (41 per cent). Three-quarters say they play alone at home on occasion; however, only twelve children (6.5 per cent of our sample, nine boys and three girls) say they play video games alone in arcades, and eighteen children (9.8 per cent, nine of each) in other places. Those aged fourteen to sixteen are slightly more likely to play with friends at home ($p < 0.103$) or in arcades ($p = 0.005$; more frequently boys: $p < 0.003$).

The mediating role of video games in the relationships between children and parents was also explored through the fact of playing together or chatting about them. Only 8.8 per cent of children in our sample say they play 'often' with their father or mother, and 17.8 per cent speak 'often' or 'very often' with either of them about video games they play. Almost a third (30.9 per cent) say they play 'seldom' but almost twice this (60.2 per cent) 'never' with parents; while very similar percentages chat with them 'seldom' and 'never'.

Turning to the Likert-scale questions, we found distinctively different perceptions and evaluations about video games between boys and girls. Though both groups report largely moderate emotions in relation to playing video games, boys' reported emotions are stronger than girls' in all cases, with four being significantly higher: getting anxious or nervous when anticipating playing ($p = 0.017$); getting angry when told to stop playing ($p = 0.001$); enjoying playing very much ($p < 0.000$); and feeling aggressive after playing certain video games ($p = 0.001$). In fact, more than 1 per cent of children in our sample (seventeen boys and three girls) report feeling clearly aggressive after playing some games.

Answers relating to self-control indicated that most children feel they have the capacity to put limits on their video game-playing. Most children disagreed with the statements 'Sometimes I am unable to stop playing' and 'Sometimes I don't do my school homework because of video games'. Nevertheless, two items present significant differences between boys and girls: boys more frequently say they play too often ($p = 0.012$), and more frequently claim to save money from other things in order to be able to buy video games ($p = 0.039$). Girls more often report not minding whether they win or lose ($p = 0.036$). Boys also answered the four items concerning fantasy-related thoughts with more intensity than girls, although opinions were very moderate. Significant gender differences appear in three items: thinking of the video console as a friend ($p = 0.057$); trying to imitate characters ($p = 0.012$); and wanting to be like a video game hero ($p < 0.000$). Speaking to the video console or to the computer while playing does not reveal any gender-related difference.

When children in our sample evaluate their preferences, again boys express themselves in slightly stronger ways than girls. They are more likely to prefer video games to other games ($p = 0.001$), and more likely to enjoy video games to watching TV ($p = 0.001$) and video games involving fighting and war. However, only 16.6 per cent of the whole sample claim to prefer video games to TV. Boys and girls agree that some video games are boring, and that they would leave the video game should some alternative come along.

Video games seem to have a more influential role in boys' social relationships than in girls'. On the one hand, boys more often choose video games in order to play alone, to the extent that they have a moderate feeling of being less in touch with friends because of video games. On the other hand, boys more than girls also choose video games more often to play or to chat about them with peers.

Both boys and girls report relatively low evaluations of the utility of video games. They are not considered very useful as learning tools (mean = 2.14. s.d. = 1.30), nor in terms of their help with the development of reflexes (mean = 2.70. s.d. = 1.50). However some aspects do differ between boys and girls: girls more frequently agree that playing video games is time wasting (p = 0.001), while boys more frequently agree that video games help them learn to compete (p = 0.034).

The relation between the idea 'playing video games is time wasting' and the evaluation 'video games are useful for learning' exhibits some ambivalence, in that these do not appear to be taken as opposing statements. For instance, almost half the children in our sample do not agree that playing video games is time wasting, but only one-eighth at the same time agree they are useful for learning. The opposite also happens: almost one-quarter think video games playing is time wasting, but only one-sixth at the same time believe they are not useful for learning (see Table 3.6).

Table 3.6 Relationship between children's views of video game playing as useful and/or time wasting

			Children's level of agreement with statement: 'Video games are useful for learning' 1 (total disagreement) to 5 (total agreement)					
			1	2	3	4	5	Total
Children's level of agreement with statement: 'Playing video games wastes time' 1 (strongly agree to) 5 (strongly disagree)	1	N	16	3	15	7	9	50
		% of total	9.0%	1.7%	8.4%	3.9%	5.1%	28.1%
		Standard residuals	−1.7	−0.9	0.6	1.5	2.8	—
	2	N	17	4	11	5	1	38
		% of total	9.6%	2.2%	6.2%	2.8%	0.6%	21.3%
		Standard residuals	−0.4	0.1	0.4	1.2	−1.1	—
	3	N	31	4	12	1	1	49
		% of total	17.4%	2.2%	6.7%	0.6%	0.6%	27.5%
		Standard residuals	1.4	−0.4	−0.2	−1.5	−1.4	—
	4	N	8	5	5	0	2	20
		% of total	4.5%	2.8%	2.8%	0.0%	1.1%	11.2%
		Standard residuals	−0.6	2.1	−0.1	−1.3	0.4	—
	5	N	15	2	3	1	0	21
		% of total	8.4%	1.1%	1.7%	0.6%	0.0%	11.8%
		Standard residuals	1.5	−0.1	−1.0	−0.5	−1.2	—
Total		N	87	18	46	14	13	178
		% of total	48.9%	10.1%	25.8%	7.9%	7.3%	100.0%

Finally, we asked children's opinions of a few other questions. Boys and girls equally agreed that video games are expensive (mean = 4.40. s.d. = 1.10); that there are too many of them on the market (mean = 3.90. s.d. = 1.35), and that they are not just 'games for boys' (more than twice the number of children disagreed than agreed). One last opinion showed significant differences: boys consider themselves much more well-informed about video games than do girls (p = 0.001), with twice the number (11 per cent boys; 5.5 per cent girls) believing themselves 'extremely' well-informed about video games.

INITIAL COMPARISON OF RESPONSES

We can offer the following summary comparisons between the answers of parents and children.

- Children in general only slightly disagree that they like video games best when there is fighting or war, while parents emphatically disagree that their child likes this kind of game best.
- Parents in general slightly agree that playing video games is time wasting, although there are important differences in the opinion among them. On the whole, children slightly disagree with this statement.
- Children in general only slightly disagree that they play video games to forget problems. Parents emphatically disagree that this is a reason for their child to play.
- The opinion that there are too many video games on the market is expressed much more strongly by parents than by children with a similar view.

A second level of comparison can be developed by contrasting the pairs of answered questionnaires (that is, each parent with his/her child). At this level some additional differences can be observed. For example, the emotions reported by children and those attributed to each child by his/her parents when playing video games are very similar, with only one significant exception: playing video games is used to 'forget problems' much more frequently according to children than their parents believe. Children's self-control when playing video games is apparently reported in similar ways by parents and children if we observe the overall results. However, as soon as we analyse the answers of each parent/child couple, three significant differences appear, all of them showing that parents perceive more self-control than his/her child attributes to him/herself. Parents are more likely than their children to state that the child does not mind whether they win or lose (p = 0.016), that he/she is easily able to stop playing (p = 0.036) and that the school homework gets done (p = 0.025).

In relation to preferences, we found some similar and some different positions when comparing parents and their children. Parents usually agree that their child would leave the video game should they have something better to do and that some video games are very boring for the child, and children respond similarly. Most parents disagree that their child prefers playing video games to watching TV, and most children also disagree. But children are much more likely to say that they like video games better than other games and that they prefer games best when there is fighting and war than their parents seem to believe.

We finally compared general opinions about video games. There is no difference between parents and their children over the opinion that video games are expensive, and both equally disagree that the child possesses a lot of information about video games. However, parents are more likely to think that there are too many video games on the market ($p = 0.002$) and children are less likely to think that video games are more for boys than for girls ($p = 0.024$).

VIDEO GAMES IN THE SPACE BETWEEN PARENTS AND CHILDREN

In this research we have been dealing with data from two groups of people: parents and children. Although each child in our sample was the son or daughter of a father or mother who answered a questionnaire, results make it evident that, in relation to video games, we have two clearly differentiated groups:

- One group is composed mainly of children who have a positive attitude towards video games, mostly moderate but sometimes enthusiastic. Only 2.7 per cent of the children in our sample (two boys and three girls) said they do not like video games at all.
- The other group is composed mainly of adults, with extremely diverse attitudes towards video games, going from a kind of fundamentalist denial of any possible positive characteristics – even when recognizing they have never personally tested a video game – to those who play games often with their children, or who play with their children while apparently never speaking about such activity.

Surprisingly, many perceptions, attributions and opinions related to video games are rather similar in the two groups, and are usually very moderate. That gives us the impression to us that respondents are trying to present video games as something not very important, not to be worried about or taken too seriously. In each group we find people wanting to stress that they and/or their children are not too obsessed with video games.

Nonetheless, other perceptions, attributions and opinions related to video games are clearly dissimilar if we compare the two groups. One basic point appears to be the perception of how frequently or regularly one plays. We explored the comparison in several ways and all of them show different ways of understanding this idea by parents and by children. One of the most surprising cross-tabulations we derived can be seen in Table 3.7, where we compare the answers of children to the question 'How many days a week do you play video games?' with those of parents to the question 'Does your child play video games?' Over one-quarter of the children in our sample say they play less than one day of a week (26.8 per cent; more frequently girls than boys). Yet only four children in this group (2.2 per cent of the sample) say they do not like playing; stranger, no child in this group belongs to the group whose parents say they never play. We can only assume that their answer means they do not play regularly.

By contrast, all the children whose parents say they never play, themselves claim to play between two and seven days per week. Perhaps some are hiding the activity from their parents; more likely, they only play when at friends' houses or in arcades. In the latter case, of course, the child may seek to ensure that parents do not know anything about this activity. One possible conclusion is that absolutely all children in our sample seem to play, although some seek to bias or minimize the frequency in different ways.

Perception of playing or chatting with parents about video games is not always identical if we compare parents and children. Most children and parents give identical answers when separately asked whether they play video games with each other (72.8 per cent) or chat about them (59.7 per cent). Almost half (49.4 per cent) of parents and children agree they never play together, and 40.2 per cent agree they never chat about video games. However, 5 per cent of parents say they play 'often', and 6.9 per cent that they chat 'often', while the child perceives such interaction as occurring 'seldom' or 'never'.

It is perhaps unsurprising to observe that children who do not play regularly are more likely than those playing one to seven days a week to agree that 'Playing video games is time wasting', or to disagree that they 'like video games best when there is fighting and war' ($F = 3.469$; $p = 0.003$) and that they play video games to forget their problems ($F = 2.214$; $p = 0.44$). However, by contrast, parents of these children are less likely to agree with the first statement and more likely to agree with the latter two (see Table 3.8).

Girls and boys are not very dissimilar in their experiences with video games, although they have some different attitudes in regard to playing them. Girls are more likely to say that they do not like video games much, but are no more likely to say that they do not like them at all. Girls report more moderate feelings about video game-playing and seem not to be so fond as boys of chatting about their experience of playing, although they have a greater preference than boys for playing with peers. They report less fantasy-related thoughts than boys when playing, less influence of video games in their social relationships, weaker preferences related to video-game playing, less attributed utility, and tend to consider themselves less well-informed (although some girls consider themselves extremely well-informed). It is important to point out that girls in our sample are not more likely than boys to believe that video games are designed more for boys than for girls.

Table 3.7 Children's and parents' assessments of the amount of time per week the child spends playing video games

			Very Often	Often	Seldom	Never	Total
			Parental report of frequency of child playing video games				
Child's report of their own frequency of video game playing, days per week	Less than one	N	20	27	1	0	48
		% of total	11.2%	15.1%	0.6%	0.0%	26.8%
		Standard residuals	4.9	−0.9	−2.3	−1.4	—
	1	N	4	40	1	0	45
		% of total	2.2%	22.3%	0.6%	0.0%	25.1%
		Standard residuals	−1.0	1.8	−2.2	−1.3	—
	2	N	0	31	8	1	40
		% of total	0.0%	17.3%	4.5%	0.6%	22.3%
		Standard residuals	−2.4	0.8	0.9	−0.5	—
	3	N	0	13	4	2	19
		% of total	0.0%	7.3%	2.2%	1.1%	10.6%
		Standard residuals	−1.7	0.1	0.7	1.5	—
	4	N	0	2	3	2	7
		% of total	0.0%	1.1%	1.7%	1.1%	3.9%
		Standard residuals	−1.0	−1.2	2.0	3.3	—
	5	N	0	4	2	0	6
		% of total	0.0%	2.2%	1.1%	0.0%	3.4%
		Standard residuals	−0.9	0.0	1.2	−0.5	—
	7	N	2	3	7	2	14
		% of total	1.1%	1.7%	3.9%	1.1%	7.8%
		Standard residuals	0.0	−2.1	3.5	2.0	—
Total		N	26	120	26	7	179
		% of total	14.5%	67.0%	14.5%	3.9%	100.0%

CONCLUDING REFLECTIONS: FUTURE DIRECTIONS FOR THE RELATIONAL PLANET

On the basis of this admittedly exploratory research, we must be cautious in drawing conclusions. We do not know to what extent parents and children have understood the almost identical questions in the same way, and we do not know to what extent such questions were really relevant to the aspects of communication we wanted to assess. Nevertheless, many of the results we have obtained can be considered enlightening. It is clear that children's point of view is not necessarily the same as that of adults'. But that does not mean that it is better or worse, right or wrong; it is the perspective of the child, and something we would wish to take seriously. But how should we take it seriously? How take advantage of children's motivation for new technologies and communicational media to increase good relations among the people of our planet?

Table 3.8 Relationship between parents' and children's views about video games and the child's reported frequency of video game playing per week

Child's report of their own frequency of video game playing, days per week		Level of agreement with statement: 1 (strongly disagree) to 5 (strongly agree)					
		'Playing video games wastes time'		'My child/I prefer(s) violent video games'		'Playing video games helps child to forget problems'	
		Children	Parents	Children	Parents	Children	Parents
Less than one	Mean	3.2	3.0	2.0	1.5	1.9	1.4
	N	48	45	48	42	48	42
	Standard deviation	1.5	1.7	1.5	1.2	1.3	0.8
1	Mean	2.8	3.6	2.1	1.5	2.3	1.6
	N	43	44	44	42	44	42
	Standard deviation	1.1	1.2	1.4	0.9	1.3	1.1
2	Mean	2.1	3.3	2.7	1.6	2.6	1.8
	N	39	39	40	39	40	39
	Standard deviation	1.2	1.5	1.5	1.1	1.5	1.3
3	Mean	2.4	3.2	2.8	2.3	2.9	2.8
	N	18	18	19	18	19	18
	Standard deviation	1.1	1.2	1.5	1.5	1.4	1.5
4	Mean	1.0	3.1	4.0	3.3	3.4	1.9
	N	7	7	7	7	7	7
	Standard deviation	0.0	1.3	1.3	1.7	1.7	1.2
5	Mean	2.5	3.3	2.3	2.0	2.7	2.2
	N	6	6	6	6	6	6
	Standard deviation	1.5	1.6	1.8	1.7	1.6	1.5
7	Mean	2.0	3.5	3.2	2.3	2.4	2.2
	N	14	13	14	12	14	13
	Standard deviation	1.1	1.5	1.3	1.6	1.6	1.2
Total	Mean	2.6	3.3	2.5	1.8	2.4	1.8
	N	175	172	178	166	178	167
	Standard deviation	1.3	1.4	1.5	1.3	1.4	1.2

Social and technological changes have raised new questions about the direction of the changes we really want in our societies. That means that important new debates on values have appeared the last few decades in Europe, some of which are closely connected with adult–child relationships. In one of the European *Eurobarometre* surveys with representative samples of all countries of the European Union (Commission of the European Communities 1990), it appeared that adults believe that the values that must be promoted most strongly among children are those of responsibility and tolerance. Some traditionally highly-appreciated values, such as hard work, saving, religious faith or fighting spirit, were much lower in the rankings (Casas 1998, 1999). In other arenas, particularly those more politically or macro-socially oriented, it seems that at present in Europe one of the outstanding values, increasing in perceived importance is quality of life. As a value, quality of life points to a new set of goals: those combining material and non-material values, and those trying to improve both material and non-material situations in society.

Are video games related in some way to values such as responsibility, tolerance or quality of life? Should they in fact be related to such important adult values? Many adults seem to consider video games unimportant stuff. Most children seem to consider video games important in some way, but they often hesitate to make such statements in front of adults, and we hesitate about children's perspective in considering them important in some way.

From debates in the media we may think there is an increasing preoccupation among parents regarding the values transmitted by video games (sometimes against human rights and human dignity). We, the adult society, could develop social pressure to bring to the market other games showing other values; but we can also use the existing ones to engage in a critical dialogue about them with our children. Instead of that, children often feel that they cannot really speak with parents about their playing activity and the only dialogue they may have is among peers.

We have the impression that most video game-playing is a lonely activity. On the one hand it may happen in the future that through the internet, online playing among several people will become much more widespread. But, on the other hand, exactly as happens with TV, we have been so concerned with what is happening 'inside' (the contents of TV films and programmes, the contents of video games) that we forget to give importance to what is happening 'around' these activities. To whom are children explaining their often very vivid experiences? Who are they asking about their worries? Who are they sharing their perceived values with? If the answer is 'only with peers' it may happen that we adults are forgetting some of our responsibilities towards the new generations.

REFERENCES

Casas, F. (1998) *Infancia: Perspectivas psicosociales*, Barcelona: Paidós.
Casas, F. (1999) 'Children, media and the relational planet', *Child Studies* 1: 119–146.
Commission of the European Communities (1990) 'Public opinion in the European Community', *Eurobarometre* 34 (August), Brussels.
Levis, D. (1997) *Los videojuegos, un fenómeno de masas*, Barcelona: Paidós.

4 'Technophobia'

Parents' and children's fears about information and communication technologies and the transformation of culture and society[1]

Gill Valentine and Sarah Holloway

INTRODUCTION: CONTEMPORARY LUDDITES?

There is a long history of different groups being threatened by the advent of particular new technologies. Perhaps most famously, in the early nineteenth century a group of weavers from Yorkshire, known as Luddites, sabotaged machines that were being introduced as part of the large-scale mechanization brought about by the development of industrial capitalism. Their actions led to the introduction of a parliamentary bill that imposed the death penalty for the crime of breaking machines. It was not the technology *per se* which the Luddites were opposed to, but rather the changes its introduction wrought; the relocation of work from home to factory threatened the cultural stability of their craft-based communities and way of life (Bryson and de Castell 1998). The Amish community in Pennsylvania, USA, are a more contemporary example of people who shun technologies, such as the radio and the television, the telephone and electricity, all of which are regarded as a threat to their efforts to articulate and maintain a distinct community identity and practices (Zimmerman Umble 1992).

In the same way that technology transformed society in the nineteenth century, so many contemporary academic and popular commentators argue that Information and Communication Technologies (ICT) are set to wreak widespread social, cultural, economic and political change in the twenty-first century. The American computer company Microsoft claims in some of its commercial promotions that we are entering an 'information age' in which the world will never be the same again. 'Distance learning, digital libraries, electronic voting, e-mail, video conferencing, remote banking, online chat, video-on-demand, home shopping and telecommuting are among the lures for the "early adopter" of the "connected" home computer and the souped-up TV' (Brook and Boal 1995: ix). The appeal of this technological advance is that it promises to deliver greater efficiency, speed, power, control, knowledge, pleasure and the potential for economic wealth and personal development. 'Cyberutopians' (Papert 1997) imagine a future in which ICT can act as an antidote to community decline (Rheingold 1993), enable us to escape the limitations of our physical bodies (Heim 1993), promote social inclusion (Owen 1990) and enhance global communications and relationships (Wellman and Gulia 1996); while 'cybercritics' (Papert 1997) suggest that in casting new social relations ICT will not only create new opportunities but also new vulnerabilities and dangers.

Children, as symbols of the future themselves, are seen to have the most to gain or lose as we enter the information age. To this end both the UK and the US governments have placed an emphasis on the need to develop children's technological competence in order to equip them for life in a wired world. Their policy initiatives have largely centred upon providing access to hardware and software at school for all children, in order to attempt to prevent the emergence of a society of technological 'haves' and 'have nots' (Social Exclusion Unit 1998). Yet technology does not impact in set ways upon children or adults but rather emerges as a different tool for different groups of users. While ICT is being embraced by many children and adults, others are fearful of the way that these technologies may transform society and their own social relations and identities, and are apprehensive about their own abilities to develop technological skills. Indeed Marshall (1997) suggests that the prefix 'cyber' is associated with many fears about the future. For example, cybernetics, with computers surpassing or replacing the human mind; cyborgs, with the blurring of humans and machines. The anxieties of these contemporary Luddites are often expressed as technophobia or an irrational hatred of computers. As a result, while governments may aim to promote universal technological competence, many children choose not to take advantage of the opportunities that they have to use PCs.

This chapter addresses parents' and children's phobias about ICT and the transformation of culture and 'society'. It begins by exploring how the fears of parents and teachers may shape children's attitudes towards and access to ICT, and then goes on to consider the technophobia of children themselves. The chapter draws on material collected as part of a two year ESRC-funded study of children's use of ICT at school and home. The first stage of the research was based in three secondary schools.[2] Two of the schools are in a major urban area in South Yorkshire, the other in a rural coastal town in Cornwall. The two urban schools are divided in terms of their intake: whilst Highfields draws mainly on a middle-class catchment, the parents of children at Station Road are primarily working class. The Cornish school, Westport, has the socially mixed intake often found in rural schools.

Within the schools we undertook a questionnaire survey of 753 children aged eleven to sixteen, asking about their use of computers and the internet in both school and home environments. This was followed by observation work in a number of case-study classes and focus group discussions – based mainly on existing friendship groups – which covered children's experiences of IT within the school environment. Semi-structured interviews were also carried out with the IT teachers and head teachers from these schools.

On the basis of this work in schools, thirty children and their families were asked to participate in a further stage of the research. This involved separate in-depth interviews with the parent(s) and the children of the household regarding the purchase of home PCs and internet connection; use of computers and the internet by different household members, different competence levels, issues of unity and/or conflict around shared use; ownership, location and the control of the domestic PC and whether being online had affected household relations.

ADULTS' FEARS FOR CHILDREN

Fears about the future

There is an inevitability in the public imagination about the relationship between new technologies and the future of work. ICT is popularly understood to be about to lead to the transformation of work and the production of value (if it has not already done so). Most notably, in the technology saturated workforce of the future, it is widely envisaged that ICT skills will be a prerequisite for most labour markets, and that the most technologically competent will be able to convert their intellectual capital into both economic and cultural capital (Marshall 1997). Kroker and Weinstein (1994: 163) for example, suggest that computer literacy will be the key to comfortable future membership of the 'virtual class'. Computer companies have been quick to stress this connection in their advertising for adults, which often plays upon the potential future economic rewards of the internet-connected PC as an educational tool (while targeting children with advertisements that emphasize its more pleasurable possibilities as a tool of play). Not surprisingly, the parents we interviewed expressed an almost universal fear that their children might miss out on the technological skills necessary for tomorrow's labour market if they did not have a home PC.

INTERVIEWER: And why did you kind of think of buying one?
MOTHER: Basically we needed one, or Alan felt he needed one for school. Because he felt he was missing out. A lot of children had got them. He's in his GCSE year. They're getting all this information off the system and as good as anyone can be you can't hold enough books in your house to hold the same information that a child can touch a button and get off the system. So that child is at an advantage. And I felt that my child was at a disadvantage 'cos we hadn't got one. So I've had to go out and buy a second-hand cheapest model I can get hold of just so he could be one step on the ladder if you like.

(Mother, Westport)

Marshall (1997: 71) labels this fear of disconnection from the impending information economy 'technophobia of the projected future' and argues that one consequence of it is the rapid expansion of ICT into the space of the home in the late twentieth and early twenty-first centuries. He understands this phobia to be a more or less middle-class phenomenon. He writes: 'The computer's integration into the home is connected to education desires so that the family's children can maintain their class position through a vague conception of computer literacy' (Marshall 1997: 75). Yet the evidence of this research is that parents from the predominantly working-class school, Station Road, are just as fearful as the middle class parents from Highfields that their children might end up on the wrong side of a technologically polarized world. As a result some go to great lengths – borrowing money or selling possessions – to purchase a PC. Others are frustrated by their inability to provide their children with the opportunity to develop their technological competence.

MOTHER: I'd give my right arm to get him a PC, I mean like I say my husband's unemployed and we've no money what-so and I would sell my soul to get him a PC. If there were any way we could get him one, I would get him one … and it's all he wants, poor sod. What can we sell, and we ain't got owt to sell and get him one, have we?

[Edit]

INTERVIEWER: So how important d'you think computers will be to the, all of your children's [aged between three and fifteen] futures.

MOTHER: Oh incredibly important, that's why we really, really wanting to get one, I mean little 'un's three and they just, that's all they're gonna need to know, ain't it, when all said and done, by time little 'un gets to secondary school, our way of thinking there won't be any pens and things.

FATHER: No there won't be.

MOTHER: So I think it's vitally important that they learn, that, well before much longer every home's gonna have one anyway but, I think it's vitally important that the earlier you can get them on them the better it'll be.

(Mother and Father, Station Road)

MOTHER: They were, well they were blackmailing me really. They said they couldn't do their work at school because they needed a computer to do it on. Homework, they desperately needed one for homework 'cos they couldn't finish their homework, 'cos all their friends had one. [Edit] They just, it seems to be whatever shop you go in or office they've got one haven't they, do you know what I mean? Everybody seems to have got them and every job you seem to go into apart from being a cleaner like me, at some stage or another they want, they want you to be able to use a computer.

(Mother, Station Road)

In this sense adults' fears about ICT are not about the present but rather about their children's future in what they imagine will be a society transformed by technology. The internet-connected PC therefore emerges for them as an educational or work tool to enable their children to develop their skills and identities in line with a rapidly changing society. In contrast, children tend to be oriented towards the present rather than the future. While they show widespread recognition that ICT will play an important part in most future forms of employment, and different children do valorize the internet-connected PC in different ways, primarily it emerges for them as a tool of fun rather than work. For example, for some groups it emerges as a tool for playing computer games, for others as an information source about sports, pop and film heroes and heroines, while some prefer to use it to communicate with friends and family (Bingham *et al.* forthcoming). In households where parents stress only the educational value of the PC, children are often reluctant to use it; in some cases even projecting their hatred of homework onto the machine itself, resenting it as 'boring' or difficult. Mr Akram explains how his son would not use the PC for educational purposes until he succumbed to putting games on it:

> when he [his son] mentioned that he wanted a computer it was specifically for games … initially I just got the word-processing bit, but over the period of time I've had to introduce a little bit of games onto it because he wasn't using it, then he went off it, so just to get him back on it again I bought a few games.
>
> (Father, Highfields)

Indeed, parents who are motivated by a 'technophobia of the projected future' can, in their enthusiasm for the potential educational benefits of ICT, unwittingly sow the seeds of technophobia amongst their offspring.

Fears for the present

While many parents and teachers have learnt to use PCs at work or in evening classes, a significant proportion have not had, or have not taken up, opportunities to become computer literate. For these adults, their desires for their children or pupils to become technologically competent and to have access to PCs at home and school are tinged with ambivalence because of their fears about their own lack of skills and knowledge.

Adult non-users are fazed by the jargon (bytes, RAM, surfing and so on) that surrounds computers and are intimidated by their lack of understanding of how a PC works (Lupton 1995). It was to counter the way that such fears alienated potential customers that Apple Computers, with the Macintosh, first substituted user-friendly icons for textual commands, to both humanize the PC and symbolically represent the incomprehensible workings within the computer (Haddon 1988). Similarly, computer companies and retailers are investing in telephone hotlines and programs in which the emphasis is on friendliness and the human face of the technology, in order to try to overcome technophobia because it deters people from buying machines (Lupton 1995).

Some parents are fearful that the technology is only understood by the younger generation and that they are being left behind. Mrs Slade describes her fear:

> But I think in, in those of us who are sort of over forty it's just unknown territory to us, um, depending on, I mean, obviously some adults, older people, I mean go, work in offices where they, they see stuff or use it. But I think for the, the vast majority of us it's absolutely unknown territory.
>
> (Mother, Highfields)

In discussing this reversal of traditional adult and child relations parents often draw upon wider discourses about the supposed 'naturalness' of children's technological competence (Holloway and Valentine, 2000a). Mr Baines argument that 'Kids aren't [frightened of it] by their very nature, they'll just dig in and experiment' (Father, Highfields) echoes essentialist representations about children's ability to pick up ICT skills through their fearless enthusiasm for learning through trial and error in contrast to the more cautious approach of adults. While some parents take advantage of their children's technological competence by asking them to provide support for their own learning, other parents avoid or dismiss ICT rather than admit to being less competent than, or in need of help from, their children (Holloway and Valentine 2000a). Mrs Grayson describes her children's superior ICT skills and how she likes to keep 'it', the PC, out of sight and out of mind:

> MOTHER: … I say well I don't know how to do it. Todd can you do this or Karen can you do this, and they usually can. It does make you feel quite inadequate...
> [edited from a different section of the same interview]
>
> (Mother, Highfields)

> MOTHER: [it's] upstairs in the small bedroom next to the bathroom, in between the bathroom and the toilet there's a small [room].
> INTERVIEWER: So has it always been there …?
> MOTHER: No, it's always been there. I feel very strongly and I still do that it won't ever come in a living room. I like 'it' out of the way.

In this way, for some parents their fears about their lack of ICT skills and the implications this has – both for their identity as an adult/parent and familial power relations – are expressed as an aversion towards 'it', the PC.

This sort of technophobia is compounded in the classroom, where the teachers' identities and authority often rest upon their ability to win the respect of their pupils by demonstrating their superior knowledge and competence. Teachers are under pressure to integrate new technologies across the curriculum yet many of them are reluctant or ambivalent about doing so because they lack training or the hands-on experience of how to use ICT, and in a demanding job have little time to spare to adapt their teaching to incorporate the technology (Bryson and de Castell 1998). With minimal technical or troubleshooting support available, some are not surprisingly fearful of encountering problems using ICT in front of pupils whose technological competence may outstrip their own. Mrs Grayson, a teacher, explains why she avoids using ICT:

> Yeah well I don't think, I mean, I mean when I said to you [the interviewer] I don't use them at school, if at all possible I will avoid them because they create more hassle for me than they do anything else. [Edit, later she returned to this theme] … you don't actually know what's happening in this box, that it's happening and what, and you're getting the result out that you want …

Given the potential threat that ICT may pose to some teachers' identity, professional status, day-to-day practices and authority within the classroom, it is not surprising that many are accused of being contemporary Luddites for resisting its wider incorporation within the curriculum.

Part of some parents' and teachers' technophobia stems from their fear of a lack of technological competence and therefore the ability to regulate their offsprings' or their pupils' online activities. PCs, and the internet in particular, bring dangers of connectivity (Valentine and Holloway 2001). Writing for example about the use of the viral metaphor in relation to computers, Lupton (1994) comments on the way that computers are often spoken of in embodied terms as subject to invasion by contaminating and potentially deadly viruses. She later writes that:

> Just as in AIDS discourses gay men or women have been conceptualized as 'leaky bodies' who lack control over their bodily boundaries so, too, in this 'cybercrime' discourse, computers are represented as unable to police or protect their boundaries, rendering themselves vulnerable to penetration. Just as humans in late modernity must both rely on trust relations but also fear them, computers can no longer 'trust' other computers to keep secrets and respect personal boundaries.
>
> (Lupton 1995: 109)

Some parents who use home computers for work purposes expressed fears that their children or their friends might introduce viruses into the PC and corrupt their files. However, the most significant fear of invasion was not that the PC itself may be contaminated but rather that the family home might be assailed by dangers brought into the home via the internet-connected PC. The relatively unregulated nature of cyberspace means that soft and hardcore pornography, racial and ethnic hatred, neo-Nazi groups and paedophiles can all be found online (Squire 1996; Sardar 1995). This has prompted a 'moral panic' in the US, UK and Australian media that the internet provides a potential gateway for unsuitable material and dangerous people to invade the family home (Lumby 1997; McMurdo 1997).

ICT emerges in different ways in different households depending on the parents' differential understandings of the technology and conceptions of online and offline space; family regimes and parenting styles and differential levels of social and technological competencies between household members. While some parents envisage that the internet-connected PC is a barrier from harm because the lure of computer games keeps children indoors and there-fore away from dangers in offline space, other parents absorb and reproduce media fears. These parents assume a distinction between online and offline space in which their children are understood not to know about or have access to pornography in other spaces such as the home and school. For them, the internet-connected PC emerges as a dangerous tool that potentially enables online hazards and evils to pollute the home (Valentine and Holloway 2001; Holloway and Valentine 2000b). Mr and Mrs Read explain their fears about the internet:

FATHER: Well I think they can access things what you don't want 'em to access.
INTERVIEWER: Right.
MOTHER: And I'd rather umm, I'd rather know what they are doing. Not you know, knowing that they're craftily going into something. I'd rather them not have it and temptation's not there.
INTERVIEWER: Yeah. So do you mind me asking, but what don't you want them to find on the internet?
MOTHER: Well there's all, you've heard all these things …
FATHER: [speaking over Mother] There's all like pornography.
MOTHER: Pornography you know.
FATHER: You've the files on like cases in America aren't there? … Where they've gone to meet somebody and it's end up being a bloke or some-thing like that. It'd happen turned out to be a kid, like you don't know. You can be speaking to somebody but you don't know who it is. They just give a name, they can tell you anything can't they? 'Alright, well meet me.' 'I'm meeting someone downtown.' Like you don't know who it is.
(Mother and Father, Station Road)

Marshall (1997) suggests that these adult fears are actually fears about chil-dren's knowledge and the waste to which they might potentially put this understanding. Well-publicized cases of computer hackers – who are usually teenage boys or young men – accessing secret files or creating computer viruses fuel adult fears that children's technological competence is dangerous knowledge out of control. Indeed, Marshall points out that the flip side of adults' fears that their children may be disenfranchised from the information age is that their children may become obsessed with using technologies in wasteful or inappropriate ways, spending excessive amounts of time and money playing computer games, hacking, chatting online, etc. Some parents fear that these online activities will become a substitute for offline hobbies and relationships (Valentine *et al.* 2000a, 2000b), that children will develop technological competence at the expense of learning basic skills such as spelling or mental arithmetic, and that they will get into 'trouble' online. The upshot of these fears is that children (particularly boys) will not fulfil the educational or employment goals which their parents have for them. In this sense, fears about technology and waste resonate with other moral panics about male youth subcultures (for example, Cohen 1973) in public space (Marshall 1997).

In some cases such fears about children's futures in an information age are translated into a suspicion of, or anxiety about the technology itself. ICT is understood by parents to be a powerful tool which can lead their children astray. These fears can in turn be transmitted by parents into schools. For example, in Highfields, parents' complaints about the way some children may be accessing unsuitable material online has contributed to a school culture in which children's access to the internet-connected PCs is restricted and highly regulated. In this way, parental fears about ICT can inhibit the opportunities children have to use technology. In turn, a lack of opportunities to develop a familiarity and comfortableness with the computer can, as we discuss in the next section, give rise to children becoming technophobic.

Even some adults who are familiar and competent with ICT expressed concerns about its use. Increasingly we invest trust in PCs, relying on them for an expanding range of work and domestic tasks while having little understanding of how they work. The intimacy with which internet-connected PCs are bound up with many adult lives provokes fears of dependency and vulnerability. As Lupton writes:

> The relationship between users and PCs is similar to that between lovers or close friends. An intimate relationship with others involves ambivalence: fear as well as pleasure. As we do with people we feel are close to us, we invest part of ourselves in PCs. We struggle with the pleasures and fears of dependency: to trust is to reap the rewards of security, but it is also to render ourselves vulnerable to risk.
>
> (Lupton 1995: 110)

These risks include panics about technological failure and computer viruses which can potentially threaten users' abilities to perform their jobs, manage their finances, communicate with friends and so on.

To summarize this section, adults' technophobia is not a fear of ICT *per se*, but rather a fear of the computer as a symbol of the future transformation of society. First, adults' techno-fears are fears of a projected future society from which they, or more particularly their children, may become disenfranchised if they lack the requisite technological skills to participate in its economic and civil life. Second, adults' techno-fears are fears about the present in which the emerging competence divide between the ICT skills of some parents/teachers and their children threatens to puncture their identity, status and authority as adults. These adults are torn; on the one hand pushing their children to develop ICT skills in order to avoid their fears of the projected future, while on the other hand fearing the consequences of their inability to control or regulate the children's knowledge and online activities (which include the risk of online dangers invading the home and children using the technology in inappropriate ways that might threaten their educational or employment futures). Third, adults' techno-fears are fears about their own or others' dependency on ICT and the blurring of boundaries between the self and the 'other' of the PC that this represents.

For some adults, techno-fears become projected onto the hardware itself, being expressed as an irrational hatred of the PC. In these technologically determinist imaginings the internet-connected PC is regarded as something external to the social relations and context within which it is made sense of and used. It is regarded as powerful, having the ability to impact on and transform both society as a whole and the lives of households and individuals. In the face of these perceived threats the most common forms of resistance employed by adults are avoidance – to steadfastly remain non users; and/or regulation – to attempt to limit and control others' ICT use, particularly their children's online activities.

CHILDREN'S FEARS

Implicit in the US and UK government drives to provide hardware and software for all within schools is an assumption that all children will want to learn to use the technology, will want to make the same uses of it and will learn and advance to the same level of competence. Yet the evidence of our research is that not all students take up the opportunities they are offered to use ICT at school or at home. However technology-rich or technology-laden the classroom, some children remain technophobic.

The academic literature suggests that there are strong gender differences in both the level and type of use to which children put ICT (Turkle 1984). Numerous studies report that girls are more fearful of technology than boys and that they receive less time on computers at school and less attention from teachers than their male counterparts (Collis 1985, Culley 1988). While girls demonstrate competence at applications such as word-processing and e-mail, it is boys who tend towards programming and game playing. Turkle (1984) describes boys as the 'hard masters' of technology.

Our research suggests that there is not just a straight divide according to gender. Even within the categories 'boys' and 'girls', the internet-connected PC emerges as a different tool for different groups of children (Holloway et al. 2000). For example, the groups in one class at Highfields included the following categories:

computer competent girls who use the PC both at school and at home in a task-oriented way to complete work and who rarely use ICT as a fun or leisure activity, although they are interested in the communication possibilities offered by the internet;

techno-boys who are highly computer literate and enjoy programming as well as hacking and games playing, although their skills are not appreciated by their peers who label them 'boffins' and 'geeks';

the lads who use the PC for playing games in and outside school and lark around on the internet trying to access porn and 'dissing people' in chat rooms;

Luddites who find computers stupid and boring, are reluctant to use them even in IT lessons and who have limited ICT knowledge or skills. It is this latter group which we wish to concentrate on in this section of the chapter.

Hannah, Lotty and Julie are in year eleven at Highfields. Like the adults cited above they are aware of the potential importance of ICT in a future information economy but unlike the adults they do not connect this vision of the future to their need to develop technological skills in the present.

JULIE: For what? [would PCs be useful]
LOTTY: Well like all the, most jobs now.
HANNAH: Yeah.
LOTTY: need computers for … with all this technology coming out they'll be useful. That's why my Mum wanted me to go on it [the PC].
[Edit]
HANNAH: Yeah there's more, more jobs to do with computers, but umm, don't know, I don't want to do computers on a job.
INTERVIEWER: You don't?
HANNAH: No, not at all.
JULIE: I wouldn't touch [one] with a bargepole.

(Year 11 girls, Highfields)

Clearly the girls are reluctant to use ICT and resist the opportunities they have at school to develop their technological competence. Their technophobia is predicated on three fears: about performance, about control and about identity. All of these are oriented to the girls' experience of the present rather than any vision of the future.

Fears about performance

Those children who have access to a PC at home have the opportunity to develop their technological competence and keyboard skills away from the surveillant and often ridiculing or hostile gaze of their peers. As a result these children are commonly more confident and comfortable with the technology in the classroom than those who do not have a home PC.

Of Hannah, Lotty and Julie only Hannah has a PC at home and all three describe their parents as afraid of new technologies. Julie claimed her father is so technophobic that he makes his secretary use his computer for him. Not surprisingly, perhaps, given the atmosphere of fear and avoidance which all three girls encounter at home, Hannah, Lotty and Julie are anxious about using computers in IT lessons because of their lack of keyboard skills and understanding of how the PC works. Lotty and Julie feel particularly disadvantaged both in IT classes and in other lessons because they have no opportunity to practise ICT skills at home or to type up their coursework for other subjects. Lotty explains:

> Cos no one else gives you a chance ... cos if you don't have a computer at home you can't do your other coursework then you've got IT [lessons] and then you've got other subjects that you have to use a computer for as well.

Their fears about their lack of skills are compounded by the social context of the classroom, where the girls know that they might be laughed at or teased by the boys if they cannot perform at the level and speed of their peers. In this respect they illustrate Brosnan's (1998) argument that the classroom can reinforce anxieties about performance differences. Rather than being stigmatized as the classroom 'dunces' the girls resist using the technology altogether, refusing to do the work or finding ways to subvert the tasks set. It is a position which commands more social status and respect amongst their peers than trying and struggling. According to the girls it is also a tactic which is to some extent endorsed by the male IT teacher.

JULIE: I don't even use them.
INTERVIEWER: You don't even use them?
JULIE: No I can't use them.
INTERVIEWER: So what do you do, just like turn up [at the IT lessons]?
JULIE: And yeah do stuff. [Edit] He [teacher] says bring some other work in cos I'm not gonna learn how to use computer [laughs], cos I don't like them.
INTERVIEWER: Yeah, why is that?
JULIE: Cos I can't use them [laughs], they bore me.

(Year 11 girl, Highfields)

In this way, the classroom, rather than challenging emerging divisions between those who have a PC and those who do not, actually becomes part of the process through which a technological fluency gap is produced.

Fears about control

PCs are supposed to be user-friendly – in other words to be malleable or controllable. Yet they are often seen as incomprehensible, alien, and as a source of anxiety, impotence and frustration. Lupton (1995) suggests that our fear of technology often originates from an inability to understand how it works or how to fix it. Such fears are evident among Hannah, Lotty and Julie, who are all deterred from learning computing skills through experimentation because of a fear that they might break the machine.

HANNAH: ... because you're scared of breaking the computer most of the time [laughs].
LOTTY: Yeah...know that one [laughs].
JULIE: That's what I'm like anyway.

(Year 11 girls, Highfields)

Fears about 'control' run deeper than an anxiety about damaging the technology. Rather, PCs are often credited with the intentionality to deliberately obstruct or frustrate their users. Ross (1991) observes that notices are often pinned on office walls near to computers, photocopiers and other machines attributing them with the ability to sense the moods of users and to respond to their degree of urgency by breaking down. He writes: 'the notice assumes a degree of evolved self-consciousness on the machine's part. Furthermore, it implies a relation of hostility, as if the machine's self-consciousness and loyalty to its own kind have inevitably led to resentment, conflict and sabotage' (Ross 1991: 1–2, cited in Lupton 1995: 104). The girls employ similar sentiments in the following account of Hannah's work experience:

HANNAH: When I was on me work experience this girl wiped off everything about this important case that was coming up in about two weeks. If I'd, I'd, I'd I don't know I just wouldn't like that. All she did was just press like a button with her little finger. I mean they could ...
JULIE: And it just wiped everything.

(Year 11 girls, Highfields)

Hannah's explanation that 'all' the girl did was 'press like a button with her little [and therefore most insignificant] finger' implies the user's innocence and lack of responsibility for the loss of the document, while Julie's comment that 'it' just wiped everything clearly attributes blame for the loss on the maliciousness of the computer. The girls' technophobia is not therefore just about the fact that they feel they do not have the knowledge or confidence to 'control' the computer but also that the technology itself might have the potential power to undermine them. Lupton suggests that it is the blurring of the boundaries between human and machine inherent in ICT which inspires feelings of anxiety and fear:

There is something potentially monstrous about computer technology in its challenging of traditional boundaries. Fears about monsters relate to their liminal status, the elision of one category of life and another, particularly if the human is involved, as in the Frankenstein monster ... While there is an increasing move towards the consumption of technologies, there is also anxiety around the technologies' capacity to consume *us*.

(Lupton 1995: 106)

Fears about identity

People are not passively inscribed into existing power relations, rather social relations in everyday environments such as the school must be negotiated, accepted and created. Yet authors (Callon 1987; Latour 1993; Star 1995) within the sociology of science and technology argue that in order to understand these relationships, meanings and identities we need to look not just at the associations (and disassociations) between humans, but also between humans and *non-humans* (Law 1994). For example, there is no school or peer relationship without participation between humans and objects. Objects can define actors, the space in which they move, the ways in which they interact, allocating roles and responsibilities and vesting them with a moral content. In other words 'objects have political strength. They may change social relations, but they also stabilize, naturalize, depoliticize and translate these into other media' (Akrich 1992: 222). Computers are just one of the many 'objects' within the classroom that lead to an arrangement of pupils and things.

Notably, the PC is an object which binds some children together, creating 'relationships'. Within Hannah, Lotty and Julie's class, for example, ICT plays an important part in the life of one particular group of computer literate boys, shaping their social networks with other boys who share their interests in programming and computer games (Holloway *et al.* 2000). In doing, so the computer vests this group of boys with a particular moral content, defining them as 'sad', as 'boffins' and as 'geeks' as the girls describe:

INTERVIEWER: Who are the people that, that, that like are really good at it?
HANNAH: People who come in at dinner times and after school and play on computer games when they go home.
INTERVIEWER: Right so what, what kind of people are they?
[Laughter]
LOTTY: Sad people [laughter].
[Edit]
HANNAH: Well they're not very good looking.
JULIE: No.
LOTTY: Not good looking and they don't care what they look like and they're immature.

(Year 11 girls, Highfields)

In popular culture 'techies' are commonly represented as being physically unattractive, wearing glasses, having bad skin and poor fashion sense. Their bodies are regarded as a product of their obsession with computers: of too much time spent staring at a screen (Lupton 1995). In other words, the PC can define the properties attributed to its users. As Hannah, Lotty and Julie explained above, the bodies of cyberenthusiasts are 'inscribed upon and constructed through the computers they use' (Lupton 1995: 103). Indeed, the girls' descriptions elsewhere in their interview of the boys as 'addicts' conjure up images of technology, like drugs, literally invading and transforming the boys' bodies.

In this way, within the context of the school, computers define the techno-boys as sexually undesirable, aligning them with non-hegemonic performances of masculinity – as 'freaks' and 'homos' (Holloway *et al.* 2000; Valentine *et al.* 2000b). In turn the association of the PC with 'sad geeks' naturalizes its status as a non-heterosexual, boring and socially undesirable object. As a result the girls imagine a binary division between online and offline activities and spaces in which online activities and spaces are regarded as 'dull', 'boring', 'nerdy' and irrelevant, in contrast to offline activities and spaces such as going out clubbing.

JULIE: … [referring to using PCs] it's just I've got better things to do with my life.
LOTTY: Yeah.
[Laughter]
INTERVIEWER: I wonder what they are [laughing]?
HANNAH: Yeah I wonder what they are as well [laughs].
JULIE: Won't get into that.
INTERVIEWER: What are these better things to do, go on?
JULIE: Well going out.
LOTTY: Clubbing. Yeah.
HANNAH: Yeah.
JULIE: And other things.
LOTTY: I mean I went out last night, I mean I wouldn't have stayed in to use a computer. If I'd got a chance to go out I'd go out.

(Year 11 girls, Highfields)

In other words, the interaction between technology, bodies, identities and peer group relations is 'complex and continuous and all the elements combined are transforming of, and transformed by each other' (Ormrod 1994: 43).

Not surprisingly perhaps, because of the way in which the meanings of PCs have emerged within the girls' peer culture, Hannah, Lotty and Julie are fearful of being seen to take an interest in ICT because of the potential threat it poses to their identities and social relationships. If they show an interest in technology their embodied identities might be re-coded by their peers as undesirable. As they explain below their participation in the heterosexual culture of the school is at stake.

INTERVIEWER: So how come you can't be, how come you can't be the type of lass that likes going out and the type?

[laughs]

JULIE: To use a computer.

HANNAH: You just wouldn't tell anyone that you were using the computer.

INTERVIEWER: Oh right, you wouldn't tell anyone?

HANNAH: No.

INTERVIEWER: So why not? [edit]

HANNAH: It's a boffin's thing to do isn't it?

JULIE: I mean computer boffins, that's what people, well ...

[Edit]

INTERVIEWER: But you wouldn't want anybody to think you were a computer boffin.

HANNAH: No.

LOTTY: No.

JULIE: No.

INTERVIEWER: No, why not?

HANNAH: Cos then you don't get, you don't get invited out or anything like that.

JULIE: Yeah.

LOTTY: You don't pull all these people at little school discos and all that kind of, I don't know ...

(Year 11 girls, Highfields)

In this way the girls' fears about the threat ICT poses to their identities demonstrates how intimately and complexly the bits and pieces, such as computers, that are part of our everyday worlds are involved in our social relations (Wenger 1998).

To summarize this section, children's technophobia is not a fear of computers *per se* but a fear of how ICT may transform their individual social identities and relationships within the everyday context of the school and their peer group cultures. Use of technology is a social act, such that the PC plays an important role in changing or stabilizing social relations in the classroom. As a consequence some children are fearful: first, about the social consequences of their performance relative to the technological competencies of their peers; second, about their ability to control the PC; and third, about the ways in which their identities might be read by their peers if they show an interest in technology.

In these children's imaginings, online and offline worlds are sharply divided, rather than mutually constituted. The online world is understood to be a socially stigmatized location positioned in opposition to the heterosexual economy of the classroom and the club. As such, the children valorize what they understand as the 'real' world over online activities and so actively resist engaging with technology.

CONCLUSION

The emphasis within US and UK government policy on ICT is the need to provide access to hardware and software for all children. The evidence of this chapter suggests that this is a naive approach because it assumes that all those who have access to the technology will take up the opportunities that they have to engage with it and that they will develop the competence to use it. Rather, the interviews with parents, teachers and children presented within this chapter demonstrate that ICT emerges differently for different individuals and groups of users. While many users of all ages take to and become adept at using internet-connected PCs, others are fearful of them and resist their incorporation into their lives.

However, both adults' and children's fears are not necessarily fears of the machine *per se* but rather are fears about how the technology might transform their social identities and relationships and in doing so change their worlds. Adults' techno-fears are, first, fears of a projected future society from which they, and their children, may become disenfranchised if they lack the appropriate technological competence to participate in it. Second, they are fears about the consequences which the emerging competence divide between adults and children may have for their own identities and their ability to prevent their children putting their technological skills to waste.

In contrast to adults' techno-fears, which are future-oriented and large-scale, being concerned with how society as whole may be transformed by ICT, children's technophobias are focused on the present and are at the local scale of classroom peer group relations. At the root of children's anxieties about computers are concerns about their performance within the classroom, their ability to control the technology and their social identities.

Both adults' and children's fears are quite determinist, in that they assume that technology will impact on their lives in particular ways with negative consequences, despite the fact that in practice the PC emerges as a different tool for different groups of users. On the one hand, ICT is conceptualized by some interviewees as something external or autonomous, rather than constitutive of humans and our worlds, which is endowed with the power to effect change upon our lives at different scales (Bryson and de Castell 1998). On the other hand, computers are conceptualized by other interviewees not as external, but rather as effecting change by blurring the boundaries between 'self' and 'other'.

If UK and US governments are serious about trying to promote an inclusive society in the information age they need to ally their efforts to provide access to hardware and software for all with a recognition of the need to tackle technophobia, particularly amongst the young. Currently, adults' techno-fears about the projected future mean that they are presenting ICT to children as something with which they must become competent because it will be important to them in a future society. In doing so adults are suggesting that PCs will impact on children's lives in potentially negative ways. Yet, children are not future-oriented, nor concerned about the broader transformation of society. Rather they are more worried about the present and the peer group social relations within which they have to negotiate and manage their own identities. In order to encourage children to take up the opportunities which they have to use ICT rather than to resist it, adults need to promote the use of technology in ways which relate to the social context of children's everyday lives and peer group cultures. For example, by emphasizing the educational uses of ICT for word-processing, spreadsheets and programming, adults contribute to the technology emerging as a tool which is considered to be boring and the preserve of 'boffins' and 'geeks'. In contrast, by encouraging children to use e-mail and the internet – online activities which children understand as connected to their offline lives and activities – adults can contribute to helping ICT emerge as a 'cool' tool in more children's eyes. This in turn will encourage them not to see technology as a threat to their identities but rather as something exciting and relevant to their offline world. So that the fact that technology, identities and peer group relations are transforming of, and transformed by, one another will be regarded by children as offering them a range of positive possibilities rather than presenting a threat to their identities.

NOTES

1   We are grateful to the Economic and Social Research Council for funding the research (award no. L129251055) on which this paper is based. Thanks also to Nick Bingham who was employed on this project as a Research Assistant.
2   The names of the schools and interviewees have been changed to protect their anonymity.

REFERENCES

Akrich, M. (1992) 'The description of technical objects', in Bijker, W. and Law, J. (eds) *Shaping Technology/Building Society*, Cambridge: MIT Press.
Bingham, N., Holloway, S. and Valentine, G. (forthcoming) 'Bodies in the midst of things: re-locating children's use of the internet', in Watson, N. (ed.) *Reformulating Bodies*, Macmillan: Basingstoke.
Brook, J. and Boal, I. (1995) 'Preface' in Brook, J. and Boal, I. (eds) *Resisting the virtual life: the culture and politics of information*, San Francisco: City Lights Books: vii–xv.
Brosnan, M. (1998) *Technophobia: the psychological impact of information technology*, London: Routledge.

Bryson, M. and S. de Castell (1998) 'New technologies and the cultural ecology of primary schooling: imagining teachers as Luddites In/Deed'. *Educational Policy* 5: 83–95.

Callon, M. (1987) 'Society in the making: the study of technology as a tool for sociological analysis' in Bijker, W., Hughes, P. and Pinch, T., (eds) *The Social Construction of Technology Systems*, Cambridge: MIT Press.

Cockburn, C. (1985) *Machinery of Dominance*, London: Pluto Press.

Cohen, S. (1973) *Folk Devils and Moral Panics: The Creation of The Mods and Rockers*, St. Albans Paladin: Granada.

Collis, B. (1985) Sex-related differences in attitudes toward computers: implications and counsellors, *School Counsellor* 33(2): 120–130.

Culley, L. (1988) 'Girls, boys and computers', *Educational Studies* 14(1): 3–8.

Giacquinta, J., Bauer, J. and Levin, J. (1993) *Beyond Technology's Promise: an Examination of Children's Computing at Home*, Cambridge: Cambridge University Press.

Haddon, L. (1988) 'The home computer: the making of a consumer electronic', *Science as Culture* 2: 7–51.

Heim, M. (1993) *The Metaphysics of Virtual Reality*, New York: Oxford University Press.

Holloway, S. and Valentine, G. (2000a) ' "It's only as stupid as you are": children's negotiations of technological competence at home and at school', *Social and Cultural Geography*: 1.

Holloway, S. and Valentine, G. (2000b) 'Multi-media(ted) homes: children, parents and the domestic use of ICT'. Paper available from S. Holloway, Dept. of Geography, University of Loughborough, LE11 3TU.

Holloway, S., Valentine, G. and Bingham, N. (2000, in press) 'Institutionalising technologies: masculinities, femininities and the heterosexual economy of the IT classroom', *Environment and Planning A* 32: 617–633.

Kroker, A. and Weinstein, M. (1994) *Datatrash: The Theory of Virtual Class*, New York: St Martin's.

Latour, B. (1993) *We have never been modern*, London: Harvester Wheatsheaf.

Law, J. (1994) *Organising Modernity*, Oxford: Blackwell.

Lumby, C. (1997) 'Panic attacks: old fears in a new media era', *Media International Australia* 85: 40–46.

Lupton, D. (1994) 'Panic computing: the viral metaphor and computer technology', *Cultural Studies* 8(3): 556–68.

Lupton, D. (1995) 'The embodied computer/user', in Featherstone, M. and Burrows, R. (eds) *Cyberspace, cyberbodies and cyberpunk: cultures of embodiment*, London: Sage 97–112.

Marshall, D. (1997) 'Technophobia: video games, computer hacks and cybernetics', *Media International Australia* 85: 70–78.

McMurdo, G. (1997) 'Cyberporn and communication decency', *Journal of Information Science* 23(1): 81–90.

Ormrod, S. (1984) 'Let's nuke the dinner' in Cockburn, C. and Furst Dilic, R. (eds) *Bringing home technology gender and technology in a changing Europe*, Milton Keynes: Open University Press.

Owen, T. (1990) 'Waiting to connect: the writer in electronic residence', *Computing teacher* 17(5): 46–49.

Papert, S. (1997) *The Connected Family: Bridging the Digital Generation Gap*, Georgia: Longstreet Press.

Rheingold, H. (1993) *The Virtual Community: Finding connection in a computerised world*, London: Secker and Walbury.

Ross, A. (1991) *Strange Weather: Culture, Science and Technology in the Age of Limits*, London: Verso.

Sardar, Z. (1995) 'alt.civilisation.faq:cyberspace as the darker side of the West'. *Futures* 27: 777–794.

Social Exclusion Unit (1998) *Bringing Britain Together*, London: HMSO.

Squire, S. (1996) 'Re-territorialising knowledge(s): electronic spaces and virtual geographies' *Area* 28: 101–103.

Star, S. L. (1995) *Cultures of Computing*, Oxford: Blackwell.

Turkle, S. (1984) *The Second Self: Computers and the Human Spirit*, New York: Simon and Schuster.

Valentine, G. and Holloway, S. (2001, in press) 'Virtual dangers? Geographies of parents' fears for children's safety in cyberspace', *Professional Geographer*.

Valentine, G., Holloway. S. and Bingham, N. (2000a) 'Transforming cyberspace: children's interventions in the new public sphere', in Holloway, S. and Valentine, G. (eds) *Children's Geographies: playing, living, learning*, London: Routledge.

Valentine, G., Holloway. S. and Bingham, N. (2000b) 'The Digital Generation? Children, ICT and the everyday nature of social exclusion', Paper available from G.Valentine, Dept. of Geography, University of Sheffield, Winter Street, Sheffield, S10 2TN.

Wellman, B. and Gulia M. (1996) 'Net surfers don't ride alone: virtual communities as communities' available at http://www.acm.org/ccp/references/wellman/wellman.html.

Wenger, E. (1998) *Communities of Practice*, Cambridge: Cambridge University Press.

Zimmerman Umble, D. (1992) 'The Amish and the telephone; resistance and reconstruction', in Silverstone, R. and Hirsch, E. (eds) *Consuming Technologies: media and information in domestic space*, London: Routledge: 183–194.

Part II

Technologies in/as interaction

5 Fabricating friendships

The ordinariness of agency in the social use of an everyday medical technology in the school lives of children[1]

Ian Robinson and Amber Delahooke

In the class Ryan comes up to me: 'I got my asthma pumps [inhalers] today'. He shows them to me, taking them from his pocket one at a time, a blue one and then a brown one. 'How do you know which one to take?' I ask. He says: 'I use the blue one first.' Sophie said to me, 'One day when we was in Miss Stone's class, yeah, he [Ryan] had an asthma attack in the playground and his pump was at home.' Georgina says, 'He was all grumpy.' 'What happened?' I ask. Georgina says, 'He couldn't breathe – he was goin' like this.' [demonstrates]

Later in the day Ryan, surrounded by a group of children, takes out one of his pumps. One of them said: 'Amber, Ryan just did it – his pump – go on Ryan, do it again.' Ryan takes it out and squirts it. 'Look it comes out of that hole,' he says, and shows us all. Then he takes it apart and puts it back together again with everyone crowding round and watching avidly. I say, 'You shouldn't waste it.' He says, 'I've got more at home.'

Ryan goes out with Sophie, then comes back and keeps puffing when I'm not looking. 'Look Amber you missed it,' say the girls. Georgina comes over and covers my eyes so that I can still see while Ryan puffs. 'How come it didn't come out of your mouth that time?' she asks. He does it a few more times [all with the blue pump] and lets it puff out of his mouth like smoke. The girls all look on in excited wonder, but keeping their distance.

Dramatis Personnae: Amber/me/I – Amber Delahooke, co-author; Ryan, Sophie, Georgina – schoolchildren; Setting – a London primary school.

INTRODUCTION: THEORIZING THE ARGUMENT

Children constitute their identities and personhoods in relation to one another as much as in relation to adult worlds, which of course provide powerful conditioning frameworks of practice. Children's own worlds of work and play are also powerful and ubiquitous, and despite the apparently constricting adult and professionally-constructed worlds within which they live, opportunities for reconfiguring adult worlds or of substantially subverting their category systems are often evident. In this respect childhood asthma is a social as much as an individual disease, in which any manifestation of its presence through practices or 'things' associated with it becomes germane to social interpretation and action. Thus the view that children are always, or almost always, set socially apart from one another by a condition such as asthma – and the means needed to control it – is largely based on a misunderstanding of the nature of childhood relationships. We argue that apparently extraneous and anxiety-provoking medical technologies such as asthma inhalers can far more easily be incorporated, almost comfortably, into children's everyday worlds than might be thought possible.

At a more general level the broad argument is that children, like others, have a continuing capacity to subvert the ways in which adult others in particular construct and deploy material objects, as well as attempt to condition how and when they may be used. As a counterpoint to the view that, in particular, children's worlds are largely dominated by their temporal and spatial framing by adult others, and that the assumed 'normal' trajectory of childhood is largely built upon their sequenced presence or absence at particular times and places (James *et al.* 1998: 37–80), the possibilities which exist – and are taken up – for children in modifying, reconstructing or sidestepping this formal and neatly patterned sequence of events are of particular interest. Such possibilities are of even greater interest where there are intersections of ostensibly powerful professional processes conditioning the lives of children. One of these intersections exists where educational and medical concerns about children and their activities take on, or centre on, a material form, which acts as the site and setting through which the processes of the management of childhood become explicit. In such situations it becomes possible to see more clearly how and in what ways the enterprise of the education of children in the broadest sense, and the enterprise of medicine, in its focus on assisting the production of a 'healthy' body/mind, appear coincident or discrepant. It also becomes possible to see, and consider, the ways in which children manage the range of expectations and assumptions of significant adult others, and/or indeed create their own patterns of management to which they may bring a wide range of beliefs and practices tangential to those of the adult world. It is this latter set of issues, concerned with children's own patterns of interaction, which forms the core of this chapter, rather than the analysis of how medical and educational views and perceptions interact with each other. Nonetheless these medical and educational views and perceptions constitute an important context of children's own interactions, and are often put forward with both the authority of professional status, and the power of position.

Following from an earlier analysis (Hepper *et al.* 1996) which demonstrated ethnographically that children's identities and personhoods need not always become the prisoner of significant medical diagnoses or their subsequent (medically-endorsed) therapeutic management, we here extend this line of analysis to pursue an even broader argument. The argument is that in the world of children's work and children's play – which are often for various reasons difficult to distinguish from one another – sickness and its management are integral to, rather than separate from, the world of health, for both are part of mutually interacting constructions of children's identities in relation to one another. Such an argument appears close to a truism in being so baldly stated. However, generally in adult perceptions, and in the practice of research, the fundamental implications of this argument have not been pursued. This situation derives from a vertical view of childhood (Nader 1980) in which interrelationships between adult and child are assumed to be the conditioning features *par excellence* of most significant aspects of children's lives; moreover these relationships are considered to operate almost entirely through a one-to-one (parent–child; teacher–pupil; doctor–patient) process. In other words the social nature of children's activities and interactions is merely seen as a background feature within which these individual relationships are located, rather than as something fundamental through which identities are constructed and personhoods created. By thinking about 'things', that is, material objects such as everyday medical technologies, and the ways in which they weave in and out of children's lives at work and play, the centrally social nature of children's worlds can be further unravelled, and furthermore the nature of children's agency can be experienced and analysed.

THE PROCESS OF CONSTRUCTING SOCIAL CHILDHOODS: ANALYSING CHILDREN'S PLAY AND CHILDREN'S WORK

Broadly based on James' (1993) view that participation in the cultural activities of childhood is a key element in children's establishing particular identities in relation to one another, this analysis is based on the observation of the local worlds of children in primary school settings as they work and play, or – to confound these categories – as they play at work and work at play. Indeed one theme of this analysis, as of some other recent examinations of childhoods, is that it is difficult to disentangle the two. Thus, one of the major casualties of current anthropological and sociological approaches to children's worlds is an imagined view of childhood as a time of unfettered and 'natural' play which, by definition, exists before the idea and practice of work is insinuated into (by then) almost adult lives.

In the vertical management view of Western childhood, before the 'new wave' of studies, adults were often considered to be seeking – frequently vainly – to impose the idea and rigorous chronological practice of 'work' on a child's world which was embedded in the apparent and (from an adult's point of view) timeless ephemera of play. Therefore children's play, perceived to have myriad and constantly shifting forms and objectives, was considered to operate in a parallel and analytically invisible universe to that in which adults lived, and to be almost unamenable to the same kinds of serious study as that which could be applied to adult activities, except in relation to its qualities as 'quaint folklore'. Of course in the new sociology and anthropology of childhood play has been considered in a very different way.

In particular, play has been not so much constructed in a parallel universe of time but in one which is ordered and sequenced by the objectives of others in an adult universe, even in relation to activities outside school (Hillman *et al.* 1990). It becomes part of the formal curriculum of childhood. However as James *et al.* (1998) have recently argued, such an approach, which is almost the exact inverse of the view of play as children's own insulated folklore, allows for almost no agency for children in the process of play. This is why they argue, following Sutton-Smith (1977), that his idea of play as 'adaptive potentiation' is a way forward for 'it permits a child-centred focus on children's activities, exploring what play might mean to children as a form of social action, rather than simply following adult definitions of play'; it also 'facilitates seeing the agency of the players' (James *et al.* 1998: 91).

There remain, however, important paradoxes at the heart of current adult concerns with play and childhood. The first and most obvious is that at the same time as childhood is seen as a discretely different time of life, its particular and special content almost disappears – not least in the perceived fusion of work and play. Second, whilst there is a substantial preoccupation with enhancing the creative and imaginative components of childhood, there appears to be a fear of allowing children to undertake such activity without the guidance or control of others, which strategy, if implemented, then leads to a further fear that children have somehow lost the capacity themselves to invent their own new ideas and worlds. Thus children's peer-based imagination and pretence in play is considered by adults to constitute a world of danger as well as a world of promise. Such ambivalences are understandable for at their heart is a set of contradictions about the relationship between childhood and adulthood, in which both linkage and separation are part of the conceptual equation.

CHILDREN'S PLAY: THE POSITIONING OF MATERIAL OBJECTS IN CHILDREN'S WORLDS

It is clear that play has been subject to increased commodification, at least in the Western (Northern) world, and not only in relation to its spatial and temporal chronology and broad content, but also in relation to arrays of material elements around which and through which the trajectories of children's social interactions are often rendered visible. These material elements can be of any kind, operating through the continuing transformations which the many-sided prisms of pretence and imagination can bring to bear on the most ordinary and everyday objects (Goldman 1998). The role of such elements in children's play has of course had a long history, preceding what is now considered to be a more formal conceptual and operational separation of the world of children from that of adults. In this history many material things have been employed within what, with hindsight, we consider as 'play', in which innovative, multiple and imaginative uses are a key component. As Ennew (1994) documented in her review of the historical context of children's toys, stone balls used for rolling and soft papyrus balls that could be thrown have been recorded in Ancient Egypt; sheep's bladders and stitched leather preceded the construction of 'bouncy' balls once rubber came into more everyday use in the nineteenth century; marbles, sometimes made of semi-precious stones, have been used since at least since 4,000 BC and yet may still be, as 'a currency more precious than money' for children (Newsom and Newsom 1978: 240). Clockwork and mechanical toys also have a long history, only recently supplemented by battery-driven and electronic games.

This retrospective vision of the deployment of material objects for children in many forms is one which emphasizes their indigenous and craft-like nature as constantly subject to local re-evaluation and imaginative interpretation. In contrast, despite some key historical evidence to the contrary, the twentieth century world of childhood has become considered as a world separated from history, especially in relation to the marketing of the material to and for children. Ennew (1994: 139) further points out in her analysis that 'as children have become progressively separated from adults in the modern world so children's games and toys have become specialized and commercialized'.

In this process fears have continued to surface about the stultifying effects of pre-formed, mass-produced, extensively marketed products for children, in which alternative imaginative possibilities might be pre-empted, swamped or destroyed. Given such fears the concern is that children's play is, as a consequence, somehow 'empty', and now requires a further injection of adult assistance to counteract the negative effects of such mass production by teaching children 'how to play'. This concern was noted by Opie and Opie in 1969, some time before the advent of the apparently novel and different gaze of the new sociology and anthropology of childhood. They noted that the widespread belief at that time was that children:

> have few diversions of their own, that they are incapable of self-organiza-
> tion, have become addicted to spectator amusements and will languish if
> left to rely on their own resources. It is felt that the enlightened adult is
> one who thinks up ideas for them, provides them with 'play materials',
> and devotes time to playing with them ... Yet our vision of childhood
> continues to be based on the adult–child relationship. Possibly because it is
> more difficult to find out about, let alone understand, we largely ignore
> the child-to-child complex, scarcely realising that however much children
> need looking after they are also people going about their own business
> within their own society, and are thus fully capable of occupying them-
> selves under the jurisdiction of their own code.
>
> (Opie and Opie, 1969: v)

One of the very recent and interesting systematic post-Opie considerations of children's play is that of Goldman (1998) in his book *Child's Play*, in which a sophisticated and theorized analysis of the role of imagination and pretence precedes a very detailed analysis of children's play amongst the Huli of Papua New Guinea. We refer briefly to this analysis because, in working from the child's-eye view of the world, we believe that one of the dangers of many present analyses is the assumption – indeed construction – of such a dimensional difference between the children's world of new and particularly electronic technologies in the First (or Northern) World, and that of primitive 'old' technologies in the Third (Southern) World, that the latter has nothing to say to the former. Indeed if one works from an intrinsic and essentialist view of these new electronic technologies – rather than from a child's-eye view – this is probably true, for in such an approach by definition the technologies determine the field of study. The importance of Goldman's work lies not just in its reminder to us that our world view is indeed a relatively ethnocentric one about children and childhood. It also reminds us, in relation to the particular argument of this chapter, that in the world of material things, or technologies, there may be crucial continuities as well as discontinuities in how such things are incorporated into children's worlds. Perhaps the most striking feature of Goldman's argument, in the light of claims made about the particular – indeed unique – capacity of (for example) the internet to allow a special kind of experimentation with identities, gender or otherwise in a world of imagination and pretence, is that other settings of many kinds have always allowed children to exercise their agency in similar ways. The technology is different, but from a child's-eye view all different material forms constitute resources with which, through which and from which identities are processually constructed, (trans)formed, played with, used, and discarded. Goldman emphasizes that pretence and imagination are based on a systematic reading of what constitutes 'normal' everyday life, as well as in a subsequent deconstruction and reconstruction of it. In this respect:

> two forms of systematic knowledge [are employed] (1) their [children's] typifications of cultural identities and roles, social events, ways of speaking and ways of acting, and (2) what they have internalized about pretend playing itself. To invoke both these resources of socio-cultural themes and a cognitive model of pretence-making, children engender fictions or representations. They dissemble reality by recreating it as an event … These 'events' come to relate to non-pretend reality as an 'other' because of a predilection in our everyday acts of reference to talk about these players of being *in a world of their own*.
>
> (Goldman, 1998: 2–3, emphasis in original)

Goldman's argument, based on and developed through a very different theoretical perspective from that of the Opies, none the less broadly reinforces their views about the complexity of children's play as well as its imaginative components. However Goldman, rather than considering children's play as complex but entirely distinguished by its indigenously quaint and separate nature, sets his analysis firmly within an array of approaches – especially those in anthropology – which seek to dissect the nature of the social world, how children know and constitute their identities within it, and at the same time influence that social world itself. Since the Opies undertook their work, the investigation of children's ordinary lives with one another has reached an almost industrial level. In the face of considerable residual adult fears and concerns about what happens when children are 'doing nothing' (that is, when they are not engaged in adult approved or scrutinized activities), an increasing number of research projects have investigated sophisticated kinds of activities with highly complex patterns of peer-constructed social order (Corrigan 1979; James 1993; Ennew 1994; Strandell 1997). Indeed they have found, as Opie and Opie (1969) indicated, people (children) going about their own business within their own juridical code.

CONCEPTUALIZING THE ROLE OF EVERYDAY MEDICAL TECHNOLOGIES IN CHILDREN'S LIVES

It is a particular aspect of children's business centred on the relationship to children's lives of 'technologies' – in particular what might be considered everyday 'medical technologies' – which we now wish to explore briefly, as part of a set of analyses which we are now developing. 'Medical technologies', in the sense in which we are using the term, are defined as material objects which have been specifically designed and constructed within a therapeutic (mainly Western, science-based, medical) paradigm to assist, modify, ameliorate or replace embodied functions or components which are considered to be – in the same paradigm – deficient, ineffective or damaged. In the everyday world of Western (and particularly British) children such material objects might be, for example, glasses, hearing aids and asthma inhalers. This definition does not of course imply that such material objects are always, or even at all, used in the ways that the definition implies, or that there are not other competing definitions of their nature, value or use, even within their originating therapeutic paradigm.

Two lines of argument are of particular interest to us. The first is about the role of 'things', of 'technologies' and more generally of the material world in relation to social life. This issue has been revisited with increasing vigour by social scientists and others in the past few years. Previous widespread and overdetermined debates on the extent to which such technologies might be considered to have 'caused' particular forms of society, or *vice versa*, have become more complex as different theoretical perspectives focused on an array of different kinds of ways in which the relationships between things and society, or more particularly between things and human actors, might be conceived.

Prout (1996) has argued, although very cautiously and with several major caveats, that actor network theory might offer another way into what had become a relatively routine – if not sterile – debate on the relationship of children to, and with, technologies. Actor network theory appeared to offer a way out of the dualism inherent in the usual conceptions of technology and society by considering both non-human and human entities as actors who mutually constitute society. Although the practice of the theory of actor networks is extremely problematic, it is at the very least helpful in promoting what must be a continuing analytical dialogue focused on the issue of how children often relate to one another and interact through the medium of objects or things which can be seen to have 'social lives'. In an earlier analysis, Appadurai (1986: 5), while not working within an actor network framework, stated a view that could be seen to add a complementary dimension: 'Whilst from a *theoretical* point of view human acts encode things with significance, from a *methodological* point of view it is the things in motion that illuminate their human and social context' (emphasis in original).

The point that Appadurai makes about 'things in motion' brings us to the second line of argument about the relationship of material things to the social world, which is linked to ideas of exchange in social life. Exchange is a richly symbolic activity, and an important source of metaphors about social relations and the social order (Davis 1992). The debate within social anthropology about the key features of exchange and exchange systems has been lengthy and continues, but Davis has argued that perhaps the most useful way of understanding such systems is through an emphasis on their symbolic, moral, ritual, political and legal meanings. He notes that there is always an underlying pattern to exchange in all cultures: 'the slogan is "other things are never equal, and are always patterned"'. Consequentiality is located not in the workings of economic laws but in the social rules of power, symbol, convention, etiquette, ritual, role and status' (Davis 1992:7–8). Davis' account allows the incorporation of fluidity, ambiguity, complexity and instability, as well as creative manipulation as part of the essence of exchange.

These two approaches, one centred on non-humans as actors – or at a more minimal level as having social statuses, capacities and influences – and the other centred on exchange as an integral component of social life, provide a fruitful (if rather complex and sometimes competing) way to understand the role of material things in children's lives, as we see children engaged in the business of everyday activities.

THE METHODOLOGICAL CONTEXT OF THE STUDY

The ethnographic research on which this chapter is based was originally designed to investigate the place of what we have described as 'everyday medical technologies' in the lives of seven to nine year old children in primary school settings in North London. Following agreement to allow participant observation in two primary schools, Amber Delahooke spent almost twelve months (1995–6) during term time in individual classes in these two schools. Both schools were in an Inner London Borough, but each had a different management and educational ethos, upon which the proportion of pupils of non-English birth appeared to have a significant bearing. In one school, from which most of the ethnographic material for this chapter is derived, more than 60 per cent of the children were of non-English birth, and for the majority of these children English was a second language. Many were from families granted refugee status in Britain. The ethos of this school was understandably more explicitly multi-cultural, and directed on a day-to-day basis to acknowledging the importance of developing the standard curricula, but in the context of recognized social, linguistic and ethnic diversity. The other primary school had a far lower proportion of such children, and appeared to operate on a more formal basis with less latitude for deviation, in all kinds of ways, from what was a more proscribed (and less 'multi-cultural') pattern of teaching and educational management.

Originally more than one class was chosen for observation in each of the two schools, but over the course of the year one class in the school with the higher proportion of children of non-British birth became the main focus of attention. The diversity of children's backgrounds and ethnicities in this particular class provided a very rich environment in which the negotiation of relationships between children themselves, and between children and adults (particularly teachers), could be observed. The class was of additional interest as a greater proportion of these children compared to other classes were, for various reasons, subject to medical assessments during the year in which classroom observation was undertaken, and were incorporating various medical technologies (such as spectacles and measured dose inhalers) into their lives.

It was usually announced initially – and bluntly – by class teachers that the ethnographer was researching children's health. However as it had also been agreed that her role in the class was one of providing reading assistance, she was quickly integrated into the daily life of the class. In the class with the higher proportion of children of non-British birth, and indeed in the other classes to a lesser extent, the children appeared to accept her as an 'honorary child', exchanging confidences with her and using her to negotiate about and among other friends. The ethnographer's relationships with the class teachers were often more difficult, as she studiously withdrew from the disciplining roles normally expected of adults in classroom situations, and also withdrew from giving the teachers information about children's activities which they (the children) had given to her in confidence. Extensive and detailed fieldnotes were compiled initially in a small notebook in class, which the children frequently asked to see, and were shown. The fieldnotes were subsequently written up in full every day after school.

The fieldwork material spanned a very wide range of activities and interactions, in relation to which those focusing specifically on medical technologies were only a part since a key concern was the social placing and contextualization of those technologies in the broader patterns of children's lives at school. However, to develop and focus the present analysis the fieldnotes from this twelve-month study have been systematically interrogated for any material in which medical technologies, and in particular measured dose inhalers, have been the object of children's concerns, actions, interactions or negotiations. In this respect, and somewhat to our initial surprise, most of the material has not related, as others might have expected, to robust and bureaucratic child–teacher relationships, in which proprietorship in school of the inhalers, and the conditions for their classroom use are the main focus of interactions. The material was far more centred on child-to-child interactions about the meaning and use of the inhalers, in the context of their own complex and broader social world. Although it may be argued that the managerial conditions in the schools in which we researched were more lax, or less authoritarian, than in other schools, we do not believe that – even if this were so – it vitiates our general argument about the significance of children's own beliefs, practices and interactions. In addition it is clear that much previous research, even if it has not been targeted precisely on medical and educational concerns about inhaler use and management, has had those concerns at its heart, thus tending to bypass those aspects of children's social worlds that we are highlighting here.

It is worth noting finally that the study on which this chapter is based is one of a number in which we have been ethnographically exploring, on a long-term basis, children's perceptions and relationships in the everyday world, not only in school settings, but just as importantly beyond those settings, in order to investigate the social placing of such ideas as 'medical technologies', 'health', and 'vulnerability' in their lives (see Frankenberg *et al.* 2001).

FABRICATING FRIENDSHIP: A SOCIAL ACCOUNT OF MEASURED DOSE INHALERS IN EVERYDAY SCHOOL SETTINGS

During the fieldwork Amber's attention was drawn to the huge diversity of objects or things that were introduced by the children into the school environment. Despite all adult attempts to limit distractions from school work, and to enforce rules dividing 'work time' from 'play time', the children managed to maintain a complex of activities centred on these things throughout both work and play time. It became clear that any and every material thing could be incorporated into the repertoire of continuous exchanges, through a mutual sharing of experience, often made explicitly social through what Christensen (1993) has noted in her work on childhood illness and injury is an injunction to others to 'look!'

In such a process exchange may not be so much a matter of physically transferring an object from one person to another, but a means of generating and consolidating shared knowledge – a knowledge which may be constructed through exchanges in the form of mutual access to privileged information. Things are thus the medium through which a wide range of social interactions between children often takes place. We have a substantial body of ethnographic data on many kinds of 'things' and 'technologies' in children's lives in a range of formal and informal settings at school which raise a wide range of conceptual and methodological issues, but for present purposes our particular concern is with medical technologies centred on children's control or management of asthma.

Although it may seem a rather obvious comment after reading our introductory ethnographic example, children – like the rest of us – use material things in ways which, depending on the perspective, either resist or expand the catalogue of uses or roles which other actors (such as their designers, manufacturers or professional prescribers and suppliers; both doctors and other medically-focused professional staff) intend or even imagine. Thus, in relation to the points in the ethnographic example above, this was the only time Ryan ever brought his inhalers into school while one of us was researching there. It is clear that he did not bring them in to school at all for health reasons, but used them as his 'things to show' for that day in a performance which both excited and impressed his classmates. The other children all wanted to see what he could do with those things, and what properties they had themselves. In this particular case both Ryan's skills in manipulating the object, as well as some of its own properties, jointly enhanced his social position *vis-à-vis* his peers in ways similar to those we have noted with other material objects.

One interesting and important symbolic feature of the social transactions illustrated in the opening ethnographic example was the role and understanding of colour, which is illustrated again in this section of ethnography:

[Towards the end of term, as the children prepare for a Christmas play:]

In comes Edinoto [one of the class] to collect the class for a play practice being performed tomorrow. Drew [who plays the king in the play] hands me [AD] his Ventolin [measured dose inhaler] in its box which he has been holding in his hand all this time. He says 'Could you look after this for me while we're rehearsing … I'm on a brown pump [inhaler] now, I've got a brown one – that's one more pump before black and black's the worst – it's my lungs … I know it's my lungs – at least I think it is – I think they're cracked – 'cos on the X-ray I saw this line across my lungs … but I missed my appointment – so my next one is on January 4th …' The Ventolin he gives me [AD] is actually a blue one …' Aaron, Sophie and others [from the class] are present during all this.

The boys in the first ethnographic example, and in this second example, point to the importance of colour and its power to convey particular meanings to the children. From an adult medical perspective the blue and the brown inhalers are designed to perform different functions. The blue inhaler is an asthma inhaler for immediate relief, and is used on an 'as needed' basis, working quickly to dilate the airways if they constrict in the course of an attack. The brown inhaler, by contrast, has an anti-inflammatory action, and works over the course of a daily regime of periodic application. For the boys the different colours signify different 'strengths', and thus inform them of the relative seriousness of their asthma. So a brown pump is stronger than a blue one, and in addition is the one before black, which is the worst.

The inclusion of a black pump into the scheme alerted us to the fact that, as a keen student of karate, Drew – in the example above – was reading the colour coding of the inhalers according to the principles of karate, in which its practitioners attain different colour belts to signify their relative competence. Thus Drew's category system was both explicitly clear – at least to him and to many of his class mates – and had the significant effect of translating worse (in terms of the status of his asthma) into better (in terms of competence at karate). While the boys' understanding of their pumps seems from an adult perspective to bring together rules from two seemingly distinct cultural contexts, from the children's own point of view and in their experience, it is an entirely rational, completely contextualized and well-considered conceptualization. Thus the colour of the pumps [inhalers] forms a shorthand way of linking into many elements in the everyday world of children's lives, as the next example demonstrates.

Drew tells me [AD] about his asthma, with Ryan, who also has the condition, sitting in on the conversation:

Drew says, 'Sometimes I can't breathe … When I had bad asthma and I only had the blue pump, it took over two pumps to stop it. I think now the blue ones would work – now, I haven't had an asthma attack for a long time now. I've got a brown pump at home. My doctor never gave me two brown pumps, or I would have brought one to school.'
Drew tells me [AD] he keeps a blue one in the staff room, 'Cos if I had an attack at play centre [in a separate part of the school] and it [the blue inhaler] was in the classroom I wouldn't be able to get it.' However, in my inspection of the pump box in the staff room I did not find one for Drew.
Ryan says 'I've got two brown pumps. When I was three I got asthma.' Both can remember their first asthma attacks, they tell me. Drew tells me how once he and Ryan both had an asthma attack at the same time:

'We're like twins with asthma we are, you and me Ryan – and Ryan had to use my pump 'cos he didn't have one. I get asthma when I run a lot, don't you Ryan? I haven't seen you have one for a while.'
'Yeah,' says Ryan, 'I get it when I run a lot,' and he tells me how he ran around his block loads of times at the weekend and didn't get an asthma attack. 'I got a white pump, have you got a white pump?'
'Yeah,' says Drew. 'What, a white one with blue bits on it? Plastic?'

Drew and Ryan form a common bond – become 'twins' in Drew's term – through their experiences with their respective symptomatic difficulties which are linked through their knowledge and use of inhalers. Although this point suggests that inhalers as particular material objects have some special status amongst children over and above other objects, in the next example, Chillel and Carly, two girls in the class being studied, have a rather down-to-earth view of their place in the rough and tumble of school life.

> Chillel tells me [AD] that she gets asthma – she has two pumps and takes them both twice a day – she forgot this morning though. And she doesn't bring them to school. I ask her what it's like having asthma. 'It gives me a blocked up nose in the night time,' she said. But she likes using the pump: 'It's good.'
> Carly said, 'I'd like to use a pump.'
> Chillel: 'It's not fun when you get a blocked nose every day.'
> Carly says, 'My brother never gets a blocked nose.'
> Carly tells us how her brother had his pumps nicked at school.
> I ask, 'Why?'
> 'People who don't like you nick your stuff,' Carly says.

Chillel and Carly's comments, and the ways in which asthma inhalers relate to the children's lives in these accounts, suggest that their role as objects – or in terms of actor network theory, as actors in the everyday world of peer group relationships at school – is one of sheer ordinariness. The inhalers are incorporated in daily life, in conversations, and in other interactions, using category systems and values which are employed in relation to many other familiar objects, settings and circumstances which have nothing at all, and yet everything, to do with asthma and its management. Thus, our perspective on children's deployment of measured dose inhalers fits well with Strathern's comments on the use of technology in domestic settings:

> One is invited to relish the 'discovery' that people are more free than the technologies suggest – that they resist colonization – and turn these devices to their own uses. Far from being dominated, they deploy them to creative ends, and to ends of their own making: the active consumer.
>
> (Strathern 1992: ix–x)

CONCLUSION

This brief analysis is set in the context of major concern with what many consider to be an epidemic of asthma in the United Kingdom. In particular, within a range of disciplines ranging from the social to the medical sciences, recent research has focused on two apparently contradictory elements. The first is the statistical ubiquity of asthma. It appears to be 'everywhere' in children and childhood at present – for example, according to the National Asthma Campaign (NAC) Audit of 1997/8, one in seven children have asthma symptoms requiring treatment; its incidence has increased threefold since 1992 (Rona *et al.* 1995), and there will be approximately four children in every primary school class with asthma (Strachen *et al.* 1994). The second is asthma's contrasting extraordinariness. It is considered to disrupt 'normal' childhoods and 'normal' relationships between children not only by virtue of its symptoms, but also by virtue of the situational and technological means of controlling or managing it (Creer *et al.* 1992; Celano and Geller 1993; Malveaux and Fletchervincent 1995). Thus on the one hand it is a statistically integrating component of many childhoods in the UK, but on the other hand it appears, in much literature, to set individual children with asthma socially, as well as medically, apart from one another.

The assertive, and often largely negative, social and educational implications of the medical diagnosis of asthma are based on its being considered not so much as a generic disorder of childhood, whose sheer extensiveness may provide beneficial social opportunities, interactions and support between children, but as a diagnosis of (many) isolated individual children whose lives are transformed in a personally unmitigated and malign way, set against the assumed 'normal' childhood of individual others. In this process of individualizing the social dimensions of childhood, the agency of children is substantially lost (Hepper *et al.* 1998). For such 'sick' children become doubly socially disabled, both by virtue of the initial medical diagnosis which catapults them explicitly into a formal medical domain as continually monitored patients of adult others, and by virtue of the special educational surveillance and direction which is considered necessary for them in school settings. However, this analysis suggests that it would be unwise to consider all or most children to be so imprisoned by their asthma and its management that their own social worlds are completely fractured.

The incorporation of measured dose inhalers as part of their ordinary everyday worlds of play was possible for the children studied in this ethnographic account, even where their cultural backgrounds – considered conventionally – were extremely diverse, with over half the children having a language other than English as their first language, and many being of refugee status. 'Child's play', in Goldman's (1998) words, allows for the possibility, through imagination and pretence as well as through other reference devices of analogy and metaphor, of children incorporating into ordinary interaction those everyday medical technologies on the same basis as other more explicitly childhood 'things', all of which are thought and talked about, and acted on and with, as well as often being exchanged. Children's play needs to be seen not as a quaint folkloric oddity set apart from the 'real' understanding and knowledge of the world, but as the essence of a social life in which – as in this case – the individualizing elements of medical and educational imperatives can be retextured and reintegrated into that life through the collective agency of children.

This process does not mean that the 'proper uses' of the technologies – those considered to be appropriate by their designers, manufacturers and professional advisors – are not understood by children; rather, that such use is limited and particular, and is only a small part of the rich fabric of children's social lives. In terms of the title of this chapter those uses are part of the process of fabricating friendships through systems of exchange, sometimes literally as when one person uses another's inhaler, but more often to demonstrate, through symbolic exchanges and displays, the usual kinds of prowess and controlled access to privileged knowledge which is part of the agency – the active process – through which the formation, cementing and consolidation – as well as, from time to time, the dissolution – of those friendships occurs.

NOTES

1   We would like to acknowledge the informative role of earlier discussions with Alan Prout and Pia Christensen on issues associated with medical technology and childhood, prior to the design and undertaking of this project. We would also like to acknowledge the invaluable support and assistance of our colleagues Ronald Frankenberg and Kirstin Schmidt in the CSHSD (Centre for the Study of Health, Sickness and Disablement, Brunel University) during and following the completion of the fieldwork, and that of Sally Kendall, now of the University of Hertfordshire. The fieldwork for the project was supported by a grant from the Brunel University – Buckinghamshire College Joint Fund.

REFERENCES

Appadurai, A. (1986) 'Introduction: commodities and the politics of value,' in Appadurai, A. (ed.) (1986) *The Social Order of Things*, Cambridge: Cambridge University Press.

Celano, M. and Geller, R. (1993) 'Learning, school performance and children with asthma: how much at risk?' *Journal of Learning Disabilities* 6: 23–32.

Christensen, P. (1993) 'The social construction of help amongst Danish children,' *Sociology of Health and Illness* 15(4): 488–502.

Corrigan, P. (1979) *Schooling the Smash Street Kids*, London: Macmillan.

Creer, T. L., Stein, R. E., Rappaport, L., Lewis, C. (1992) 'Behavioural consequences of illness: childhood asthma as a model,' *Journal of Asthma* 23: 261–269.

Davis, J. (1992) *Exchange*, Milton Keynes: Open University Press.

Ennew, J. (1994) 'Time for children, or time for adults,' in Qvortrup J., Bardy M., Sgitta G., Wintersberger H. (eds) *Childhood Matters: Theory, Practice and Politics*, Aldershot: Avebury Press.

Frankenberg, R., Robinson, I. and Delahooke A. (201) 'Countering essentialism in behavioural social science: the case of the 'vulnerable child' ethnographically examined.' *Sociological Review* 48(4): 587–611.

Goldman, L. R. (1998) *Child's Play: Myth Mimesis and Make-believe*, London: Berg.

Hepper, F., Robinson, I. and Kendall, S. (1996) 'Significantly different or successfully unique?' An asthmatic child's construction of social identity,' *British Medical Anthropology Review* 3: 5–10.

Hepper, F., Kendall, S. and Robinson, I. (1998) 'Empowering children through ethnography?, in Kendall, S. (ed.) *Health and Empowerment*, London: Arnold.

Hillman, M., Layboum, J. and Whitelegg J. (1990) *One False Move: A Study of Children's Independent Mobility*, London: Policy Studies Institute.

James, A. (1993) *Childhood Identities: Self and Social Relationship in the Experience of the Child*, Edinburgh University Press.

James, A. and Prout, A. (eds) (1990) *Constructing and Reconstructing Childhood*, Falmer Press.

James, A., Jenks, C. and Prout, A. (1998) *Theorizing Childhood*, Cambridge: Polity Press.

Malveaux, F. J. and Fletchervincent, S. A. (1995) 'Environmental risk factors of asthma in urban centres', *Environmental Health Perspectives* 103(S6): 59–62.

Nader, L. (1980) 'The vertical slice: hierarchies and children', in Britain, G. M. and Cohen, R. (eds) *Hierarchy and Society: Anthropological Perspectives on Bureaucracy*, Philadelphia: Ishi.

National Asthma Campaign (NAC) (1998) *National Asthma Audit 1997/8*, London: National Asthma Campaign.

Newsom, J. and Newsom, E. (1978) *Seven Years Old in the Home Environment*, Harmondsworth: Penguin.

Opie, I. and Opie, P. (1969) *Children's Games in Street and Playground*, Oxford: Oxford University Press.

Prout, A. (1996) 'Actor network theory, technology and medical sociology: an illustrative analysis of the measured dose inhaler', *Sociology of Health and Illness* 18(2): 198–219.

Rona, R., Chinn, S. and Burney P. (1995) 'Trends in the prevalence of asthma in Scottish and English schoolchildren 1982–1992', *Thorax* 92: 992–3.

Strachen, D., Anderson, H., Limb, E., O'Neill, A. and Wells, N. (1994) 'A national survey of asthma prevalence, severity and treatment in Great Britain', *Archives of Disease in Childhood* 70: 174–8.

Strandell, H. (1997) 'Doing reality with play', *Childhood* 4(4): 445–464.

Strathern, M. (1992) 'Foreword' in Silverstone, R. and Hirsch, E. (eds) *Consuming Technologies: Media and Information in Domestic Spaces*, London: Routledge.

Sutton-Smith, B. (1977) 'Play as adaptive potentiation', in Stevens, P. (ed.) *Studies in the Anthropology of Play*, New York: Leisure Press.

6 Situated knowledge and virtual education

Some real problems with the concept of learning and interactive technology

Terry A. Hemmings, Karen M. Clarke, Dave Francis, Liz Marr and Dave

INTRODUCTION

Information and communication technology (ICT) is now at the heart of educational policy, and museums are increasingly relying on their position as resource providers and mediators within the National Grid for Learning. Based around the internet, this mosaic of information networks will enable schools to share resources wherever their location. Educators within museums, however, have by definition always identified their functions as being an integral part of both the local and national pedagogical landscape. In the UK, national science museums have a long didactic tradition, providing educational and informational resources for a diversity of visitors.

Many museums, and particularly science museums, now have galleries designed to appeal to children. Oriented around the notion of experimentation and discovery, most large museums provide displays specifically designed to provide an 'interactive' experience. Essentially, this pedagogic approach provides for a process of self-discovery, whereby knowledge is gained experientially rather than didactically. Interacting with objects, it is claimed, provides an active context for more intrinsically meaningful activity. It is argued that direct, 'hands-on' involvement encourages enquiry oriented towards an understanding of abstract conceptual matters. This contrasts with the didactic instructional model of teaching and learning where information regarding, for example, the history, function or use of an exhibit is transmitted to the passive onlooker.

In this way 'interactivity' is claimed to have positive educational outcomes (Government Green Paper: *The Learning Age* 1998). Clearly, it is also the key feature that separates computers from other media in enhancing learning. Hence communication that is computer-mediated is distinct from other forms of communication in that it enables active involvement, whereas books, radio and television are activities oriented towards the passive receipt of information. This policy is exemplified in the work of the CTI (Computers in Teaching Initiative), which was launched in 1989 with the mission 'to maintain and advance the quality of learning and increase the effectiveness of teaching through the application of appropriate learning technologies'. In order to support and promote changes in teaching practice, a university-based network of twenty-four discipline-specific support centres has been established. Each is hosted by a relevant university department, 'ensuring that the work of the CTI remains focused on the real priorities of teachers and learners'.

No concept so characterized educational thinking in the late 1990s as did interactivity. Intertwined with this notion of interactivity is the concept of the 'virtual', which also bids to become one of the most over-used terms of the late twentieth century as its use spreads with the growth of the internet. The gist of the concept of the 'virtual' appears to rest on the assumption that the use of electronic technologies allows the user to interact with elements in a space engineered and defined by the technology; elements and spaces that need not necessarily bear any relationship to how we understand embodied spatial and temporal locations (Hughes *et al.* forthcoming). So embedded in the notion of the digital age are these ideas that there is little questioning their value or utility.

The idea that computer mediated communication (CMC) produces educationally relevant interaction relies utterly on some description of use. In this chapter we argue that there are relatively few descriptions that allow us to identify what is being spoken of when interactivity is promoted as a concept. As sociologists, our conception of interaction is predicated on the view that all social behaviour is inherently interactive. Consequently, questions concerning the value or otherwise of interactivity rest on evidence concerning precisely what interaction is taking place. Museums, and particularly interactive galleries, therefore provide a real-world site for capturing and analysing the complex interplay between the social, organizational, cultural and political factors relevant to the design and use of virtual technologies.

Our concern here is that enquiries into the putative impact of innovative technology within the educational arena have, for the most part, drawn upon various theories of the teaching and learning process. Theory-dominant perspectives, whatever their merits for enabling us to derive generic concepts and thus generic systems, provide little analytic purchase on the problem of practice. In this way, we are arguing for an ethnomethodologically-informed ethnographic approach to the study of learning, applied specifically to the problem of new technology in learning.

THE STUDY

Our analysis is based on a two-year ethnography of the work of museum staff and visitors' activities at two locations: the Museum of Science and Industry in Manchester (MSIM) and the National Railway Museum in York (NRM). During fieldwork both museums were in the process of introducing new information systems. Consistent with our previous arguments, we want to suggest that the effectiveness of such systems will largely depend upon the extent to which they are informed by an understanding of what kind of information-related educational work is undertaken, by whom, and how this work is organized as an interactional, situationally-accomplished activity.

A set of general observations progressively raised an interest in education as part of the organizational life of the museum. In turn, this led us to try to understand how education took place here, as elsewhere, in the context of a set of organizational imperatives. These included, for instance, the structuring of visits so they could remain orderly and could take place within pre-determined time slots, and yet nevertheless constitute an experience that incorporates collaborative working, situated learning, and working with technologies. Our focus here, then, is specifically informed by the sense in which these visits are educational. There is, of course, an immediate sense in which they are evidently so, because they are visibly and accountably treated in that way by most visitors but more noticeably by museum staff and school groups. Nevertheless, embedded in much educational research is the idea that some conceptual or theoretical work goes on when education is done, over and above what is immediately visible. Groups of schoolchildren on educational visits were observed, using videotape, engaging with one interactive activity in particular called 'Wheels on Rails'. We describe 'Wheels on Rails' more fully below. Suffice it to say for the moment that the policy issues we mention above make interactive galleries a perspicuous site for understanding the relationship between what actually goes on rather than what ought to be going on. We should perhaps stress that we are studiously indifferent, as befits an ethnomethodological perspective in policy matters, but nevertheless believe that careful description of interactions constitutes an invitation to consider the relationship between ethnographic data and policy. The impact on policy matters we have outlined above, which concern what to do for various practitioners, depend for their force on careful consideration of what happens. Our contention is that much of the argument concerning policy is in practice, for the most part, supported by only empirical and analytic glosses.

Our interest here does not lie in any theory of the education process but in the practice of education. We are particularly interested in the structure of an educational experience such that it can be said to have a 'beginning', a 'middle', and an 'end', and how it is that interventions take place in such a way as to produce that structure. In short, what is it that observably makes the experience 'educational'? In pursuit of this interest, and as part of an ongoing ethnographic study into the work of the museum, we spent several months observing and analysing interaction with displays in the NRM. The part of our work we discuss here concerns the 'Magician's Road', a set of interactive exhibits intended primarily, but not exclusively, for groups of schoolchildren visiting the NRM. 'Magician's Road' is a self-contained gallery consisting of a collection of hands-on, interactive apparatuses and facilities of the 'press on this button' or 'play with this device' kind, designed specifically with schoolchildren in mind. What we do next, therefore, is draw some early conclusions about educational use of artefacts, representations and text by examining three examples of 'groups' at work with an artefact, taken from a series of organized visits observed at the museum. The examples are all situated at one particular interactive exhibit which forms part of the 'Magician's Road' ('Wheels on Rails'). Again, we are trying to show in this context that providing educational resources involves a great deal more than simply providing images, text, and links between them.

Our interest was prompted by our growing recognition that visitor understanding and use of exhibits was not in any strong sense determined by the artefacts themselves. After all, the case made for the educational power of new technology is in some instances determinist, in that it speaks of the 'effects' of new technology in these environments, and in certain respects, museum sites represent an early and physical version of the educational promise held out for new technology such as the internet. The collection of 'interactive' exhibits at NRM consists of a *mélange* of apparatus, representations, texts, and physical artefacts oriented towards some experimental result. In other words, and without stretching the analogy too far, it seemed to us that 'hands-on' experimentation of this kind was not too far removed from some of the claims made for hypertext as an educational medium and resource. Equally, education in arenas such as museums is a policy issue, as is evident in recent debates over the function and value of 'edutainment'. That is, explicitly or otherwise, it seemed to us that some vision of how the educational experience should be conducted was embedded in these artefactual arrangements, and was purportedly visible in the work of the organized visit. Lastly, the visiting groups were being exposed to an experience which educators saw as less structured, more open and more discovery-based than the typical classroom enterprise, and moreover which was taking place 'away from home'. That is, ordinary presumptions concerning the teachers' and children's roles in the process might be problematized and negotiable according to perspectives on the task in hand. In sum, we were interested in gaining a precise view of what actually happened when 'education' was being done in the context of a museum visit.

Here in the 'Magician's Road' gallery was an arrangement of artefacts, instructions and representations in a physical location away from a classroom, which arguably shared characteristics with what is anticipated for the use of electronic media: the ability to 'interact' with representations, the prospect of 'non-linear' search and retrieval of information, and a pupil-led or discovery-based approach to use. It seemed to us that understanding how visiting groups would actually use the artefacts and instructions to achieve an educational outcome, and what variations in that outcome might be observed, could tell us something about the practical potential of electronic media. In particular, it allows us to identify ways in which 'theories of learning' and 'organizational matters' are played out, in and through the modalities of organization represented by the structuring of visits, and of the text and artefacts themselves. Second, because children of various backgrounds and ages are regular visitors, it provides an opportunity to look at what an 'educational experience' looks like for the children and teachers concerned, and how they might achieve this experience against an organizational background where artefacts and representations are foregrounded as the 'relevant' matter. Simply put, we are in a position to say something about how educational practices might be accomplished when oriented to a representational structure.

In the 'Magician's Road' gallery, groups of children were invited to 'play' with the exhibits, and yet the rhetoric of museum staff and of visiting teachers very much suggested the centrality of the educational experience. The first point to be made, and it is easily forgotten when we gloss the visit as 'less structured' than the classroom, is that visits are nevertheless structured or organized. We suggest that there are broadly three ways in which some level of organization can be discerned: the scripting of the site visit; the organization of text; and the design of the artefact.

First, therefore, one of the evident characteristics of these visits was that they were 'scripted', and scripted in keeping with an educational theory. In other words, organization of visits to the 'Magician's Road' is structured with a view to providing lessons to be learned. This is exhibited in a variety of ways including, for brief mention, the fact that before children are let loose on the exhibits there is a quite formal instructional sequence where children are gathered on a carpeted setting that looks like a railway platform and an 'Explainer' delivers a more or less scripted speech which anticipates the activities which will follow. In brief, school groups are met by the Explainer, who commences with the injunction that they must not move from the carpet until instructed. The Explainer delivers a speech that provides the schoolchildren with some initial expectations as to what they will experience as well as some potential relevancies. Some talk concerns health and safety, rules the children must follow, and so on, but there is also reference to the activities that are possible. Thus, and for instance, the 'Explainer' carries a wheeltapper's hammer which is used to exemplify what can be done by dint of questioning: 'Do you know what this is for?' This invariably leads to a way of providing an explanation concerning the purpose of wheel tapping. The questioning is progressively widened by the Explainer to include reference to the flat trajectories of railway lines, the principles of friction, the need for railway cuttings and tunnels and so on. A key instruction is also provided by emphasizing to the children that they need to read the text that accompanies the interactive exhibits. In other words, the work being done is that of providing the schoolchildren with some initial expectations as to what they will experience as well as some potential relevancies. Similarly, at the end of the visit, children are gathered again, and reinforcement work is done. There is thus a level of organization which we can term the structuring of the 'site visit'.

How this organization is provided and exhibited, as in scripts for the Explainers, depends both on a set of pedagogic beliefs which can be discerned in the structures, and on organizational concerns. For instance, school visits are scheduled and this requires that they be completed within a fixed amount of time. Overrunning the time allocated for visits (forty to forty-five minutes) often has practical repercussions, particularly during busy periods when demands on the schedule and staffing arrangements provide little in the way of slack. While our analysis highlights the interaction surrounding the particular exhibit called 'Wheels on Rails', in certain respects its relevance serves to draw attention to the nature of competencies brought to the setting by participants (the data we discuss below is taken from several hours of videotape taken of groups of children using the exhibit). Before they approach an exhibit, pupils have been made aware that there are lessons to be learned here and suggestions have been made as to what those lessons might be. Similarly, they have been made aware that it is the museum Explainers who seem to take centre stage when explanation is to be done, rather than their teachers.

The exhibit consists of a piece of apparatus constructed to represent a scaled-down model of railway track. The apparatus is some four metres long and half a metre wide. The parallel track is gently inclined downwards with a right-handed curve at the far end. In front of the track is a table, on which are to be found six sets of axles with a wheel at each end.

Seen in section, each set of wheels has a distinct and differently shaped wheel profile. Immediately beside this table is a stand clearly displaying text and a number of simple line-drawn illustrations, all designed to provide a description of the function of the apparatus together with an explanation of its relevance to the principles of mechanics which are fundamental to the operation of the railway. By definition, there is an organization to the text for use. The instructions for the 'Wheels on Rails' exhibit consist of three sections. The first consists of background information explaining the importance of wheel action to the development of the railways. Thus, in the first and second sections we find the following words:

> As railways developed so different materials for wheels and rails were used and differing ways developed to make sure that the wheel stayed on and was guided by the rail.
>
> The earliest railway vehicles had plain wheels and used a guidance pin reaching down between the tracks – very much like the power pin on today's Scalextrix racing cars. Later L-shaped rails were used to guide plain wheels and it was only with the development of the edged rail and flanged wheel that the forerunner of today's wheels and rails appeared.
>
> Today's rail is made of steel and is laid in continuously welded lengths which may be well over a mile long. The guidance for the wheel is provided by the coned profile and a flange; together these ensure that the wheels remain on the straight track and safely negotiate corners.

Simple line-drawn icons of the wheel sets in profile are also provided, as are illustrations and labelling of the flanged wheel which immediately follow this. What is significant here is that the desired outcome to the experiment is provided more or less immediately.

In the first section, the relevance of the 'coned' profile and the flange of the wheels is established. That is, the instructions are not provided so as to allow children to 'discover' the correct set of wheels, but are designed to allow children to confirm the result given. The second section outlines the instructions for use, and explicitly describes the 'Wheels on Rails' exhibit as an 'experiment'. This section begins with these instructions:

> The experiment consists of a length of curved track (in a basket frame) and a number of sets of model wheels, each with a different coned profile and without flanges. Carrying out the experiment is very simple. Select a wheel set, take it to the upper end of the track and release. You should find that the wheel set with the markedly coned profile is particularly suitable for negotiating straight and curved track.

Adjacent to this text is another line-drawn icon identifying the profile of the 'correct' set of wheels. This is followed by an explanation in diagram and text form, which emphasizes the variable circumference of the wheels as they touch the inside and outside rails respectively. The third section of the display board is taken up with text relating to principles of 'cant' (camber) and the relevance of speed restrictions. The fourth section refers to the wheel tapping experiment, and points out that 'real' railway wheels have this coned profile and a flange. The instructions/explanation finish with text outlining the ways the apparatus may be appropriately related to parts of the National Curriculum. These instructions may be regarded as more or less exemplary as they are clearly laid out to establish, in order, what lesson is to be learned – that of the importance of wheel shape – how it can be learned – by rolling each set of wheels down the track and confirming that only one set of wheels will negotiate the bend – and an explanation – that variable circumference enables the wheels to stay on. The instructions also provide relevances to other experiments on offer, notably the wheel tapping experiment, and to other organizational concerns, notably links to the National Curriculum.

The displays themselves also contain an organization that in theory was designed to lead the children towards certain kinds of enquiry. That is, in each instance the exhibits are designed in such a way as to invite conclusions. One feature of the 'Wheels on Rails' exhibit, for instance, is the way in which it echoes experimental conditions, in that before children are allowed to descend on the exhibit the sets of wheels are always arranged vertically on a table adjacent to the rail. This 'end upwards' colonnade view provides for ready recognition that each wheel has a different profile, and their placement next to the rail is an invitation to place them on the rail. As we shall see, however, the level of organizational competences demonstrated by the children exceeds what is anticipated by the layout of the exhibit.

Taken together, these differing modalities of organization explicate the things to be done. Initially a set of relevances is outlined by the Explainer, including not only educational but also organizational relevances. Thus, while organization of the first set of interactions obviously suggests 'things to look for' for the children, it also provides for the relevance of the time allowed to visit the 'interactives' and for the role of the accompanying teacher. The organization of the instructions provides a 'lesson to be learned' and equally, by placing the answer early in the text, allows for it to be learned quickly. As the designer of the exhibit commented, 'on a busy day, there's hundreds of kids coming through here and you can't let them stay forever ... so the design can't be too complicated, we have to keep them moving round.' Again, therefore, there is an organizational imperative embedded in the organization of the text. Finally, the organization of the exhibits provides 'things to be done in a certain way'. In effect the exhibits are designed and constructed in such a way that they replicate a number of known experimental outcomes. Again, organizational matters are relevant here, since the number and placement of the wheels is designed to facilitate an immediate appreciation of the purpose of the experiment. These modalities of organization, of course, do not determine activity. Taken together, they create a structure of relevance out of which children may decide on appropriate behaviours, along with adults accompanying them.

The organization of visits to the 'Magician's Road' is structured with a view to providing lessons to be learned and methods or routes for doing the learning, and at the same time provides for a recognition of other relevant matters. Thus it is clear that a theory which is both educational and organizational is in place, one which recognizes the importance of pedagogy but which, even so, orients to matters such as 'how long do they have?' and 'who is in charge here?' Thus, we argue that the layout of the exhibit we discuss and the instructions for use associated with the exhibit not only embody a theory concerning the nature of the lesson and how it is to be learned but also some suggestions as to how the outcome should be achieved processually. However, as we shall see, they neither guarantee that these are the lessons learned nor that the process will take a given form. The character of the lesson and of the process is an achievement of the parties to the interaction. Moreover, it is an achievement that is evidently variable.

We use three contrasting scenarios as examples. Our interest was in how the 'lesson to be learned' from the assemblage of instructions, text and artefacts might be accomplished in a variety of ways and in particular how 'timely intervention' by the adult was a significant feature in what kind of lesson was learned. In the course of several hours of videotaping we discerned some consistency in the lesson achieved, according to the style of adult intervention.

Example 1

Four girls arrive together accompanied by an adult. The adult male watches throughout but does not speak at any time.
Girls A, B, and C collect the wheels from the table. The girls do not read the instructional plaque.

Girls A, B and C stand at the head of the track. Girl D stands at the foot.
Girls A and B roll all six wheels at intervals of about eight seconds, in
each case allowing the previous set of wheels to complete their trajectory before rolling the next. Rolling all six wheels takes approximately
forty seconds.
Girl D brings three sets of wheels back to the head of the track. She rolls
two sets in turn, the 'nearly right' set and the 'right set'. She does not
roll the third set.
Girl C retrieves the 'right' set and returns to the head of the track,
placing them on the track. Girl A leaves. Girls B and C leave.
Girl D watches the wheels roll down the track and then leaves.
Total elapsed time: one minute ten seconds.

A number of observations can be made about this interaction. The first and
most obvious one is that the available instructions have at best a peripheral
relationship to the activities of the group, since we were unable to identify any
time at which any girl in the group read them. Regardless, the girls arrived as
a group, and organized themselves to 'do' the experiment as a group. The
adult style was non-interventional in that at no time did this adult speak or
proffer suggestions as to the appropriate lesson to be learned.

All four members of the group 'took a turn' although the initial organization allowed for only two to do so. Only two sets of wheels were rolled more
than once and only the 'correct' set of wheels was rolled three times. Strik-
ingly, not one of the girls was heard to speak during their visit to this exhibit.
The pupils organized themselves to achieve the successful completion of the
experiment without reading the instructions, asking the adult, or discussing
the result amongst themselves. It appears that, for this group, successful
completion here is establishing the right set of wheels. That this is done more
than once is in keeping with Lynch observations (1993a) that replication is as
much about establishing that the experiment has been done right as it is about
guaranteeing that the results are right. Nevertheless, this has a consequence in
terms of what we can say about the nature of the lesson that has been learned.
There is no visible evidence of any kind that an explanation has been arrived
at, in the absence of any evidence that the instructions have been read, and any
discussion following the completion of the task.

Example 2

Teacher and six pupils arrive.
Teacher instructs pupils to note title and brief description of exhibit.
One pupil picks up a set of wheels and is told to put them down.
Teacher walks to foot of rails. Time elapsed: fifty seconds.
Pupils each pick up a set of wheels and roll them in turn.
Pupils: 'Ohhhh'
'Nope'

'No'

Time elapsed: one minute thirty seconds

Teacher: 'The fourth set of wheels is the right one?'

Pupil: 'Yesss ...'

Teacher picks up 'right' set. Points to them and gives them to pupil.

Pupils roll two sets of wheels unsuccessfully. Time elapsed: two minutes.

Teacher: 'OK, what have you found out?'

Pupil: 'Only one set worked ...'

Pupil: 'These nearly worked ...'

Teacher: 'Sorry? There's only one right set ... who's got the right ones?' Takes 'right' set from pupil. Points to another set. 'These? ... did you say these nearly worked? ... what's the difference?'

Pupils hold one set against the other. Teacher points to different shape.

Pupils are instructed by the teacher to sketch the shape of the 'right' wheels. One pupil rolls the 'right' and 'nearly right' wheels again.

Teacher picks up the 'nearly right' wheels and shows them to the pupils. They are sketched as well.

Teacher holds up both sets.

Teacher: 'Is this one as sharp as that?'

Pupil: 'No ...'

Pupils continue to sketch.

Teacher: 'So ... gather round in a circle.' Moves to plaque.

Teacher: 'OK ... why did it win ... why did this one manage to go round the corner?'

Pupils proffer various explanations. One pupil takes the 'right' set to the bend and shows the teacher.

Pupil: 'That stops it ...'

Teacher: 'What do you mean, it stops it?'

Pupil: 'Well, when it goes that way ... in there ... it pushes against the rail.'

Teacher: 'Right ... and it works, doesn't it? You always find it works. Where's the other one? ... surely this one would work as well, wouldn't it?'

Teacher picks up another set.

Teacher: 'So why doesn't it?'

Teacher rolls set of wheels.

Teacher: 'Why is this one coming off?'

Pupil: 'Oh, I know ... I know ...'

Teacher shakes his head and rejects explanation.

Teacher: 'Right, back to your shape ... why does this one stay on?' Gestures with 'right' set. Shows 'nearly right' set of wheels.

Teacher: 'As that one comes off [pointing to left-hand wheel], why doesn't this one [points to right-hand wheel] keep it on?'

Pupil: 'It can't turn ...'

Teacher: 'Pardon? Pardon?'

Pupil: 'It can't turn ...'

Teacher: 'It can't slide up and down. This one can.

It can't slide up and down. This one should, shouldn't it?

But it can't ... because it can't slide up and down.'

Teacher: 'Which one do you think was designed first?'

Pupil: 'That one ... 'cos you see wheels like that [pointing to the 'right' set] on trains now.'

Teacher: 'OK, on to number two ...' [Begins to walk towards the next exhibit]

Total time elapsed: eight minutes thirty seconds.

A number of points can be made here regarding the structuring of the activity. The teacher determines the appropriate time to begin experimentation and actively prevents experimentation until descriptions of conditions have been made. Without speaking, the teacher provides a cue for the experiment to begin by moving to the foot of the rails. Again, all the members of the group at some point roll wheels. Teacherly intervention takes place again when the right set of wheels has been unambiguously identified. The 'experimental' work lasts for two minutes, but the interaction around the exhibit lasts for another six minutes. The teacher initiates a discussion by asking 'what have you found out?' and more or less at the same time ensures that the 'right' set of wheels are identified and retained. A candidate answer is provided to the effect that only one set worked, immediately followed by a second pupil observing that a 'nearly right' set of wheels also exist. The teacher establishes that there is only one 'right' set and shows it to the group, but also uses the 'nearly right' set as a focus for comparison. Comparison becomes an explicit step in the lesson, first by pupils holding one set against the other, and then making the comparison formally by drawing the wheels in profile. The teacher confirms that pupils recognize the difference by referring to the 'sharpness' of the wheels.

There is a distinctive third phase when the teacher asks the pupils to gather round and moves to the display board. The teacher clearly identifies 'explanation' as the third phase by asking 'why' questions and listening to proffered explanations. Pupils use the apparatus and wheels as pointers for their explanations and the teacher refers back to the comparison of 'right' and 'nearly right'. He confirms that the right set 'always works' and asks why the second set does not, at this point rolling the second set again. No reference is made at this point to the other four sets of wheels that have all been rejected. The point here is that this third phase involves clearly establishing that one set of wheels is capable of movement in a way that the other set is not. An explanation is proffered, amplified and rephrased by the teacher, and an evolutionary connection made. The teacher signals the end of this interaction.

Example 3

Three unaccompanied pupils finish experiment, and two leave.

The third tries a final set which falls off the track. Shrugs shoulders and begins to replace wheels on table.

Explainer arrives.

Explainer: 'Did you find the real one?'

Pupil: 'Yeah' [Points]

Explainer: 'Why?'

Pupil smiles.

Explainer puts 'right' set on tracks and commences explanation, showing the principle of variable circumference.

Another pupil arrives.

Explainer puts wheels on table and second pupil picks up a set and moves to rail.

Third pupil arrives and picks up a set.

Explainer continues to explain.

Explainer: 'Let me show you how ... see ... it moves over as it goes-round ...' First girl nods.

Second pupil puts another set on which immediately falls off. Tries again.

Third pupil collects correct set and brings it back up.

First and third pupils leave.

Second pupil tries another wrong set.

Fourth and fifth pupils arrive.

Fourth pupil picks up a set of wheels, fifth pupil leaves.

Second pupil tries two more sets, identifies correct set and says, 'it's them ...' to Explainer and tries them again.

Pupil: 'Yep. Places wheels on table and leaves.

Sixth pupil arrives and touches Explainer on arm.

Seventh pupil arrives.

Sixth and seventh pupils pick up wheels and roll in turn.

Seventh pupil rolls right set as Explainer commences explanation.

Eighth pupil arrives.

Explainer points to wheel tapping experiment.

Sixth and seventh pupils continue to roll.

Ninth pupil arrives, and picks up wheels.

Explainer picks up right set and puts them on table.

Seventh pupil leans across and picks up wheels, trying them again.

Explainer draws attention to 'right' wheels and 'nearly right' wheels and discusses them with pupils seven, eight and nine.

Explainer leaves.

The three remaining pupils try the right set again.

Two pupils roll two wrong ones together. The wheels fall off and they leave.

(Timing these sequences as 'one' episode proved impossible.)

Here there are similarities to example 2, in that explanation becomes a much stronger focus of the interaction, but differences too, in that the constitution of the group is no longer clear, and thus, the beginning and end of the experiment is less apparent. The Explainer arrives just as two out of the three pupils who constituted the original group leave. The third girl is in the process of doing some checking work as the Explainer attempts to initiate explanation. Here we see the Explainer orienting to the exhibit as a focus for explanation, rather than the group, with varying consequences. Explanation is completed for the first pupil, but not, it seems for the third as she leaves with the first pupil as soon as the explanation is deemed complete for the first pupil and her only. The fifth pupil similarly leaves without any explanation proffered (and indeed without any attempt at experimentation). The second pupil, in apparent indifference to explanations that have been going on around her previously, establishes the correct set and confirms it. The pupil has been present during an explanation, but has manifestly not been a party to it. Nevertheless, no explanation is given to this pupil. The sixth pupil, on arriving, signals her readiness to commence the experiment by touching the Explainer on the arm, as a seventh pupil also arrives. Again, the rolling of the right set signals completion, and explanation commences at this point. An eighth pupil is disposed of during the course of the experiment, presumably because the Explainer at this point is trying to maintain some coherence as to who is actually doing the experiment, and thus who can be a focus for the explanation. The arrival of a ninth pupil problematizes this arrangement, so the Explainer takes the right set of wheels and places them on the table, again signalling that the experiment has been successfully completed. This cue is not accepted, since the seventh pupil again rolls the wheels. The Explainer successfully engages the three pupils currently present in an explanation, to her satisfaction, and then leaves.

Summary of findings

In sum, we see a number of similarities and differences in these interactions.

1   Children orient to the task to be undertaken as experimental, despite the existence of instructions and information concerning the 'right' result. That is, the instructions are often only cursorily perused, if at all, and the 'doing' is typically construed as the physical activity of rolling the wheels. In exactly the same way, failing intervention on the part of an educator, children tend to see the task as complete when the 'right' set of wheels has been identified to their satisfaction.
2   That is, we observe the completion of the activity to be either the selection and operation of the 'right' set of wheels, often punctuated with triumphal gestures, or as taking place after some 'checking' or verification of the result, normally against the 'nearly right' set of wheels, unless there is an intervention by teacher or Explainer such that task completion becomes the completion of a satisfactory explanation.

3   We assume, in keeping with Lynch's argument (1993b), that the checking we see typically is very much checking that the experiment has been 'done' properly, which explains why it is normally only two sets of wheels, or one alone, that are involved in completion.

4   In keeping with children's interpretation the task is construed as a physical one; groups of children self-organize such that they can all participate in the activity. One feature of this organization is the principle that everyone takes a turn, again failing an adult intervention. The 'everyone takes a turn' principle seems to supersede the 'task is completed when the right set of wheels is identified' principle, in that children regularly take their turn, if not previously taken, after the 'right' set has been identified.

5   There is no single text, artefact, or procedural arrangement that can successfully produce the desired educational outcome. Whatever the theory of learning that is in place, and whatever organizational imperatives are embedded in the instructions, it is the timely and appropriate intervention of the educators that produces a redefinition of the outcome. The instructions, artefacts etc. do not determine the educational outcomes.

6   Teachers and Explainers intervene selectively, and according to their assessment of the lesson being learned, but may do so in more than one way. We identify in these examples two strategies. The first is the group orientation strategy, where the group activity is accomplished as the identification of the conditions of the experiment – successful completion of the wheel rolling – and followed by a period of question and answer such that a satisfactory explanation is produced. In this style, the teacher's intervention can be called 'strong' in that there is a consistent move, by gesture, posture and explicit instruction, through distinct phases. A second strategy involves intervention when the task has been completed to the satisfaction of the pupils undertaking it, which seems to be a preferred strategy for explainers, and consists of a questioning style of the order, 'did you find the right wheels?' and 'did you understand why?' This strategy implicates a much more fluid approach to the nature of the group, as seen in example 3. Several different groups may form and disband during the Explainer's intervention, with the consequence that some children are not party to the explanatory phases. The intervention here is arrived at by the individual pupil signalling he or she has selected the 'right' set of wheels and the Explainer replacing the wheels, signalling completion.

DISCUSSION

The burgeoning interest in the use of ICT in educational and similar institutions, and the recognition that ICT has the potential to 'transform' social and organizational life, are of course not new. Certainly since Marx, the possible effects of technological development have been noted and with the advent of constructionist perspectives (see for instance Pacey 1999), the way in which technology and society are complexly interwoven has become a major research agenda. Parallel to this kind of historical approach (in that for the most part such work attempts to account for developments which have already occurred), research has gone on apace which seeks to marry sociological and psychological methods and perspectives with development itself. Interdisciplinary research communities such as CSCW (computer-supported co-operative work) and CSCL (computer-supported co-operative learning) have evolved wherein the purpose of human science involvement is less explanatory than it is constructive, in the sense that providing methodological and perspectival support for technological development – if you will, informing design – is the main agenda. Our reflections are in part informed by what we see as similar terms in the debate on the effective design and evaluation of ICT for educational contexts.

Equally, ethnomethodological studies of classrooms are not new. There is an extensive literature on the ordinary practices of the classroom, including Lynch (1993b), Macbeth (1990) and Heap (1982). Studies of group learning outside the classroom are less easily found, and yet we would argue that some of the data we describe above has a clear relevance to various arguments concerning the use of technology for collaborative learning, including that of the concept of situatedness we discuss above. We have already pointed out that in some usage, situatedness is something of a gloss, and can lend itself to some rather glib oppositions. We would point out here that being in a classroom and being in the outside world are not self-evidently one thing or another. Here we see an environment that manifestly shares some features of the classroom, but also in some respects does not. Our specific interest lies in the notion of group use of technology for education, and we can make the following points:

1   The term 'group' is itself under-examined. There is clearly a sense in which groups can be self-organizing, in that pupils constitute their groups by taking turns. Groups can also be organized by teacherly fiat, although it still seems that turn-taking is maintained. What is clear is that in some circumstances the constitution of the group can be extremely fluid.

2   There is scope within the context of a single technology for any number of lessons to be learned. That is, the technology does not determine the lesson. Children's orientation to a practical lesson, however, seems by default to be the completion of the task.

3   If we accept a 'preferred' view of the lesson, it is generated by timely intervention on the part of the educator. There is no single method for doing this, in that it can be based on a focus on the exhibit or on the group, and examples 2 and 3 show the difference. In either instance, educators need visible cues which enable them to judge that a particular sequence has been completed and that intervention is required if an explanation is to be proffered. Questions are appropriate questions, designed for children of this age group and educational background. They are, as it

were, 'pitched just right'. Providing electronic facilities for significant educational experiences means identifying the importance of beginnings and endings, the balance between discovery and 'direction through questioning', the specific ways in which questions are posed and when interventions take place. Children sometimes 'discover' the lesson to be learned when left to their own devices, and sometimes are taught the lesson when prompted by experts. How to provide these 'prompts' electronically is an important question, and may well relate to the experiences of other kinds of visitors as well although we have yet to determine this. How would an electronic representation embed 'timely intervention', 'appropriate elapsed time' etc.?

4   The educational experience can be defined in terms of 'beginnings', 'middles' and 'endings' as much as by a pedagogic theory. Indeed, understanding how these phases in the activity are accomplished requires us to see teaching and learning as the achievement of a set of organizational objectives as much as a set of pedagogic objectives.

It is perhaps stating the obvious, but the apparatus was constructed in order to exemplify a specific mechanical principle that allowed curves or bends in railway tracks to be laid. Up until this development, rail-based transport was limited as steam engines and carriages could travel only along straight lines. This 'magical' solution at the NRM enabled the designers to use technology to 'engineer' the use of the model. It also provided a practical way of explaining, by using a model, an abstract mechanical principle in a non-scientific way. In theory, technology provided both the medium and the message. However, the notion of embedding an explanation and lesson within the technology that can be understood and learned through the activity itself by the whole range of potential visitors is problematic, as our examples have shown.

As previously mentioned, the apparatus was designed and constructed to function in a specific way which would provide the 'task' and the 'lesson' – to find the most suitable shape for a railway wheel. Left to their own devices, the group of girls in example 1 completed the task without adult intervention, quickly and without speaking. What was 'going on' seemed utterly familiar to all members of this group; in that the 'doing' of the activity seems commonplace and unproblematic. However, it is all too easy to overlook these seen but unnoticed matters. Paying serious attention to the commonplace reveals the skills and artful accomplishments that these children display during their activity. Clearly, these children organize their activities in such a way as to 'bring off' the task rather than discovering the theoretical workings of the technology embodied in the apparatus. As Garfinkel (1984: 32) states, 'Every feature of sense, of fact, of method, for every particular case without exception, is the managed accomplishment of the organized settings of practical actions.'

Our final point is that understanding the nuance of the organized visit raised issues that we feel are germane to the prospect of any electronic alternative serving similar functions. Virtual educational facilities evidently provide an opportunity to extend curriculum delivery, without a massive overhead, by providing resources which allow teachers to search and select materials which are relevant to their specific curriculum needs, and by facilitating both preparatory, follow-up and self-tutoring activities. Again, there is no suggestion that this is an easy task. Whatever the medium, we believe the problems of providing pathways through information remain broadly the same. However, two problems seem largely ignored. First, the interactional dynamic observed contains lessons concerning how decisions are made as to what constitutes the beginning, middle, and end of a lesson, as well as the content of the lesson. Second, for the most part, arguments about what has constituted the education process and what will constitute it under the auspices of new technology have the status of assumptions, some of them moral. That technology may have considerable potential for the delivery of 'educational' processes is broadly unarguable, in that it manifestly provides scope for learning at a distance, for distributed group work, and so on. Nevertheless, these affordances are just that. They cannot and do not in themselves explain what goes on in the education process, but in principle allow educating to be done in different contexts, for the work of education is no more or less than what it is construed to be by the parties to it. Whatever policy recommendations are made in terms of the world as it ought to be, our point is that they must be based on careful analysis of the world as it is.

REFERENCES

DfEE (1998) *The Learning Age: A Renaissance for a New Britain*, HMSO Command Paper 3790.

Garfinkel, H. (1984) *Studies in Ethnomethodology*, Cambridge: Polity Press and Oxford: Blackwell.

Heap, J. (1982) 'Understanding classroom events: a critique of Durkin, with an alternative', *Journal of Reading Behaviour* 14.

Hemmings, T., Divall, C., Francis, D., Marr, L., Porter, G. and Randall, D. (1997) 'Situated knowledge and the virtual science and industry museum: Problems in the social-technical interface', *Archive and Museum Informatics* Special Edition.

Hughes, J., O'Brien, J., Randall, D., Rouncefield, M., and Tolmie, P. (forthcoming) 'Some "Real" Problems of Virtual Teams,' New technology work and employment 16(1).

Lynch, M. (1993a) *Scientific Practice and Ordinary Action*, Cambridge: Cambridge University Press.

Lynch, M. (1993b) *Demonstrating Physics Lessons*. Paper presented at the Institute for Research on Learning, Carnegie Workshops.

Macbeth, D. (1990) 'Classroom order as practical action: the making and un-making of a quiet reproach', *British Journal of Sociology of Education* 11(2).

Pacey, A. (1999) *Meaning in Technology*, Cambridge, Massachusetts: MIT Press.

7 The moral status of technology

Being recorded, being heard, and the construction of concerns in child counselling[1]

Ian Hutchby

Modern society is experiencing substantial changes in family form and composition. Associated with these changes is an apparent growth in parental separation and divorce. Parental separation can be a traumatic experience for children of all ages (Hetherington 1991). In certain areas of the UK, specialized child counselling services have been set up in order to provide an environment in which children can come to terms with the experience of separation, divorce, and family break-up without the possibly complicating presence of one or both parents in the room.

Hitherto, most research on counselling has been carried out within the discipline of psychology. Until fairly recently there was no attention paid to the phenomenon of counselling from a sociological perspective. Recent exceptions include the work of Perakyla (1995) and Silverman (1996) on the discourse of adult HIV/AIDS counselling. As these studies have shown, a close examination of the ways people talk in counselling can provide valuable insights into the kinds of strategies used by counsellors to help clients make sense of, or find ways of dealing with, extraordinary situations. This in turn feeds into key sociological concerns with the role of institutional practices in contemporary everyday life, and with the significance of discourse as a principal means of mediating social relations.

The work of Silverman (1996) and Perakyla (1995) focused on the counselling of adults. In order to extend our knowledge of the discursive practices of counselling in the context of adult–child interaction, I arranged with a child counselling service in London to tape-record counselling sessions for children whose parents either had separated or were in the process of doing so. The policy of the service was that parent(s) should be seen in an initial assessment meeting together with their child(ren), but subsequently children were seen by the counsellor on their own for between four and six sessions. At the end, frequently, another meeting was held in which parents, children and counsellors would all be present.

The data involve children ranging from four to twelve years of age, and include counselling sessions conducted by both male and female counsellors. The cases include single children and siblings, both male–male and male–female. In the latter cases, siblings were seen by counsellors both together and separately. In all, the data comprises over twelve hours of recorded talk.

In this chapter I focus on just one aspect of this talk: the fact that it involves a recording technology – the tape recorder and microphones – in clear visibility throughout the session. The researcher was not physically present during recordings, but the recording itself was not conducted covertly. As we will see, counsellors were often concerned, particularly at the start of sessions, to render the technology's presence visible for the child, even though the fact that the session would be recorded (as well as the research purposes of the recording) had been discussed beforehand with both parents and children. The issue I will discuss revolves around the role of the recording technology in the production of the talk, and the talk-instantiated work of the counselling session. Beginning from the concern, characteristic of much qualitative research, with naturalistic recording as an ethical issue, as well as one which possibly impacts on the 'authenticity' of what is being recorded, I offer an alternative focus on the fact of the recording as an analytic phenomenon. Looking at the moments where participants – both counsellor and child – display their orientations to the presence of the technology leads to a consideration of the ways in which the technology comes to have different forms of presence within the talk; and in which it is thus bound up with various aspects of the counselling session's distinctive interactional work.

ETHICS AND ANALYTICS

The tape-recording of discourse in non-experimental settings brings with it a range of concerns, both ethical and analytical. On the ethical level, researchers need to decide whose consent among the participants should be sought prior to the recording taking place; and who among the relevant parties should be informed about the fact of the recording and the nature of the research. In part this keys into long-standing sociological concerns with the use of overt versus covert data collection methods. Within my own perspective, conversation analysis, researchers have for many years recorded everyday conversations (usually over the telephone) with the informed consent of at least one participant (the one to whose telephone the recording device is attached). However, it is not often made clear whether those who call the data gatherer's phone are made aware of the presence of the recording device.

When young children are involved this ethical dimension takes on a greater salience. In the light of recent legislation such as the UK's Children Act of 1989, the aim of which is to give children greater voice, agency and autonomy in terms of processes affecting their lives (such as legal processes surrounding divorce), it was not thought appropriate simply to gain the consent of parents and counsellors to the recording of sessions. It was necessary also to gain the informed consent of children themselves. This was done by means of a letter, written in styles that differed according to broad age group categories, which explained some basic facts about the research project, guaranteed that the tape would not be listened to by parents, explained that the child had the right not to agree, and finally invited them to sign to say that they had read and understood the letter. In practice, the process of obtaining the child's consent[2] was done prior to the counselling period actually starting, at the initial assessment meeting.[3]

Over and above the ethical questions, however, the same considerations lead to a potentially significant analytical question: given that the recording is being carried out overtly, what role might the technological device itself play in the unfolding of the session? Do participants appear to orient to its significance in any observable ways? And if so, what are the ways in which the technology itself comes to impinge on the work of the counselling session: on the aim to have the child verbalize and explore his or her feelings about a problematic life situation (Geldard and Geldard 1998)? Is the presence of the recording technology inherently problematic; or may there be ways in which its presence can have an enabling effect?

In general, the procedure was to place the tape recorder (a small battery-operated portable machine) on a table at the side of the room, and situate two small, flat multidirectional microphones in different parts of the room (for example, one near the armchairs where participants would sit, and one near the toy cupboard from which children would choose games, often at the counsellor's invitation). For some ways of thinking, the fact that both counsellor and child were therefore fully cognizant of the presence of the tape recorder in the room constitutes an inevitable analytical problem.

Some counsellors expressed a number of concerns about this during discussions with me. For instance, would not the presence of the recording device have a detrimental effect by making it difficult to capture examples of 'authentic' counselling talk? Would it not prove problematic through inhibiting the child from speaking 'naturally'? And would it not, even, affect the counsellors themselves, making it difficult for them to produce the kind of talk they would 'normally' produce in a session?

These concerns about the authentic, the natural and the normal are of course important, particularly if one's interest is in understanding the nature of the counselling process or evaluating counselling outcomes.[4] Such interests are key to much of the work that has been done in counselling psychology in recent years (see Woolfe and Dryden 1996). But as Silverman (1996) points out, each of these emphases in different ways leads to a situation in which the phenomenon itself – that is, what actually happens in the counselling session – disappears. Silverman observes how a vast amount of counselling research seeks to develop a normative model of good counselling practice which can be assessed using either quantitative measures of 'outcomes' or qualitative measures of people's 'responses' to counselling. In either case,

> research [is] fundamentally concerned with the environment around the phenomenon rather than the phenomenon itself. In quantitative studies of

'objective' social structures and qualitative studies of people's 'subjective' orientations, we may be deflected from the phenomenon towards what follows and precedes it (causes and consequences in the 'objective' approach) or to how people respond to it (the 'subjective' approach).

(Silverman 1996: 24)

Consequently, like Silverman, my approach is to turn the focus not towards what people think about counselling but towards what they do in counselling. The aim, therefore, is not to begin with a normative model of counselling which the presence of the tape recorder may in some sense distort. Rather, by focusing on events within the counselling session as it unfolds, I want to turn the question about the possible 'effect' of the recording on the 'reality' of the session into a different issue: one which asks, what kind of presence (if any) does the tape recorder have in terms of the observable behaviour of the participants, both counsellor and child?

In what follows I present some observations on one particular session with an eight year old child in which, at the very start of the session, the tape recorder was accorded various statuses by both participants. As we will see, the attribution of presence, both physical and, in some sense, moral, to the technological device is not to be seen as a negative feature of the counselling session. Rather, it turns out to facilitate a wide range of talk about the child's responses to the breakdown of her parents' relationship. This in itself is an illustration of a more general feature of counselling talk in my data, in which counsellors use a strategy of 'picking up on' aspects of the discourse environment (not just the words that are spoken, but also objects or circumstances that are implicated in what is said) which are then translated into 'therapeutic objects'.

In texts on counselling practice (for example, Geldard and Geldard 1998) such a feature of counselling talk is referred to as 'active listening'. Active listening is intended to convey a sense that counsellors are 'able to help the child to tell her story and to identify troubling issues. In doing this the child must know that we are paying attention and valuing the information that we are receiving' (Geldard and Geldard 1998: 57).

As in other practical guides to counselling, it is not clear whether the examples Geldard and Geldard use to illustrate this technique are drawn from actual counselling sessions, from training sessions, or are invented. What is clear is that when we look at actual child counselling practice in my data, the technique is much more 'constructive' than it is simply 'active', and it also involves 'speaking', in the sense of both 'interpreting' and 'reconstructing' the child's utterances. Geldard and Geldard (1998: 57–64) recognize this; but the terms they use to describe such speaking practices, namely 'reflecting' and 'summarizing', imply a less actively interpretive and reconstructive role on the part of the counsellor than seems empirically to be the case.

Like many counselling techniques, active listening is in fact very similar to procedures involved in the production of ordinary conversation. Conversation analysts have noted that in order to manage successful turn-taking in conversation, participants need not only to be hearing, but to be listening to the talk of their interlocutor(s). As we know from the phenomenon of supermarket muzak, among other things, one can be hearing a sound without actually listening to it. The difference is that in listening, one is inevitably engaged in interpreting, in making sense of, in responding to, an utterance. Among the central questions facing participants in talk-in-interaction is: 'Why that now?'; 'What is the relevance of that particular utterance in this sequential environment?' (see Schegloff 1984). In engaging in listening to an utterance rather than just hearing it, participants are involved in a process by which their own next utterance is to be oriented to for how it proposes an understanding of the co-participant's prior utterance.

In child counselling, this practice comes to be bound up with the constitution of the counselling framework itself, in its activity of monitoring the child's talk for possible ways into a 'therapeutic' interpretation or intervention. The counsellor's active listening in relation to even minor aspects of the child's talk plays a key role in the success of the session's work: the work of inciting the child to speak about his or her experiences. As Silverman (1996: 208) remarks, the essence of counselling is that each centre, or service, 'offers an institutionalized incitement to speak according to its own practical theories'. In the HIV counselling services studied by Silverman (1996) and by Perakyla (1995), counselling was provided as part of an overall package associated with the provision of an HIV test, rather than specifically being requested or sought out by the client. One result of this was that counsellors had to develop a range of strategies for bringing counselling into play in the face of resistance from the client.[5]

In my data there is a similar need. Indeed, the incitement to speak may prove more problematic because the sessions involve young children who may not fully understand or accept the role of the counsellor, and who have often been introduced to the service at the volition of their parent(s) rather than themselves. What I will show is a range of ways that the counsellor monitors, interprets and constructs the child's utterances in order to bring into play possible 'concerns' about family relationships. Orientations to the technology play a part in this, as the presence of the tape recorder comes to be situated within three interrelated interpretive frameworks: 'being recorded', 'being heard', and 'being counselled'. These frames colour the interpretation of utterances at different points in the opening stages of the session in question.

OBSERVABILITY: 'BEING RECORDED'

The case I will discuss involves an eight year old child, 'Jenny' (not her real name), whose parents have brought her to the service because they are currently in the process of negotiating a separation. Jenny saw the (male) counsellor[6] on four occasions. My observations will focus on the first full session; the 'post-assessment' session. At various points in this session (not only at its beginning), both the counsellor and the child displayed their orientations to the presence, and the relevance, of the tape recorder and associated technological phenomena (the microphones, the reels, volume controls, LCD sound level monitor, etc.). Thus, the presence of the technology becomes 'observable' from the participants' points of view.

There is a significant distinction between orienting to the 'presence' of the technology and orienting to its 'relevance'. Orienting to the 'presence' of the device means according it a status as a physical object within the room. This may involve a variety of actions, for instance, mentioning that there is a tape recorder on the table, noticing aspects of it such as the flashing LCD lights on its recording display, asking questions about how certain aspects of it operate, and so on. Orienting to the device's 'relevance', on the other hand, means bringing its presence into play in situations where it may not be overtly oriented to in the first sense, but where it is taken by one or other participant to be implicated somehow in what is being said. Both these means of orienting to the technology are involved in the counsellor's work of enabling the child to speak about her feelings; and both will be illustrated in the course of the analysis.

The first mention of the device's presence comes right at the beginning of the session, as the counsellor and the child are engaged in selecting the places where each will sit:

(1) C19/99:1a ((Start of Session))
C = Counsellor, Male; J = Child, Female, 8yrs

```
1    C:   Sit down and we'll ta:lk about the recording >(if you
2         like) f'r a< mo:ment, (.) Where you gonna sit. >Djwanna
3         sit?< (.) Sit over there.
4         (2.2) ((Sound of footsteps))
5    C:   Oowuhhh (.) Where shall I sit. (0.2) Shall I
6         si[t over] here,
7    J:     [There.]
8    J:   No there. There.
9    C:   Which one this one o[ver he]re?=
10   J:                       [There.]    =Yeah.
11   C:   Right. (.) Okay. (1.5) Oowhhhh (0.5) So yeah. Djwan- (.)
12        If yer feeling uncomfortable, take your bag off won't
13        you.(0.3) If you want to: or leave it on you decide.
14        (3.1) ((Rustling sounds))
15   C:   So:. hhh .hh (.) So your second time he:re,
16        (3.6)
17   C:   Yeah? .thhh So an-and (.) ((banging)) I'm gonna move the
18        chair cuz I- (0.4) ca:n't see you very well. .h I's too
19        far away.
20        ((Banging))
```

21   J: Hunh hee he he
22   C: Hhh .h ((sniff)) So've [you-
23   J.   [So this is being recorded.

As they enter the room C mentions 'the recording' (line 1) and suggests that, if the child likes, they can 'ta:lk about' it. What immediately follows this, however, is not talk about the recording but a discussion about where J might like to sit, and where C should sit, the latter issue being resolved by J herself (lines 7–10). The ensuing few turns involve a series of five attempts by C to initiate the session proper, each of them using the prefatory item 'So': 'So yeah' (line 11), 'So:', 'So your second time he:re' (both line 15), 'So an- and' (line 17); ultimately moving towards the production of a first question for the child: 'So 've you-' (line 22). This question is interrupted by J herself reintroducing the issue of the recording: 'So this is being recorded.' (line 23).

There are a number of points to note about this initial sequence. First, J displays her orientation to the relevance of the recording device by picking up on C's first brief mention, even though subsequently C gives indications that he may be moving away from that topic. His attempts to initiate the session instead involve references to this as the 'second time' (that is, the first post-assessment session), and the beginnings of a question taking the form 'So [ha]ve you ...'. Neither of these give any clear indication that the recording is about to be topicalized. Rather, the impression is that it is the session itself, and perhaps some issues connecting back to the first assessment, that will be the initial topic of talk. C may, of course, have good reasons for not wanting to make too much of the presence of the recording device, given counsellors' above-mentioned concerns about normality and naturalness in the session.

Second, J's reintroduction of the topic itself utilizes the very prefatory marker 'So' used five times already by C: 'So this is being recorded.' This suggests that she may have been monitoring C's aborted attempts to produce a 'So'-prefaced sentence in the light of an expectation that these would, indeed, eventually result in an opportunity to 'ta:lk about the recording'. Having heard the counsellor's initial move away from that topic, with 'So your second time he:re,' (line 15), and then heard the beginnings of his second apparent shift, the start of the question 'So 've you-' (line 22), J comes in with her own proposed completion of the sentence: 'So this is being recorded.'

The third point is that this of course involves J, an eight year old child, taking the initiative (in the sense of taking control of the topic and, therefore, the immediate course of the session) in a discourse environment where it might be expected that the adult (a professional child counsellor) would do that. This is not meant as a negative reflection of this particular counsellor's skills. Far from it: as we will see, he is able to turn the child's displayed orientations to the presence and relevance of the recording device to good therapeutic use. It is rather to note something else: namely the fact that it is the very presence of the device that comes to furnish the environment in which the child can engage in this initiative-taking move. In other (non-recorded) circumstances, there may be other features of the environment upon which a child may draw in order to initiate his or her own line of interaction. The point with this datum is that the recording technology is shown to have something more than a mere constraining effect on the course of the talk. Even at this early stage in the session, and in this relatively minor way, the device begins to reveal its affordances as a resource for the (child's) initiation of a course of action.

Extract 2 shows how this course of action proceeds:

```
(2) C19/99:1a ((Continuation of extract 1))
22   C:   Hhh .h ((sniff)) So've [you-
23   J:                     [So this is being recorded.
24   C:   This is being re↓corded now.
25   J:   ((brightly)) ↑O:ka::y,
26   C:   Yeah.
27   J:   I sound like a ba:by.
28        (.)
39   C:   Are you worried that you sound like a baby,
30        (.)
31   J:   No↑:.,=
32   C:   Or dju think sounding like a baby's oka[y.
33   J:                                          [(Dae)
34        c↑a:↓r:e=ehh
35   C:   Yeah? heh .h Who=who thinks you sound like a baby most.
36        (0.7)
37   J:   My grandma an' grandad.
38   C:   De- An' what does s:he say tuh- to tell you that she
39        thinks you sound like a baby.
40   J:   You sound like a ↑baby.
41   C:   Does she. (0.2) .hh An' dju think she:- she l- does she
42        ↑like that or, (.) d[oes she sa]:y, that she's not- not=
43   J:                       [(       )]
44   C:   =liking it.
45   J:   She doesn't like it cuz I say it sounds like my cousin.
46   C:   A:hh
47   J:   Eh huh huh hee heuh .u .hh
```

C responds to J's topicalization of the recording by confirming that the session is indeed being recorded (line 24), after which J utters 'O:ka::y' with a playfully exaggerated brightness. What happens next illustrates another way in which the technology's presence, having been mentioned, is brought to bear on a course of action: this time, an entry into a therapeutic dialogue.

J's next comment, 'I sound like a ba:by' (line 27), is hearable in a number of different ways. For instance, it may be taken to be an expression of her self-consciousness about being recorded; or we might imagine that this is something she has either been told or decided herself on occasions when she may have been playing with recording her voice on a tape recorder. From a conversation analytic perspective, however, what is of most relevance is the understanding or interpretation that her interlocutor, C, displays of this utterance in his following turn in the sequence.

Of the many and varied ways in which anyone might respond to an eight year old child's announcement that 'I sound like a ba:by' (for example, 'Do you?', 'No you don't', 'Who says that?', 'Why do you think that?', 'What's wrong with that?', etc.), C selects one that begins quite clearly to frame the sequence up in therapeutic terms: 'Are you worried that you sound like a baby' (line 29). The significance of this is that it manifests an orientation to the child's talk as involving 'concerns'. More than that: it *constructs* J's utterance as one that may be expressive of a concern. In picking up on a hearing of the assertion 'I sound like a ba:by' that treats it as possibly expressive of a concern, rather than (for example) a factual observation, C is engaged in making relevant a counselling 'frame' for the present interaction. It is not clear, on the surface of things, whether J's turn in line 27 shows her to be oriented to the relevance of 'counselling' rather than (or in addition to) that of 'being recorded'. But C's response in line 29 clearly seeks to bring that relevance to bear on the talk.

Here, then, is a second way in which displayed orientations to the presence of the technological device can be recruited in the pursuit of other interactional projects relevant to the setting. By 'hearing' the child's reference to what she sounds like not simply within the frame of reference of 'being recorded', but also that of 'being counselled', C is able to direct the talk towards providing a first picture of J's relationship with family members (in this case, her grandparents).

There are other frames of reference which can be brought to bear upon orientations to the technology's presence. One of the most significant, itself related in different ways to the frames of 'being recorded' and 'being counselled', is that of 'being heard'.

ANALYSABILITY: 'BEING HEARD' AND THE MORAL STATUS OF THE TECHNOLOGY

The next extract shows how the counsellor's picture of the child's possible concerns about her family relationships becomes filled out quite substantially, again by means of displayed orientations to the technology's presence. What is of note here is the way that the discourse moves between the relevancies not just of counselling and 'being recorded', but also of a third possible framework: 'being heard'. Notice how, in the course of the extract, C once again orients to aspects of J's actions in respect of the tape recorder as possibly expressive of concerns, and how the technology and features of its layout (recall that there are two microphones placed in different parts of the room) come to stand in for moral evaluations of J's relationships with her two parents.

(3) C:19:99:1a

```
 1    C:   So:::, (0.8) as you say Jenny i' is being recorded, (0.4)
 2         an' look there's a microphone ther:e,
 3    J:   Boo(h)↓oo: uhih hi[h hee h*eh
 4    C:                     [uheh
 5    C:   An' another one, (.) the other side of the roo:m,
 6         (.)
 7    J:   Let's see. ((Footsteps))
 8    C:   Can you see it,
 9         (3.2)
10    J:   ((Close to microphone)) Oh ye:::ah.
11    C:   Yeah?=
12    J:   =That one can't record as much because we're over here.
13    C:   Yeh I guess so.
14         (1.5)
15    C:   So d'you think this microphone's gonna record us more
16         than the other one.
17    J:   Yeah.
18         (3.0)
19    C:   [[Wu-
20    J:   [[Cuz, if we speak really loudly that one will be able to
21         get it.
22    C:   °Yee:ah. (.) Guess so.°
23         (1.6)
24→  J:   He↑LLO:::::! hee hinh=
25    C:   =Djthink that microphone heard that.
26         (1.8)
27    C:   No:.
28→  J:   .hhh↑HE↑↑LLO:::::! (0.4) Think it heard that.
29         (3.2)
30→  C:   .hhh How l:oud dyou have t' speak at ho:me. .h t'get
31         people to hear you.
32→  J:   .hh Well my ↑da:d's: ↓de:af.
33         (0.4)
34    C:   ↑A:↓h:.
35    J:   So I >have t'go-< .h (.) This morning I w'trying to get
36         his attention cuz I saw something in a magazine that I
37         might want, .hhh an', I'm goin', ↑DA:↓:D, knock ↑knO:↓CK,
38         are you ↑thE::↓RE, (.)↑DA:↓:D, ↑DA:↓:(h)D!hhh
39         (0.8)
40    C:   An' did 'e hear.
```

```
41   J:   No.
42   C:   Not at a:ll.
43   J:   No:.
44        (1.2)
45   C:   Okay. (.) .hhhh So how d'you get his attention.
46        (0.6)
47   J:   I have to gettuh up an' go an' (.) sort of like s:strangle
48        ehhih(m) (.) .hh ba:sic'lly:, (1.6) Kick him or somethi[ng.
49   C:                                                        [What
50        abou:t (.) getting your mum t'hear what you've got
51        to s[ay.
52→  J:       [°She hears everything.°=
53   C:   =Mum hears absolutely everything.
54   J:   °°Yeh°°
```

In an incremental, turn-by-turn development, aspects of the geography of the technology here become merged with the child's picture of her problematic home life. The key to this is again the counsellor's orientation to 'counselling' in addition to 'being recorded', in his question at line 30–31. Once more, this involves a hearing of J's hails aimed at the differently located microphones – 'Boo(h)↓oo:' in line 3, and 'He↑LLO:::::!' (line 24) followed by an even louder '.hhh↑HE↑↑LLO:::::!' in line 28 – as possibly expressive of concerns: in this case, a concern about 'being heard at home'.

The main image associated with C's question 'How l:oud dyou have t' speak at ho:me' (line 30) is a common one used in child counselling and in books aimed at helping children 'get through' parental separation – that of parents continually arguing and children being made to feel miserable in the middle. Yet the very mention of this stock image in counselling at this particular point in the session seems to emerge out of clearly displayed orientations to the presence of the technology. More than that, there is a sense in which the discussion of the two microphones (one quite close by, the other on the opposite side of the room) and the subsequent discussion of the child's communicative relationship with her parents (one who often does not hear her, the other who hears everything) reflect one another.

Note that 'hearing' is a concept introduced in this exchange by C (in line 25) and subsequently picked up by J (in line 28). The child herself had initially used a more mechanical vocabulary in referring to the microphones: 'That one can't record as much' (line 12). Later she uses a slightly different term: 'If we speak really loudly that one will be able to get it' (line 20), and it might be said that 'get it' occupies a kind of intermediate status between the mechanical, inanimate 'record' and the far more animate, anthropomorphic 'hear' used by the counsellor. But the use of 'hear' in relation to the microphones is interesting because, in as much as it is taken up by J in line 28 ('think it heard that), it links into the subsequent exchange about the hearing of her parents.

Note, then, the close relationship between the way J describes her father and mother's 'hearing' of her and the way the differently located microphones have been mentioned. She asserts (in line 32) that her father is 'deaf' (though it is not clear that this is the case, especially since C, who has met the father, responds by orienting to this as 'news' as opposed to merely acknowledging what should be a mutually shared piece of knowledge), and that she has to yell at him to get his attention (lines 35–38). It is interesting to note that there is a close prosodic match between J's enunciation of 'He↑LLO::::::!' (line 24) and '.hhh↑HE↑↑LLO::::::!' (line 28), and '↑DA:↓:D, knock ↑knO:↓CK, are you ↑thE::↓RE, (.)↑DA:↓:D, ↑DA:↓:(h)D!hhh' (line 37–38). The first set of hails has a 'singsong' prosody which is reproduced in a more pronounced way in the second set. Although difficult to capture in the form of a transcript, in the hearing this makes for a markedly close link between the (here-and-now) address to the microphone and the (reported) address to the father.

There is also an intriguing relationship between the description of the mother (in line 52) and the previous discussion of the recording microphones. Invited to draw a comparison between the necessary actions in getting her father's attention and those involved in gaining her mother's, J announces, with a marked drop in volume, that her mother 'hears everything'. And when C invites a confirmation, with 'Mum hears absolutely everything' (line 53), J responds by dropping her voice almost to a whisper: '°°Yeh°°' (line 54).

Although there is no clear indication that the child is consciously making these comparisons between the different aural capacities of the two microphones and those of her two parents, the link is a striking one, particularly when we bear in mind the close sequential and temporal relationship between the respective descriptions of 'hearing' and 'being heard'. What is clear, nevertheless, is that the counsellor's introduction of the topic of 'being heard at home', on which the comparison turns, has a direct sequential link to the child's utterance in the turn that precedes it, where she refers to the microphone having 'heard that'. Again, albeit in a more ambivalent way, we can trace a relationship between orientations to the technology's presence and the production of a counselling frame for the talk.

In the following case, we see another example of the counsellor picking up on references which may orient to the technology's relevance (as distinct from merely its presence), and using that to lead the child into talk about 'concerns'. The issue here hinges on different aspects of 'hearing' and 'being heard'. It is somewhat later in the session, and the child is drawing pictures, the counsellor exploring with her some thoughts about these pictures. J has drawn a sketch of a dog, which she describes as 'very thin' and as 'a stray'. This comes to initiate a lengthy story involving many other drawings. I will just focus on the beginning stage of this story.

(4) C:19:99:1c
1   C: It's good to pretend sometimes.

```
2     J:   .h Well ACtually he was locked in a boot an' he got out,
3          (0.3) an' and the r-RSPCA found 'im 'n 'e, .hh he- .h
4          h[e-
5     C:      [He w'z locked in someone's boot?
6          (0.4)
7     C:   Goodn[ess.
8→    J:        [Y- The RSPCA found him, .hh[h He was] on TV=
9     C:                                   [Uh  huh.]
10    J:   =en he ran away=.h=an' 'e couldn't find a home.
11         (0.8)
12    C:   So:: he- did 'e=who did 'e run away from the boot or from
13         the RSPCA.
14         (0.3)
15    J:   The RSPCA[:.
16    C:            [He ran away-=]
17→   J:                         =Cuz 'e was scared of the camera.
```

Note here two things in particular. First, J's utterance in line 8, 'He was on
TV'; and second, her remark that the dog ran away 'cuz 'e was scared of the
camera' (line 17). It is not clear whether these references, at the moment of
production, are associated with J's orientation to the actual presence of a
different kind of recording technology in the room at present. However, the
next extract shows how, as the story carries on, the counsellor indeed picks up
on this very possibility (note especially line 22, and lines 24–26):

(5) C:19:99:1c (Continuation of extract 4)

```
17    J:   Cuz 'e was scared of the camera.
18         (.)
19    C:   So the people that were tryin' to- (.) help 'im, he ran
20         away from.
21         (1.1)
22→   C:   He was scared of th'camera.
23         (0.7)
24→   C:   .h Dju think 'e would've been sca:red, .hh if there was
25         no camera. (.) But if hi:s voice was being taped but not
26         being filmed?
27    J:   mYeah.
28    C:   He'd've still been scared then,
29    J:   °Mm:.°
30         (0.2)
31    C:   A:h.
32         (2.8)
33    C:   How could=how could he not be sca:red, (0.2) with his voice
34         being taped.
35         (1.9)
```

```
36→ J:  Wull, if:: he::, (0.3) yihsee he's got very good hearing.
37   C:  Ye:ah,
38       (.)
39   J:  mYeh.
40       (0.5)
41   J:  An' so[:
42   C:       [Bit like your mum.
43       (0.6)
44   J:  Yeah. .h[h ] An'::, (0.4) so::.
45   C:          [Mm.]
46       (1.7)
47   C:  What=what does that mean having good hearing.
48       (0.9)
49→ J:  He can hear the tape recorder goin', bvhvh[vhv
50   C:                                            [He c'n hear it
51       whirling round.=]
52   J:  =Yeah.
```

We again find C orienting to the child's utterances as possibly expressive of concerns, except that this time, references to the technology are not to be heard in terms of concerns about 'being heard' within the family situation. Rather, the concern is taken to be about the fact of 'being recorded' within the counselling session itself.

The pivotal utterance here is in lines 24–26, where C renders explicit a relationship that is only potentially present in the child's remarks about the stray dog's fear of 'the camera': that is, the relationship between this fictional-ized event and the child's current circumstance. More than that, C's turn invites J herself to see, and to go along with, that proposed relationship. As the exchange proceeds, it becomes ambivalent as to whether it is the imagined concerns or fears of the dog, or the real concerns of the child, that are at issue (note the continued third person reference in the child's turns in lines 36 and 49). This ambivalence is shown especially clearly in the child's turn in line 49, in which she mimics the muted sound of the actually present tape recorder in the course of describing how the dog's fears arise because of the fact that 'he's got very good hearing' (line 36). Once again, then, 'hearing' and 'being heard' are brought up as central concerns, this time in the context of a story where the concerns of a fictional character become merged with the supposed concerns of the child storyteller.

In these examples it has become clear that the technology may not be oriented to simply as a presence in the room, but more significantly, in terms of its relevance for the activities being carried out within the room. In the process, the inanimate objects of tape recorder and (differently located) micro-phones come to be attributed with a range of complex identities, linked to which are a number of moral statuses. In the course of the talk, the relevance of 'being recorded' interweaves with that of 'counselling' and 'expressing concerns', 'hearing' and 'being heard', and the status of the technology shifts as it is used to facilitate forms of counselling talk.

CONCLUDING REMARKS

One of the significant features of contemporary western culture is the increasing promulgation of the view that 'communication' is the key to solving many of the problems of everyday life (Cameron 2000). Counselling, and the associated 'talking cures' of psychoanalysis and psychotherapy, play a central role in this incitement to communicate. Child counselling services are of particular interest because they treat the difficulties children can experience as a result of parental separation and divorce as issues which not just the parents, but the children also need to 'talk about'. The discourse of child counselling exists at an interface between the increasing incitement to communicate, and the growing recognition of children's social competence and agency (James and Prout 1990; Hutchby and Moran-Ellis 1998).

Discourse itself can be conceived of as a 'technology', in two different senses: a toolkit for making sense of events, on the one hand; but on the other, an ideological resource, one which can be used to establish and maintain the relative significance of different versions of events. In counselling and psychotherapy, by this token, part of the aim is often to make 'normalizing' interventions in the client's expressed worldview. In order to 'normalize', however, it is recognized that the 'object' of the intervention (the problematic belief, interpretation, standpoint, etc.) needs to be brought into view. This is taken to be the main point of the early stages of a counselling intervention.

This chapter has shown some of the ways in which such therapeutic objects begin to be brought into view in the context (and the presence) of a different form of technology: a mechanical tape recording device. We have seen how arrays of humans (counsellor, child, and the child's non-present family members) and technologies (both the recording device and the discursive technology of counselling) become arranged in shifting configurations out of which begin to emerge glimpses of the child's sense of her situation in the family home.

There are those among the community of social researchers, as well as among the communities of socially researched (such as professional counsellors), for whom the presence of a recording device as a data collection technology renders problematic the 'normalcy', 'naturalness' and 'authenticity' of the events and actions being recorded. This tends to be expressed in the form of a view that participants' awareness of the fact that they are being recorded will tend to alter their behaviour, such that the researcher's object of analysis is inevitably distorted. Given contemporary ethical concerns over the conduct of covert data collection, particularly when it involves children or those from disadvantaged groups, such a concern raises serious questions about the viability of qualitative research based on naturalistic data.

I have suggested one way in which this concern can be countered. Rather than assuming – and worrying – that the data is inevitably distorted due to the presence of a recording technology, one thing we can do is to turn the technology's presence into an analytic phenomenon. The fact that participants in the data presented above explicitly orient to the presence and the relevance of the technology does not mean that their interaction is not 'authentic'. Certainly, had the recording device not been there, they would not have engaged in much of the talk reproduced above. But this is an interactional event involving a tape recorder; just as, on a different day, there may have been a training practitioner present as an observer, and that would have been an interactional event involving a non-participating observer. In either case, it is the event as it unfolds that is of analytic interest, rather than there being some 'real thing' that would 'otherwise' have taken place.

In treating the technology's presence as an analytic phenomenon, we have seen how the participants themselves observably orient to it as an interactional phenomenon. But more than that, it is clear that the device, far from simply 'standing in the way' of the setting's activities, becomes actively bound up with those activities through the very orientations of the participants. Instead of being a determinate and negative force, the technology reveals a whole array of communicative affordances (see Hutchby 2001) which enable both the counsellor and the child to begin communicating about the (largely implicit) matter at hand: the estrangement of the child's parents. Apart from instigating talk about what the child has been told, by adults, that she 'sounds like', the technology in its particular spatial configuration affords the child an imagined comparison with her differential relationship with her father and mother; similarly, the audible hum of the reels affords incorporation into the imagined dilemmas of the fictional characters she invents in the course of a story. Out of these affordances, as we have seen, the counsellor is able to begin, sometimes tentatively and sometimes leadingly, to constitute a therapeutic object.

APPENDIX: TRANSCRIPTION CONVENTIONS

Transcripts reproduced in this chapter use the conventions of Conversation Analysis, originally developed by Dr Gail Jefferson.

(0.5)	Numbers in brackets indicate a gap timed in tenths of a second.
(.)	A dot enclosed in brackets indicates a 'micropause' of less than one-tenth of a second.
=	Equals signs are used to indicate 'latching' or absolute contiguity between utterances; or to show the continuation of a speaker's utterance across intervening lines of transcript.
[ ]	Square brackets between adjacent lines of concurrent speech indicate the points of onset and cessation of overlapping talk.

(( ))	Double brackets are used to describe a non-verbal activity: for example ((banging sound)). They are also used to enclose the transcriber's comments on contextual or other relevant features.
( )	Empty brackets indicate the presence of an unclear utterance or other sound on the tape.
.hhh	h's preceded by a dot are used to represent audible inward breathing. The more h's, the longer the breath.
hhhh	h's with no preceding dot are used in the same way to represent outward breathing.
huh	Laughter is transcribed using 'laugh tokens' which, as far as the
heh	transcriber is able, represent the individual sounds that speakers make
hih	while laughing.
:	Colons indicate the stretching of a sound at the preceding lexical item. The more colons the greater the extent of the stretching.
–	A dash indicates a sudden cut-off of the prior sound.
.	Punctuation marks are not used grammatically, but to indicate
,	prosodic aspects of the talk. A full stop indicates a falling tone; commas indicate fall-rise or rise-fall (that is, a 'continuing'
?	tone); question marks indicate a marked rising tone.
↑↓	Upward and downward arrows are used to show a marked rise or fall in pitch across a phrase.
a̲:	Underlining of a letter before a colon indicates a small drop in pitch during a word.
a:̲	Underlining of a colon after a letter indicates a small rise in pitch at that point in the word.
Under	Other underlining indicates speaker emphasis.
CAPS	Capitals mark a section of speech markedly louder than that surrounding it.
→	Arrows in the left margin point to specific parts of the transcript discussed in the text.
° °	Degree signs are used to indicate that the talk between them is noticeably quieter than surrounding talk.
< >	Outward chevrons are used to indicate that the talk between them is noticeably slower than surrounding talk.
> <	Inner chevrons are used to indicate that the talk between them is noticeably quicker than surrounding talk.

NOTES

1   The research on which this chapter is based was supported by the ESRC, under grant R000222900, 'Responding to Family Separation' (Principal Investigator: Dr I. Hutchby). My sincere thanks to the counsellors, the children and their parents, all of whom gave consent to the recordings on which the findings are based. All names and references to places have been altered in order to protect participants' anonymity.

2 In legal terms, children under the age of majority may in fact only 'assent' to their parents' 'consent'; that is, children cannot overrule their parents' refusal of consent, though they can decline to give their own assent to something their parents have consented to.

3 For this reason, these initial assessment meetings were not recorded.

4 The same kinds of concerns have frequently been expressed about the nature of conversation analysts' claims to be basing their findings on 'naturally occurring' examples of talk-in-interaction (for an introduction to CA see Hutchby and Wooffitt, 1998). Since at least one party usually knows that the conversation is being recorded, to what extent can it be said that this is really 'naturally occurring' talk that would have taken place in just the same way had the recording not been made? There are a number of responses to this, which I do not have the space to go into in detail here (for one interesting discussion, see Drew 1989). Suffice it to say that the claim to be analysing naturally occurring data is less a claim to be observing talk that is somehow 'pure' and 'uncontaminated' than a counter to two established tendencies: the policy in structural linguistics that intuitive or invented examples of sentences may be a better (or less distorted) source of language data than the utterances produced in ordinary talk; and the procedure in social psychological research on verbal communication whereby laboratory experiments are used to generate 'controlled' examples of mundane phenomena such as arguments.

5 For an account of a similar situation in the context of Health Visitors, who in the UK are required by law to visit first-time mothers in the months following the birth of a child, see Heritage and Sefi (1992).

6 The service preferred to use the term 'specialist worker' in order to distance their interventions from those more focused around children referred by social services and educational psychologists. For simplicity's sake, however, I retain the term counsellor throughout this chapter.

REFERENCES

Cameron, D. (2000) *Good to Talk?* London: Sage.

Drew, P. (1989) 'Recalling someone from the past', in Roger, D. and Bull, P. (eds) *Conversation*, Clevedon: Multilingual Matters.

Geldard, K. and Geldard, D. (1998) *Counselling Children: A Practical Introduction*, London: Sage.

Hetherington, E. (1991) 'Coping with family transitions: Winners, losers and survivors', in Woodhead, M., Light, P. and Carr, R. (eds) *Growing Up in a Changing Society*, London: Routledge.

Heritage, J. and Sefi, S. (1992) 'Dilemmas of advice: Aspects of the delivery and reception of advice in interactions between Health Visitors and first-time mothers', in Drew, P. and Heritage, J. (eds) *Talk At Work: Interaction in Institutional Settings*. Cambridge: Cambridge University Press.

Hutchby, I. (2001) *Conversation and Technology: From the Telephone to the Internet.* Cambridge: Polity Press.

Hutchby, I. and Moran-Ellis, J. (eds) (1998) *Children and Social Competence: Arenas of Action*, London: Falmer Press.

Hutchby, I. and Wooffitt, R. (1998) *Conversation Analysis*, Cambridge: Polity Press.

James, A. and Prout, A. (eds) (1990) *Constructing and Reconstructing Childhood: Contemporary Issues in the Sociological Study of Childhood*, London: Falmer Press.

Perakyla, A. (1995) *AIDS Counselling: Institutional Interaction and Clinical Practice*, Cambridge: Cambridge University Press.

Schegloff, E.A. (1984) 'On some questions and ambiguities in conversation', in Atkinson, J. M. and Heritage, J. (eds) *Structures of Social Action: Studies in Conversation Analysis*, Cambridge: Cambridge University Press.

Silverman, D. (1996) *Discourses of Counselling*, London: Sage.

Woolfe, R. and Dryden, W. (eds) (1996) *Handbook of Counselling Psychology*, London: Sage.

8   Bubble Dialogue

Using a computer application to investigate social information processing in children with emotional and behavioural difficulties

Ann Jones and Emma Price

INTRODUCTION

In many of the chapters in this book, the main focus is on children within a technological culture: what impact technologies have on their lives and activities and what kinds of involvement and engagement children have with technologies. But the conference that led to this book was also concerned with children's social competence (see the Introduction). This chapter is concerned with a rather different use of technology in children's lives, where the focus is on children whom we might describe as 'troubled': children whose behaviour is challenging; who have difficulties in negotiating social situations and often also have emotional issues to deal with. Such children can be doubly disadvantaged: where children have difficulties in communicating and expressing themselves they are unable to benefit from the support and help they might receive through talking with other children and adults and, very importantly, their own perspectives on the situation are likely to remain unheard. We also know that emotional and behavioural difficulties (EBD) impede learning. In the UK, the Department of Education and Science's definition of children with EBD captures this aspect. They are defined as 'children who [present] ... inappropriate, aggressive, bizarre or withdrawn behaviour'; and who 'have developed a range of strategies for dealing with day-to-day experiences that are inappropriate and impede normal personal and social development and make it difficult for them to learn' (DES 1989). Such children often have low self-esteem, another barrier to learning, and teachers of children with EBD report how increasing experience of success generally helps to improve pupils' behaviour and indirectly may also help children's social and emotional development (Howard 1991).

There is widespread evidence that children with EBD also have difficulties in negotiating social situations and managing interpersonal relationships (Crick and Dodge 1994). Many such children are likely to find communicating with others about the difficulties they have – particularly with adults – an uncomfortable experience and one which they will avoid. Yet paradoxically, it is very important that we understand children's own perspectives and understanding of the difficult situations in which they find themselves. This is consistent with the recent emphasis on the child's perspective: for example, the Children Act (1989) highlights children's rights to be heard. Professionals working for local educational authorities and social services are therefore increasingly faced with the challenge of eliciting the child's perspective on issues that concern them.

In this chapter we are concerned with how we might use and harness our technological culture to support children with EBD and in particular to help them to communicate their views. Computers are a common, everyday part of many children's lives and a technology that most feel very comfortable with and find engaging. In particular, we will discuss the use of a computer application, *Bubble Dialogue*, (Gray *et al.* 1991) that can support children's communication by allowing children to construct a narrative that reflects the child's view of the world. We start with a brief review of different approaches to understanding the problems that children with EBD have in negotiating social situations. We then discuss the use of computers to help children deal with social and emotional issues in their lives (as opposed to the much more common use of computers for cognitive learning) and introduce the *Bubble Dialogue* application. This application has allowed us to investigate the dialogue that children create in role-playing social situations and in so doing we share the strong emphasis on the social as well as cognitive role of language that is adopted by classroom researchers such as Mercer (1995). The remainder of the chapter draws on a comparative study that was undertaken of the use of *Bubble Dialogue* by a group of children with EBD and children who attend a mainstream school. The study focused on the children's self-expression and the strategies they used to resolve interpersonal conflicts. The results of this study are discussed and work with practitioners (teachers and social workers) who have also been using the application to work with individual children is also briefly discussed. Their experiences will be drawn on to discuss the possibilities for using tools such as this to develop ways of analysing the child's interpretation and perspective of the world in contexts relevant to the child, which could present an opportunity to tailor help to particular children.

NEGOTIATING SOCIAL INTERACTIONS

This section gives a brief review of psychological accounts of negotiating social interactions, including the skills needed in the kinds of situations (albeit virtual) investigated in the study described later in the chapter. How do children negotiate the kinds of situations that many of these children routinely find difficult, for example being told off or held to account by a teacher, playground conflicts? Much of the research into the difficulties experienced by such children in understanding and negotiating social situations has been conducted in the US where the term 'socially maladjusted' tends to be used, but this can be seen as comparable with EBD in the UK.

Essentially there have been two main approaches to understanding children's social interactions in the psychological literature: a structural–developmental approach, as exemplified by the work of Selman (1980), and an information processing model (Dodge *et al.* 1986). For Selman, an understanding of social interactions depends on Interpersonal Understanding (IU): the cognitive ability to co-ordinate psychological and social perspectives of the self and other. Selman argues that such co-ordination develops in stages and that IU understanding increases with age. While some children are deficient in IU, others fail to apply their highest ability in some situations. The second approach, taken by Dodge and his colleagues, is an example of a functional approach, where managing social interactions is viewed as social problem-solving. Here, there are a number of mental steps, for example, encoding of situational cues, representation and interpretation and a mental search for response and selection of a response. Children can experience difficulties in social interactions when there are problems in one or more of these stages of problem-solving.

Based on this model, there is evidence from Dodge's work that rejected and aggressive children may perceive ambiguous stimuli differently from other children, and that aggressive children differ in other ways too (Dodge and Frame 1982). For example, they are more likely to interpret a situation using previous experience (rather than current information); attribute hostile intent to peers in neutral situations (Steinberg and Dodge 1983); and may be less skilled in differentiating between benign, hostile or accidental interest (Dodge *et al.* 1986).

Dodge's information processing model is probably now more influential than Selman's: one reason for this is the growing concern about the adequacy of stage models in general. However, both approaches view the cognition of EBD children as inadequate compared with children without such difficulties, and can therefore be described as 'deficit' models, which in turn have been widely criticized. For example, we know that children's responses vary according to the situation and individual (for example, one child may be hostile and another withdrawn), and neither of the models can account for this kind of difference. Demorest (1992) therefore calls for a different kind of approach and comments that 'we must adopt a framework that examines the content of children's cognitions resulting from their particular personal histories rather than ... the ways in which cognition compares with universal standards'.

Demorest (1992) has suggested a model of personal beliefs or scripts: a child will show problems in one situation and not in another because only the first taps a problematic personal belief formed from similar situations in the past. Therefore an understanding of persistently-held beliefs may be essential for an understanding of the chronic styles of relating that lead to a label of maladjustment. As noted earlier, it is certainly important that we try to get children's perspectives of these situations. It is also important that in investigating social difficulties we look at situations that are pertinent for the child. A tool such as *Bubble Dialogue*, described below, can allow us to do both of these things.

There is very often an association between low achievement and behavioural problems and so much of the work on using computers with children with EBD has been in supporting cognitive development and achievement, because an improvement here is likely to help with behavioural problems. For example, when Hopkins (1991) surveyed teachers to find out about their views on IT in EBD schools he found that they perceived IT as effective because it increases motivation, fosters self-competition and confidence and improves self-esteem. Thomas (1992) has also reported on these beneficial effects for EBD children working with computers. However, there has been little work so far in using computers more directly to assess and help develop children's emotional and social understanding and articulation.

BUBBLE DIALOGUE AS A TOOL

The computer application *Bubble Dialogue* differs from traditional role-play in important ways that are believed to enhance self-expression. It provides a comic strip environment where the participants create the dialogue between, typically, two characters. The dialogue consists of both speech and thought 'bubbles' for the characters, thus giving participants the opportunity to decide what the character says publicly and thinks privately. Because the characters are depicted on the screen, participants appear to become more distanced from the situation, and (somewhat paradoxically), this has been shown to be fruitful. For example, in early studies, O'Neill and McMahon (1991) found that 'people normally reluctant to step into roles in front of others would easily be drawn into exploring roles on the screen'. This suggests that children identify with the characters: a process whereby they empathize with on-screen characters such that they begin to project their own experiences onto that character within the dialogue. This enables a child to identify with the characters without the emotional risks often associated with doing so. In addition, the explicit inclusion of a 'thought' mechanism (that is, a thought bubble), which allows participants to give voice to the thoughts behind a character's speeches, can facilitate a rich dialogue. Less is left open to subsequent interpretation: participants can justify their case and voice their feelings within their characters' thoughts safe in the knowledge that this extra information exists in a private form. They understand, by convention, that a thought is not available to others. It does not 'belong' to the public domain of speech. Such a distinction is not easily possible within traditional spoken role-play. One important aspect of this argument is that *Bubble Dialogue* can facilitate communication and expression. O'Neill and McMahon have described the possibilities that the application offers as a methodology 'for users to make public those perceptions of context, content and interaction which might otherwise remain unformed and unsaid as well as unwritten' (O'Neill and McMahon 1991: 34).

This potential for helping children to express feelings opens up the possibility of using *Bubble Dialogue* not only as a methodological and educational tool, but also as a therapeutic tool and a tool for exploring and learning about social interactions. Applications of this sort tend to emphasize the emotional and social aspects of communication; computers in education do not typically exploit this function. However, this new focus is consistent with recent work in developmental psychology which argues that cognitive, social and emotional skills are intertwined and interdependent. It also accords with both a constructivist view of learning, and an emphasis on the importance of language as a medium for learning. These two themes are considered next.

CONSTRUCTIVISM AND LANGUAGE

A question of recent interest in the use of computers in education has been how computers can mediate, support and perhaps change the way children use language. Language has long been viewed as a vital medium for the kinds of exchanges through which children develop and learn, both socially and cognitively. Even when infants are very young, during the normal course of development, parents and infants engage in synchronized pre-verbal interactions. Through these the infant learns some of the conventions of social interaction, such as turn-taking, which he or she will make good use of later (Schaffer 1989). The importance ascribed to language is reflected in the extent to which discourse is a focus for much classroom research. For example, Edwards and Mercer (1987), in their exploration of the idea of common knowledge, argue that to discover how mutual understandings are typically created in classrooms, we must look at the patterns of conversation that occur in them.

Such research is part of a long tradition in the study of talk in school education and in the analysis of discourse. Some recent studies have focused on the use of language and new technology. Mercer and Fisher (1992) analysed the interventions made by teachers in the computer-based activities of their pupils, and Wegerif (1996) investigated how computers can help in fostering exploratory talk. Researchers who take a socio-cultural view emphasize both the crucial role of culture in our learning and the social nature of the learning process (for example, Crook 1994) and build on a Vygotskian account of learning (Vygotsky 1966, 1978). This view also emphasizes the importance of context in learning: a point argued strongly by the situated cognition school (for example, Brown *et al.* 1989). Each of these viewpoints assumes that knowledge is constructed, rather than being a commodity to be acquired, and that learning is therefore a constructive process.

The use of *Bubble Dialogue* also assumes a constructivist view of education, of the kind described above, and allows us to investigate the language that children use in constructing real-life type stories. Cunningham *et al.* (1992) suggest that it addresses a need for classroom-based techniques for promoting knowledge construction; they argue that everyday scenarios in role play are usefully transported into classroom learning because children can embed learning in realistic and relevant contexts. *Bubble Dialogue* provides a much needed resource to do this.

A STUDY COMPARING CHILDREN WITH AND WITHOUT EBD

Our particular interest in the use of *Bubble Dialogue* began with the desire to investigate its potential as a therapeutic tool for children suffering social, emotional or behavioural problems: a tool which might help them communicate and express themselves through this particular form of role play. Results from preliminary work in exploring these issues were encouraging (Jones 1996). In a subsequent study, adopted or fostered children used *Bubble Dialogue* with their adoptive parents or with social workers over a number of sessions as a supplement to other techniques already in use. Scenarios were tailor-made to suit their needs (Selby and Jones 1995). A second study on the use of the application by ten primary (mainstream) pupils (aged ten to eleven) provided baseline data and explored how this group reacted to an interpersonal conflict scenario, compared with the adopted and fostered children. Here the scenarios were decided in advance and all included a conflict or difference of views that required a resolution.

Again, the results indicated that *Bubble Dialogue* could be an effective medium in supporting children's communication, especially about difficult topics (Jones and Selby 1997). In the adoptive group there was an increase in communication when children used *Bubble Dialogue*, which continued after sessions stopped. It was also revealed that some children had unexpected difficulties with particular issues and many children were unwilling to deal with conflict in the scenarios. By contrast, the mainstream group were willing to deal with conflict and employed a range of appropriate strategies for resolving conflict. Both groups enjoyed using *Bubble Dialogue* and made appropriate use of the thought and speech bubbles. By using the same scenarios for each of the children, the mainstream group study allowed a systematic analysis of the children's strategies for resolving the conflicts, and produced baseline data which was used in the study of EBD children.

The aim of the study was to examine how children who attend an EBD school used *Bubble Dialogue*. Data was collected from ten children and as in earlier studies, the child played one role and the researcher played the other role. Four scenarios were constructed which addressed hypothetical interpersonal conflicts, as follows:

(1) Cinema scenario

Characters: Mum and her son Dan.

Prologue: Dan is going to the Saturday cinema club with his younger brother, Sam. Dan wants to see Jurassic Park, but Mum thinks he should go to see Charlotte's Web.

Opener: Mum says: 'Dan, I really don't think that film is suitable for Sam – he is only six and he will be scared by it. I think you should go to the cartoon.'

In this scenario, the researcher played Mum and the children took the role of Dan. The scenario was intended as an opportunity to investigate how the children would approach conflict resolution when in the less powerful role.

(2) Shopping scenario

Characters: Mum and her daughter Jenny.

Prologue: On Fridays, Jenny usually goes round to her friend's house after school, but today her Mum wants her to help with the shopping.

Opener: Mum says: 'Jenny, I want you to help me with the shopping after school.'

As a contrast to the previous scenario, here the researcher played Jenny while the children took the role of Mum. Similarly, this scenario was intended to find out how the children would approach conflict resolution when in a more powerful role.

(3) Bullying scenario

Characters: Tom, the bully, and Bob, the victim's older brother.

Prologue: Bob and David are eleven and nine. They are brothers. At lunch playtime Bob thinks David is being bullied. He goes over to the group and talks to the ringleader, Tom.

Opener: Bob says: 'What's been going on here?'

In this scenario, the children took the role of the older brother, Bob, and the researcher played the bully, Tom. The purpose of this scenario was to see how the children resolved conflict when dealing with another child. Also it was of interest to discover how the children dealt with a bully because bullying is an issue that many children may have to confront during their schooldays.

(4) Accidental kick scenario

Characters: John and Peter.

Prologue: John and Peter have been playing football and John has accidentally kicked Peter on the shin. Peter is upset.

Opener: John says: 'Whoops! Are you OK?'

This scenario was only used with the EBD children and replaced one of the four scenarios used in the mainstream study, which the children had not found very engaging. Dodge and Frame (1982) found that aggressive children are more likely to attribute hostile intent to peers in neutral situations. The aim with this scenario was to see how the EBD children responded to this situation, which could be interpreted in different ways, but where the prologue tells us that the kick was accidental.

THE *BUBBLE DIALOGUE* APPLICATION

Earlier we described how *Bubble Dialogue* offers a comic strip environment in which participants are encouraged to fill in speech and thought balloons for the characters depicted on screen. Each role-play situation is known as a scenario and has four main elements:

Prologue: a brief textual description which sets the scene for the scenario.

Character labels: the names that are assigned to the two characters.

Graphics: a depiction of the two characters (or groups) on the screen.

Opener: specification of the first utterance by one of the characters.

Scenarios can be developed very rapidly and there is no restriction on the situations that can be created. A graphics library is provided with the program so the creator of a scenario can select graphics for a scenario. Alternatively, graphics can be developed and imported into the package. Any changes made during the course of a dialogue are automatically saved. Scripts detailing the responses made by the characters can be generated and printed out in textual or comic strip (pictorial) format.

Once a dialogue has been created, the participants can move into review mode, which enables them to move backwards and forwards through the script, adding any comments, explanations or modifications to the original dialogue. Figure 8.1 shows a *Bubble Dialogue* screen depicting the Accidental Kick scenario, one of the scenarios used with the EBD children.

The dialogues produced by the children were the primary source of data (although children were also interviewed and transcripts of discussions taking place during the sessions were available). Analysis of the dialogues from the study with mainstream children had revealed three different ways of using the thought and speech distinction (or not) and five different approaches to resolving conflicts. The advantage of using the standardized scenarios is that it enabled a comparison of the EBD children with the baseline data, by using the categories initially developed in phase one of the study. It did mean, however,

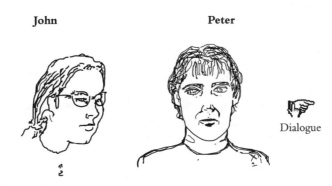

PROLOGUE

John and Peter have been playing football and John has accidentally kicked Peter on the shin. Peter is upset

John

Peter

Dialogue

Figure 8.1 The Accidental Kick scenario

that scenarios could not be tailored to children's particular needs, and so case studies were also carried out with such individualized scenarios, but are not discussed here.

THOUGHT AND SPEECH DISTINCTIONS AND CONFLICT RESOLUTION STRATEGIES

In looking at how both the mainstream and EBD children used *Bubble Dialogue*, the study focused in particular on two aspects. The first is the thought/speech distinction and the second the children's strategies for resolving the conflicts.

Thought/speech distinction

The contrast between public and private speech is a crucial dimension of *Bubble Dialogue*, because participants can use the 'thought' mechanism to reveal more than they would comfortably say out loud. We therefore needed to look at how children used thoughts and speech and whether they were making a distinction between them. The analysis revealed three ways of using thought and speech: conflicting thought and speech; disclosures or statements of judgements; and intrusions. The use of each category is briefly discussed and illustrated below.

Conflicting thought and speech is where a child would make one response in 'speech' and then indicate through 'thought' that he or she thought differently. A difference between what a character thinks and what is said out loud suggests that the participant is making appropriate use of the bubble facility to distinguish between public and private expression. Such distinctions support our suggestion that the facility for expressing private thoughts can give us some insight into feelings and thoughts that would not otherwise be revealed.

One common form of the speech/thought conflict arises when threats are issued. Here, the person says something threatening, but thinks that they will not really carry out the threat. For example, in the bullying scenario: Bob responds to the bully's taunt that there's no one tough enough to bully him with a threat, saying: 'Oh yeah – try me'.

The thought ascribed to Bob, however, is rather different and is shown in Figure 8.2.

Of the total utterances illustrating thought/speech distinctions, there were twenty-six showing such conflicting thought and speech in the EBD group and sixteen in the mainstream group.

Disclosure or statements of judgement is where the participant discloses some additional information to back up his or her position (usually within thoughts) or he/she make judgements, often concerning the other participant (again mostly done privately). For example, during the cinema scenario: Dan thinks: 'I wish I could kill my brother but he always gets away with it'. These disclosures were made by both groups of children, although the EBD group

Figure 8.2 Bob's 'thought'

made more disclosures (a hundred and two, compared with the eighty-two disclosures from the mainstream group). The disclosures were mainly restricted to thoughts, suggesting that the children judged them to be either unacceptable or too uncomfortable to say out loud.

Intrusions from thoughts is rather different because it indicates a breakdown in the public/private speech/thought distinction, where typically a child allows their character to refer to a topic which has only previously been introduced within the other participant's thoughts. An example from the bullying scenario (from a child in the EBD group) can be used to illustrate this point: Tom thinks: 'I wonder if Bob will believe me.' Bob (child) says: 'I don't believe you – I only believe my mates.'

It is possible that such intrusions indicate that the children did not really understand the distinction between thought (private) and speech (public), but it could also indicate weak role-taking skills where the participant was unable to ignore privileged information to which he or she has access, but his or her character does not. There were ten instances of such intrusions in the EBD group as opposed to only three in the mainstream group. We might expect more instances of intrusions from those children who have difficulties looking at situations from someone else's perspective. Most uses of thoughts and speech show very appropriate use of the distinction, suggesting that the children had a good understanding of it, but made occasional 'slips', which may be a matter of forgetting that a previous utterance was a thought and not speech.

The use of the thought/speech distinction and disclosures by the two groups

In both groups, most of the children were happy to use the thought bubbles although there were two exceptions from the EBD group. Interestingly, one of these was a child who explained that he did not know what other people were thinking, and was unwilling to speculate. He had been described by the teacher as a boy who could only see things from his own perspective. He would frequently use thought bubbles inappropriately and type in random keys, or utterances which were irrelevant to the scenario, and contributed to the higher number of intrusions in this group that were discussed above.

Another child from the EBD group, Aaron, used the speech bubbles to describe violent actions and tended to use the thought bubbles to comment rather than express a different view:

Bob says: 'Smack (hit)'
Bob thinks: 'Good.'
A little later:
Bob says: 'I'd hit him again'
Bob thinks: 'Yes'
Later:
Bob says: 'I would hit the person who came up to me'

Bob thinks: 'I wouldn't be thinking anything. I would just want to carry on doing it.'

Both groups of children made disclosures, but there were differences in the type of disclosure made, and the form they took. The EBD group frequently used the review mode to reveal how their *Bubble Dialogue* interactions related to their interactions in real life. For example, during the cinema scenario, Dan (played by the child) said to the mother: 'you never promise me anything.' In the review mode, when the researcher was discussing the completed scenario with him, he explained that this reflected his views in real life, and said 'I really think that.' Aaron, who used his speech bubbles to 'hit' the bully, used the review mode to explain: 'I wouldn't hit a teacher. Mainly I would hit someone who was picking on my family.'

In this way the review can provide important information about how the children view issues in real life. The mainstream children did not disclose so much in the review mode, but unlike the EBD group, they did use thought bubbles to acknowledge that the other character had made a valid point, for example, in the shopping scenario: Mum says, 'I know it's not fair on Jenny.'

Use of conflict resolution strategies by the two groups

The prescribed scenarios included situations that we expected to be salient to the children, such as bullying. Earlier analysis of the mainstream group data had revealed five strategies for resolving conflicts and the data from the EBD group was initially analysed using these categories. However, a further category, physical aggression, was needed. The data for both groups is summarized in Table 8.1.

Table 8.1 Total number of utterances illustrating the conflict resolution strategies for the mainstream and EBD groups

Conflict resolution strategy	Mainstream group	EBD group
threats	18	22
orders	3	18
bribery	2	4
bargaining	3	6
suggesting alternatives	12	17
physical aggression	0	6

Six different strategies were used for attempting to resolve the conflicts: threats, orders, bribery, bargaining, suggesting alternative strategies and physical violence. These categories are described in more detail elsewhere (Jones *et al.* 1998) but here we want to concentrate on the two categories where there was a marked difference in usage between the two groups: orders and physical aggression.

Both groups of children displayed a range of strategies for dealing with conflict so clearly the EBD children were aware of a number of possibilities. However, there were differences in the preferred strategies of the two groups. For both groups the preferred strategy was to issue threats, but whereas the mainstream group would usually disclose that they did not intend to carry out the threat, the EBD group were more likely to disclose that they did intend to carry out the threat. This is not surprising as all but two of the children were described as physically aggressive. The second preferred strategy for the EBD children was giving orders, where by contrast, the mainstream children were suggesting alternative strategies as their second preference. Finally, the EBD children also used physical violence, a strategy not seen in the mainstream group.

Earlier studies of the adoption group had revealed that they avoided entering into conflict whereas by comparison the mainstream group did not avoid conflicts. The EBD group did enter into conflict, and this was sometimes physical. Only one child from the EBD group refused to be drawn into conflict in the bullying scenario and he had previously been described as withdrawn. His thought bubbles revealed that he was angry – for example, Bob thinks: 'you look out' – but this anger was not portrayed in the accompanying speech bubble where Bob says: 'fine, thank you'. Two other children from the EBD group avoided entering into a conflict when they were in scenarios involving a child and mother, but both were very confrontational in the bullying scenario which involved two children. For example, one child said, 'Well there is no chance I'm going to see Independence Day so I might as well go and see the other film.' The researcher was surprised by this compliant attitude, which was in marked contrast to their attitude in previous scenarios, and so asked him if he would really give in so easily; he replied, 'It would be a treat to go to the cinema so I would go and see it anyway.' The other child who avoided a conflict said: 'I always put my family first.'

In contrast to the mainstream group, some EBD children tended to launch into immediate confrontation when playing the role of a mother, sometimes issuing threats. For example: Mum says, 'You are coming shopping with me or else.' This may reflect their own parents' styles of communication or the child may be projecting his or her own style onto the character. The important point is that this illustrates how *Bubble Dialogue* can be used to make children's interactional styles explicit so that they are available for discussion and reflection.

Developing the ideas of Dodge and Frame (1982) that aggressive children may perceive ambiguous stimuli differently from other children, the first scenario used with the EBD group included an event which could be perceived in different ways, although the prologue indicated that the kick was accidental. This scenario, 'Accidental kick', is shown in Figure 8.1 on page 141. Eight out of the ten children in our study expressed the view that they had been kicked on purpose, and were angry about it. Only one child resolved the conflict by forgiving his playmate. Our data, therefore, although it is a small sample, is consistent with Dodge's evidence.

Much of the work on investigating the social competence of children with social difficulties has been carried out with aggressive children, and most of the EBD children in this study were also described by their teachers as aggressive. However, two of the children were described as withdrawn and both these children were judged by their teachers as more expressive when using *Bubble Dialogue*. One of the issues in understanding children's social interactional skills is how best to assess their social competence. Typically children have been presented with hypothetical situations that may lead to peer conflicts. For example, Dodge *et al.* (1985) developed a taxonomy of situations most likely to lead EBD children to experience social difficulties. While this taxonomy has been systematically evaluated (by contrast with assessment tools in many other studies) two key issues remain. One is the extent to which the children respond to these situations as if they were real, and the second is the degree of salience that they have for individual children. Our studies of the use of *Bubble Dialogue* indicate that children do indeed enter into the role play and identify with their characters, thus maximizing the match of their responses in the application to those in their everyday lives. Regarding the second issue, *Bubble Dialogue* also allows scenarios to be tailored to children's own interests. In this chapter we have discussed the standardized scenarios in order to allow comparisons with the mainstream children but the application also allows the child to generate a scenario rather than being presented with one that is already prescribed. In addition to providing more salience and engagement, this can give the child a greater degree of empowerment.

PRACTITIONERS' USE OF *BUBBLE DIALOGUE*

A number of practitioners have expressed an interest in using Bubble Dialogue and in this section the use of the application in this context is briefly discussed. Three case studies are described: its use by a counsellor working for the NSPCC (National Society for the Prevention of Cruelty to Children); its use by an educational psychologist working in a multi-disciplinary team of social workers, psychologists and teachers; and finally its use as an investigative tool by a teacher–researcher in the EBD school that we used in this study.

Bubble Dialogue as a counselling tool

David, aged nine, was receiving counselling, following his sister's experience of abuse for which his father had been imprisoned. He was working with a counsellor whom he had known for a year, but so far he had been uncommunicative. One problem that his mother had expressed was that David tended to say exactly what he was thinking and could thus be very hurtful and rude. David used *Bubble Dialogue* in two of his counselling sessions. Unfortunately after these two sessions the counselling programme had to be halted because of a family crisis.

David's counsellor believed *Bubble Dialogue* to have been very successful. She commented that it allowed David to see that thoughts could remain as thoughts and sometimes might be best left unsaid. After using *Bubble Dialogue* a similar scenario was used on paper where David was asked to list what he thought about his mother, and what he *said* to her (and vice versa). Using *Bubble Dialogue* as a metaphor in this way enabled David to see that what he said to his mother (he hated her) was not actually what he thought about her (that he loved her and cared for her), but that whilst this remained a thought, his mother could not see this.

The thought/speech distinction for David, then, worked in both directions: it enabled him to be more reflective and consider that he might not always want to say what he thinks (that is, refrain from expressing his emotions in that way) and that on other occasions what he says is contradictory to what he feels and thinks, but that other people cannot necessarily know this.

Using *Bubble Dialogue* also allowed David's counsellor to see how David went about resolving the conflict in the scenarios. In particular, the scenarios illustrated how he was prepared to move his own position in order to resolve the situation, and also his capacity for reflecting on the other character's viewpoint. This was in contrast to his behaviour at home, where the counsellor's notes reported that David often perceived situations as unfair and did not deal with them very well, but tended to end up in fights and arguments very quickly. Using *Bubble Dialogue* allowed the counsellor (and his mother) to become aware of the insight and thoughtfulness that David could express through this tool. His mother also believed that this had a positive impact on his behaviour at home and resulted in more reflection before action.

Using *Bubble Dialogue* with impulsive children

Here, *Bubble Dialogue* was used with children who tended to have behavioural problems. Although the children were not at schools for children with EBD, many had similar problems and were disruptive at school and/or more generally. For example, one child was a persistent arsonist. The team of practitioners consisted of teachers, an educational psychologist and social workers. The educational psychologist worked both with groups of children and with individual children, using the program as an additional tool. Drawing on the social information processing models described earlier in the chapter, the psychologist thought that *Bubble Dialogue*'s features could facilitate 'unpacking' the different stages or components of social information processing. He also frequently adopted a cognitive behavioural therapy approach and felt that the application could work well within this framework. He commented: 'Features such as the review mode facilitate its use to demonstrate the sequential interactions between situation, thinking, feelings and behaviour. Additionally the review mode enables the individual to explore the effect of modifying thoughts on feelings and behaviour' (Mount, personal communication, 1997).

Bubble Dialogue was mainly used in assessment sessions and with individual children. It was reported to harness the children's attention better than the usual sessions (based on interview/discussion sessions). It was also felt that the immediate visual feedback from the typing produced a more reflective slowing of pace and increased accuracy in the more impulsive characters: 'for a couple of kids it felt like the more I let them have control over the computer the greater the depth of their reflections and/or the effort they put into the task' (Mount, personal communication, 1997).

Bubble Dialogue as an interview tool

One of the teachers at the EBD school where we carried out the study used *Bubble Dialogue* with his own class; partly to explore its potential and partly as a tool for his own research. He found it helpful in two ways: as a device for replaying, reviewing and discussing incidents, in particular to explore different outcomes and possibilities; and as an interview device. The teacher's research was in the area of bullying and he had found it very hard to elicit any information through face-to-face interviewing, but he found that using *Bubble Dialogue* opened up discussion in this area.

CONCLUSION

The work reported here provides further evidence of *Bubble Dialogue*'s usefulness for helping children to express themselves and communicate. Specifically, it also indicates the range of different styles of conflict resolution available to the EBD and mainstream groups. Some of the EBD children's preferred strategies (giving orders and physical aggression) are consistent with what we know about such children's difficulties in resolving the kinds of situations presented. However, as an assessment tool for analysing children's social competence, *Bubble Dialogue* is much richer and more ecologically valid than the tools that are typically used. It also allows us to start getting a view of the child's perspective, and allows this to be located in a meaningful context rather than requiring the child to undertake a 'test' of social competence that he or she is likely to fail. The findings from the EBD group suggest that practitioners may also be able to use *Bubble Dialogue* with children to obtain the child's perspective on events, to encourage the child to reflect on his or her thoughts and feelings about interpersonal conflicts, and to rehearse more successful conflict resolution strategies.

NOTES

1 Cognitive behavioural therapies are based on the idea that what is important about situations in determining our behavioural and emotional reactions to them is the meanings that we attach to situations.

REFERENCES

Brown, J. S., Collins, A. and Duguid, P. (1989) 'Situated cognition and the culture of learning', *Educational Researcher* 18(1): 32–42.

Crick, N. R. and Dodge, K. A. (1994) 'A review and reformulation of social information-processing mechanisms in children's social adjustment', *Psychological Bulletin*, 115(1): 74–101.

Crook, C. (1994) *Computers and the collaborative experience of learning*, London and New York: Routledge.

Cunningham, D., McMahon, H. and O'Neill, B. (1992) 'Bubble Dialogue: A new tool for instruction and assessment', *ETR&D*, 40(2): 59–67.

Demorest, A. P. (1992) The role of social cognition in children's social maladjustment', *Social cognition*, 10(2): 211–233.

DES (1989) *Special Schools for Pupils with Emotional and Behavioural Difficulties*, Circular 23/89, London: HMSO.

Dodge, K. A. and Frame, C. L. (1982) 'Social cognitive bases and deficits in aggressive boys', *Child Development* 53: 620–635.

Dodge, K. A., McClaskey, C. L. and Feldman, E. (1985) 'A situational approach to the assessment of social competence in children', *Journal of Consulting and Clinical Psychology* 53: 344–353.

Dodge, K. A., Petit, G. S., McClaskey, C. L and Brown, M. M. (1986) 'Social competence in children', *Monographs of the Society for Research in Child Development* 5(2) Serial No. 213.

Edwards, D. and Mercer, N. (1987) *Common Knowledge*, London: Methuen/ Routledge.

Gray, B., Creighton, N., McMahon, M. and Cunningham, D. (1991) 'Getting started with Bubble Dialogue', *Language Development and HyperMedia Research Group Internal Report*, University of Ulster at Coleraine.

Hopkins, M. (1991) 'The value of Information Technology for children with emotional and behavioural difficulties', *Maladjustment and Therapeutic Education* 3: 143–151.

Howard, B. (1991) *Across the Curriculum: Supporting Learners who display Challenging Behaviour*, NCET.

Jones, A. (1996) 'The use of computers to support learning in children with emotional and behavioural difficulties', *Computers and Education*, 26(1–3): 81–90.

Jones A. and Selby, C. (1997) 'The use of computers for self-expression and communication', *Journal of Computers in Childhood Education* 8(2/3): 199–214.

Jones, A., Price, E. and Selby, C. (1998) Exploring children's responses to interpersonal conflict using Bubble Dialogue in a mainstream and EBD school', *Computers and Education*, 30(1/2): 67–74.

Mercer, N. (1995) *The Guided Construction of Knowledge*, Multilingual Matters Ltd.

Mercer, N. and Fisher, E. (1992) 'How do teachers help children to learn? An analysis of teachers' interventions in computer-based activities', *Learning and Instruction* 2: 339–355.

O'Neill, B. and McMahon, H. (1991) 'Opening new windows with Bubble Dialogue', *Computers and Education* 17: 29–35.

Schaffer, R. (1989) in Slater, A. and Bremner, G. (eds) *Infant Development*, Hillsdale, N.J.: Erlbaum.

Selby, C. and Jones, A. (1995) 'Bubble Dialogue for adopted children: Five case study reports', *Computer Assisted Learning Research Group Technical Report 153*, Institute of Educational Technology, The Open University.

Selman, R. L. (1980) *The growth of interpersonal understanding: developmental and clinical analysis*, New York: Academic Press.

Steinberg, M. N. and Dodge, K. A. (1983) 'Attributional bias in aggressive adolescent boys and girls', *Journal of Social and Clinical Psychology* 1: 312–321.

Thomas, M. (ed.) (1992) *IT and Students with Emotional and Behavioural Difficulties*, NCET.

Vygotsky, L. S. (1966) 'Genesis of the higher mental functions', reprinted in P. Light, S. Sheldon and M. Woodhead, (eds) *Learning to Think*, Routledge.

Vygotsky, L. S. (1978) *Mind in Society: the development of higher psychological processes*, Cambridge, Mass.: Harvard University Press.

Wegerif, R. (1996) *Computers and exploratory talk*, unpublished PhD thesis. Open University.

Part III

Technologies and cultures of childhood

9 The extensions of childhood

Technologies, children and independence

Nick Lee

INTRODUCTION

As James and Prout (1990) argue, children have long been studied from the perspectives of adults. Thus children have figured primarily in social knowledge as the symbols and foci of adults' difficulties and concerns. 'Socialization' (for example, Parsons 1951), for example, is an answer to the very 'grown-up' problem of social order and its reproduction, while 'developmentalism' (for example, Piaget 1929) provides a set of answers to the question of what treatment children require at different ages and thus what obligations adults have toward them. Adults' expertise concerning childhood has typically been built, it is argued, through research that systematically excluded children's own points of view, research that assumed children to be 'becomings' rather than beings in their own right (Qvortrup 1994).

The 'new paradigm' (James and Prout 1990) of childhood studies is quite a departure from this tradition. New paradigm research focuses on children's views and experiences because of their own intrinsic importance, and investigates children's social autonomy and independent social competences. The new paradigm is something of a declaration of independence for children and for childhood. In order to recognize children as social actors and to reveal the part children play in producing our social worlds, it has been necessary, within the new paradigm, to see childhood and children in autonomy from adulthood, adult concerns and adult institutions.

This volume is concerned with the relationships between children and technologies. Some of the studies reported herein adopt the new paradigm approach. So let me clarify this chapter's relationship to the new paradigm approach. I will not be adopting or exemplifying the ends and means of the new paradigm; but neither will I be subjecting the new paradigm to sustained critique. Instead, I will attempt to place the new paradigm approach in a historical context. This means treating the new paradigm approach itself as a social phenomenon that needs to be accounted for. Putting the new paradigm in context will lead me to indicate some of its shortcomings as I see them, and to outline a supplementary approach to research on the question of children's independence, a question that can never be separated from issues of justice and dignity for children (see Chapter 10).

My starting point, then, is to ask why childhood is taking on 'independence' nowadays. How is it that the new paradigm seems so timely? In accounting for the new paradigm, I will of necessity also attempt to account for the growing perception that children are indeed becoming more independent in Western societies. To this end, I will addresses three key issues:

- What factors have contributed to childhood's emergence into independence?
- Why does it now seem reasonable, even necessary, to study children from their own perspective and to study childhood for its own sake?
- If children now appear to be gaining independence, how can the social study of childhood give an account of this independence as a phenomenon that is itself dependent on social factors?

As I will argue, both technologies in particular (such as television and the use of the personal computer as a telecommunications interface) and our understanding of technology in general are of central significance to these issues. I will argue that domestic technologies – especially communications technologies – have played a vital role in setting the conditions that make the new paradigm approach seem reasonable and appropriate. Further, I will suggest that our understanding of technology in general can condition the approach we take to the issue of children's independence.

Once the relationships between changing childhoods, changing views of childhood and changing technologies have been charted, I will turn to the issue of how to conceptualize new forms of autonomy and independence that are being created for and by children. Technologies, especially media technologies, are often understood as the 'extensions of man' (McLuhan 1987). I will examine different formulations of this concept of 'extension' in some detail, relate them to notions of autonomy and independent action, and draw out some of their implications for the study of contemporary childhoods in the light of 'independence'.

THE INDEPENDENCE OF CHILDHOOD: WHY NOW?

In this section I will describe how particular technologies, and social reactions to them, have played a part in making childhood appear worthy of attention in its own right. We will see that the emergence of childhood as an area of study that is independent from the study of education, the family, socialization and development (Lee 1998), and the growing recognition of children as people who have views and perspectives of their own, are very late twentieth-century phenomena dependent on late twentieth-century technological, social and economic conditions.

As I suggested above, for many years it was possible, indeed sensible, for social researchers to consider children in one of the following ways: as an appendage of the family; as the raw material of educational institution; or as recipients of lay and/or professional adult care and attention. Each of these approaches to the study of children had one feature in common: the children concerned were seen through a layer of adults (adult family members, teachers or health and welfare workers) and adult concerns. Children were often understood as being surrounded by adults, because in many ways they were. If, in the main, children were studied in the context of institutional 'cocoons', such as the family, education and welfare, then small wonder that they were also understood as being fundamentally dependent on adults. This cocooning established the conditions in which it made sense to study children through adult agendas and concerns. The institutional cocooning of children, then, had a major impact on the way children were understood. Childhood, by and large, signified a state in which one was protected from mainstream society[1] by clear boundaries, which were maintained and policed by adults on children's behalf, and for children's benefit. This cocooning of childhood has its own very specific history in the twentieth century. Once this history has been related, we will be ready to explore connections between the themes of technology, extension and independence.

HOME AND SAFETY

The high point of the cocooning of children was reached, in the UK at least, in the years following World War II. After the war's enormous displacements of children as evacuees, and of men of fathering age as soldiers, the cocooning of children could be seen as a restoration of a security that had recently been disrupted. With the passage of the Family Allowances Act in 1945, the National Health Service Act in 1946 and the National Assistance Act in 1948, and with an increasing availability of public sector rented accommodation designed for family occupation from 1945 onwards (Pickvance 1999), the UK 'welfare state' was systematized and strengthened (Miller 1999).

The welfare state had great implications for children's social position. Children were to be surrounded by many concentric layers of adult protection and guidance: first parents and their care; then the walls of the family home; then teachers and health and welfare workers and their expertise; then the State itself standing guard in case of parents' inability or failure to support their children. The personnel of each layer of the cocoon were concerned to act on behalf of children in what passed for children's best interests.

The post-war period also saw an economic boom across western industrial nations. Relatively low levels of unemployment and a relatively high degree of job security helped to reproduce a 'traditional' division of labour between adult men and women, a division of labour that had been put in question by many women's wartime occupation in industry.[2] This division of labour had a double cocooning effect on childhood. Fathers earned wages outside the family, interfacing on behalf of their children with the adult world of work and production, while mothers interfaced on behalf of their children with the adult world of consumption, keeping the household supplied with life's essentials. Childhood, then, in the immediate post-war years, was being shaped as a period of total protection. The grounds were being laid for the age-old dream of childhood as a period of innocence finally to come true.

Despite the increasing degree to which childhood was being planned, managed and opened to inspection within the welfare state, the material conditions of family life made it increasingly possible for ordinary adults to think of childhood in terms of privacy and protection. Privacy and protection meant keeping the bad news of the public world out of the family home and away from children. The 'bad news' of the sphere of production was filtered for children by the father, and the 'bad news' of the sphere of consumption was filtered for children by the mother.

THE TRIVIALIZATION OF THE DOMESTIC

In the classic feminist text 'The Feminine Mystique', Friedan (1963) noted how in the years of the post-war boom, the family home became the site of a peculiar complex of privacy and protection that amounted to a complex of secrecy. She described the lifestyle of many relatively affluent married women as involving a 'mystique'. This 'mystique' was composed of a number of practices of concealment undertaken by women homemakers. Evidence of household labour was to be hidden from the male 'breadwinner'. Effortful practices of cleansing, tidying and child-care thus became, from men's perspective, 'arcana', and simple activities like the preparation of meals were converted into feats of prestidigitation. For Friedan, as for later commentators (for example, Greer 1971), these secrets of household practice were accompanied by an interior psychological practice of concealment – the repression of female sexuality. In the post-war patriarchal home, women, in so far as they lived the 'feminine mystique', were required to 'infantilize' themselves, to engage in a work of concealment, hiding such traces of their adulthood as evidence of their labour and evidence of their sexual desire. The more concealed the labour of consumption, child-care and sexuality could be, the more innocent and protective the space of the family home could appear. An ideal home was one in which, to all appearances, nothing of great significance happened. Thus, along with the concealment of labour within the family home, along with the innocence of the home, came the trivialization of matters of consumption, of women and of children.

The boundaries of the post-war family home that allowed for the privacy and protection of childhood were clearly 'patriarchal' in their effects. We should note however that these boundaries were not the result of a historically invariant oppression of women or a historically invariant oppression of children. The form of patriarchy practised in the family home was dependent on the sustainability of men's position as exclusive interface between the family home and the world of production. As long as productive work belonged to men, and as long as men could rely on finding employment, the family home could remain a space of 'innocence' and all within it could remain trivial. The private, secret space of the family home involved an infantilization of children as much as it did an infantilization of women.

CHILDHOOD DEPENDENCY IN ECONOMIC CONTEXT

So far, I have argued that in the mid-twentieth century, it made a certain kind of sense to study children through adult concerns, and to understand children as fundamentally dependent. After all, such large-scale phenomena as nation-ally planned recovery from World War II, the post-war economic boom, and the continued focus on industrial production as the economic basis of society shaped adults' practices of home-making, so as to render children dependent and, from a certain, masculine perspective, to render child-care trivial. To say that the study of children has traditionally been influenced by an ideological 'dominant paradigm' of childhood (James and Prout 1990) is to recognize at once how accurately the traditional study of children reflected the conditions of children's lives, and how little critical distance there was between those traditional studies and children's actual conditions of existence.

The historically-specific form of patriarchy that centred on the family home as a site of secrecy and of innocence was itself dependent on the primacy of production in the economy. As long as matters of consumption and household affairs could be understood as trivial, and, indeed, performed as trivial by homemakers, the more children could successfully be cocooned and the more they could be studied as dependents of no intrinsic social scientific interest. To a large extent the range of people studied by social scientists for their independence of view and autonomy of action was restricted to those who were economically independent as producers. In the course of the decades between World War II and the present day, however, the balance between the significance of production and consumption in society was to change. As we shall see in the following section, this change, with all its impli-cations for changes in the nature of the family home and in children's social position, was assisted by the spread of domestic technologies, including television.

CONSUMER SOCIETY

The idea that Western society is best understood as 'consumer society' is a well-worn cliché, but it is one worthy of close examination. It is unlikely that 'consumer society' could mean a society made up exclusively of consumers. So what can the phrase mean? We have seen that the 1950s and 1960s were, for Western industrial societies, a period of relative prosperity with relatively high levels of stable employment. This meant that many ordinary families had the resources to purchase or to rent consumer goods such as washing machines, refrigerators, vacuum cleaners and television sets. Some of these devices were designed to cut down on domestic labour, to allow for higher standards of household order for a smaller expenditure of effort. Washing machine, refrigerator and vacuum cleaner reinforced the 'mystique' of the household. Each in their own way made it easier to conceal the traces of the domestic labour of consumption. Steamy sinks of suds were replaced with a humming white box. Another white box decreased both the speed and the visibility of milk turning sour. The vacuum cleaner collected dust from carpets and other fabrics without sending a cloud of residual dust into the air.

As well as promising a more leisurely existence, however, these devices increased the diversity of goods (foodstuffs and clothing) that could be stored, preserved and maintained within the family home. Washing machine, refrigerator and vacuum cleaner, then, were vital pieces of equipment for expanding the range of purchasing choices. The focus of the labour of consumption expanded from the gathering and maintenance of necessities to the formulation of decisions over what to purchase. A home fully equipped with 'white goods' was well equipped to take part in the consumption of a wider range of products. As Easlea (1973) points out, this expansion of consumption was itself a significant contributing factor in the post-war economic boom.

A 'consumer society' then, is one in which the family home, increasingly open to the storage and maintenance of a wide range of goods, comes to function as a key, active relay in the economy. In a consumer society, consumption within the family home becomes a matter of serious interest. Even as the family home became more closely integrated into the market – the adult worlds of consumption and production – the key technologies that allowed for this integration made the family home cleaner and more efficient; a safer, purer space, more innocent still of the visible traces of the bad news of the adult world 'outside'.

So far, we have seen that domestic appliances made the family home appear an even more efficient cocoon for children while also increasing the degree and range of penetration of the family home by the market. Any disparity we might detect between the image of the independent, carefree, leisurely consumer family and the economic function of the family home is thrown into sharp relief by the medium of television. Television was the ideal form of entertainment for a cocooning family. It could be enjoyed without leaving the home and enjoyed in tandem with families' enjoyment of other home comforts made available by domestic appliances. But, whether through the set design of fictional programming, or through advertisements, the television acted as a 'shop window', presenting the bounty and diversity of the consumer society to consumers in their own homes. Television was a technology that brought news of the outside world into the home, the news that the family home and family division of labour had been designed to filter for children's consumption. While being a key element of the cocoon, television brought about a penetration of that cocoon. Television, then, interfered with the household structure of secrecy and with the trivialization of the domestic. This was to have significant implications for childhood and children's social position because the conditions of consumer society provide opportunities for children to demonstrate independence of mind relative to their carers.

Postman (1983: 80) summarized the effects of television on childhood as follows: 'Without secrets, of course, there can be no such thing as childhood.' Postman's thesis is that television shattered the secrecy and privacy of the home, thereby destroying 'childhood'. In advancing this thesis, Postman equates childhood with 'innocence' of the 'bad news' of the world. On Postman's account, television, the 'total disclosure medium' (1983: 81), makes all images of the adult world freely available to children. Postman, then, is in tune with the ideology of childhood innocence that was made sustainable by cocooning practices. Postman, perhaps, underestimates the extent to which new forms of media-hygiene (bedtimes, restricted viewing, the UK's nine o'clock watershed) have been developed by programme makers, programme schedulers and by parents, and may also underestimate the degree to which children themselves select which programmes they want to watch. But even if television did not bring about the 'end of childhood' as he suggests, by bringing a 'shop window' into the home and by hailing all viewers, regardless of age, as consumers, television gave children a power they had not previously enjoyed.

I have argued that in a consumer society the family home is a key economic relay. Children in the family home are exposed to the news of choice and availability of goods. Children have always played an economic role as recipients of the benefits of adult labour and have received the effects of activities undertaken on their behalf by caregivers. Those making purchasing decisions always had to bear children in mind. But children's exposure to choice and diversity through the medium of television means that, within consumer society, children's desires have to be borne in mind when purchasing decisions are made. Exposure to choice gives children a position from which to have a say in purchasing decisions and thus to have a significant impact on the economy. In this context, children are no longer trivial. This complex interaction between technologies, the family home as a site of consumption and consumer choice, and the changing place of the family home within the economy, helped to lay the foundations for our contemporary views of children as being capable of sustaining independence.

If it now seems reasonable, even necessary, to view children as 'beings' rather than as 'becomings' (Qvortrup 1994), then this is partly because, in a consumer society, one can play an active part in the economy even before one has been deliberately trained or educated so to do. To be an effective producer requires that one have a stock of experience, knowledge and skill only available through a relatively lengthy process of 'becoming', such as education or training. To be an effective consumer one need only have preferences to express, and the social skill to impress those preferences on others. These preferences may become more subtle and differentiated over time, but they can be formulated, announced and impressed on others from a very young age, as many parents will know.

In sum, I have argued that the development of consumer society – itself intimately related to the development of domestic technologies – has created a field of interaction and decision-making in which children can 'have a say' alongside adults, regardless of their perceived or attributed levels of competence. Consumer society, then, involves a partial 'de-differentiation' of the states of adulthood and childhood.

This does not imply that the 'cocooning' of children by adult organizations has come to an end. After all, schools and social service departments still exist, and still call upon their staff to act on children's behalf in (what passes for) children's best interests. The notion of childhood's independence, then, emerges within a 'mixed economy' of maturity and immaturity. Throughout the middle years of the twentieth century, temporally-based variations in children's status as independent 'beings', in which children seemed more independent as they aged, became increasingly supplemented by spatial variations between the different social locations, such as home and school, in which children found themselves.

The changing role of the family home in the economy changed children's position in the adult world, helping to make it possible for today's students of childhood to see children as 'beings in their own right'. But the existence of a 'mixed economy' of maturity and immaturity in children's lives also ensures that children's independence can be encountered by new paradigm researchers as something that needs to be argued and fought for. Certain contexts allow us to think of children as independent, but the variety of contexts in which children find themselves helps to maintain controversy over their degrees and types of independence.

EXTENSIONS AND DEPENDENCE

In the previous section, we charted a course through the changing technological, economic and social policy conditions that have influenced the relative credibility of the basic understandings of childhood that are available to the research community. We have mapped attempts to 'cocoon' children onto styles of childhood research that assumed children to be fundamentally dependent on adults. We have also suggested that 'cocooning' yielded a particular type of family home, which, with the rise of consumerism, became a crucial relay in Western economies. Within the family home, children, in so far as they were consumers, were to gain an independence of voice that had significant impacts on the adult world. In short we have seen how closely the changing image of childhood has followed the deployment of particular technologies and social reactions to them.

Throughout the argument so far, I have tried to demonstrate that if it now seems both possible and sensible to view children as independent, this change of view is itself dependent on social factors. One item from the agenda I outlined in my introduction to this chapter remains outstanding. I have yet to indicate how an understanding of technology in general can influence our approach to the study of childhood, dependency and independence. I will now argue that seeing children's lives through the concept of 'extension' can add a valuable supplement to the research strategies formulated so far within the new paradigm.

The new paradigm works toward the promotion of the view that children are capable of independent action. The hope is that the promotion of this view will lead to an expansion of those areas of life in which children are accorded the respect due to them as human beings. Building on my account of children's changing circumstances, I now suggest that if the view of children as independent is to become an actionable influence on policy and practice, it needs to be accompanied by a detailed understanding of the social conditions that underlie instances of childhood dependence and independence. Thus I will argue that the concept of 'extension' (McLuhan 1987; Strathern 1992) can be of assistance in understanding the conditions that lead to specific instances of childhood dependence and childhood independence.

Retreat into the present?

Viewed from the present day, the change in childhood's image looks like a dramatic reversal from dependence to independence. It is tempting to see technologically-mediated changes in children's opportunities for social or economic participation as 'revolutionary'. Postman (1983) certainly takes such a view, seeing television as the engine of childhood's destruction. Postman clearly deplores the results of what appears to him to be a technologically-driven revolution in inter-generational relationships. Though the new paradigm expresses rather different values from Postman, tending to celebrate, rather than lament, changing relations between adults and children, to some extent it also shares his 'revolutionary' model of social change. The new paradigm, after all, was first expressed in the form of a manifesto for childhood research (James and Prout 1990).

Research agendas can be subtly influenced by implicit commitments to basic models of social change. If a change is revolutionary, then it is a change from one social arrangement to another that is entirely different. This limits the extent to which historical comparisons can be made between successive social arrangements. This is because seeing change in terms of the 'before' and the 'after' maximizes the contrast between successive social arrangements but minimizes the attention we can give to similarities and overlaps between them.

A reduced capacity to make historical comparisons can, arguably, reduce our ability to see our own research in historical context. As history is divided into 'before' and 'after', and the differences between these states of affairs are emphasized for rhetorical effect, the possibilities for discussion become trapped in the present and circumscribed by the contest between the different sets of values that are prevalent today. The argument over what childhood should be like and how children should be described can come to obscure our understanding of how childhood comes to be what it is – more or less dependent or independent. Further, the less attention we can give to understanding change over time, the fewer useful lessons we can learn for guiding practical change in the present. Thus, an over-emphasis on promoting a specific set of values concerning childhood may prove self-defeating. So what could help forestall a damaging 'retreat into the present' (Elias 1987) on the part of the new paradigm of childhood studies? What might help sustain childhood studies' ability to inform practical change?

On Postman's (1983) account, children's fundamental dependency is no longer respected. Technology is perverting nature and thereby destroying 'childhood', the institution that has developed over many years for the security and socialization of the young. For Postman this is likely to have a deleterious impact on society. In the terms of the new paradigm, the fundamental ability of children to act independently has long been either ignored or systematically suppressed by the influence of another 'dominant' paradigm. Today, notions of freedom and inter-generational equality, particularly freedom and equality of speech, are challenging the existing institutions that are built on that 'dominant paradigm' of childhood. Change in the image of childhood is akin to liberation.

I would suggest that in both of these accounts, the factors that are used to account for children's dependency are different in kind from those that are used to account for children's independence. If the condition of the young is in both cases understood to be defined by the balance between only two basic types of social force, small wonder that the revolutionary model of change remains influential. My argument so far, then, suggests that childhood studies need ways to account for observed instances of both children's dependence and independence in the same terms. This leads us to the concept of 'extension'.

What is 'extension'?

> In a culture like ours, long accustomed to splitting and dividing all things as a means of control, it is sometimes a bit of a shock to be reminded that, in operational and practical fact, the medium is the message. This is merely to say that the personal and social consequences of any medium – that is, of any extension of ourselves – result from the new scale that is introduced into our affairs by each extension of ourselves, or by any new technology.
>
> (McLuhan 1987: 7)

McLuhan's *Understanding Media*, originally published in 1964, is often understood as an early work of 'media studies', something that ought to be read by students of the press or of radio and television programming. However, alongside chapters on the press and television, this volume also contains work on speech, clothing, housing and weapons, things not normally understood as 'media'. When McLuhan uses the term 'media', he means anything that mediates between persons, between persons and machines or between persons and the natural world. At root, McLuhan is concerned with patterns of relationship; how relationships of mediation alter the pattern of what it is possible for us to do. When McLuhan tells us that 'the medium is the message', he is trying to refocus our attention away from issues of what is communicated through media, and towards issues of how the availability of various media changes the range and character of what can be done. When, for example, McLuhan examines newspaper publishing, he is less concerned with the content of the particular stories that newspapers carry than with the impact that the news industry has on the shape of politics. For example, in a description of what we would nowadays call 'spin-doctoring', he writes: 'it is the instant consequences of electrically moved information that make necessary a deliberate artistic aim in the placing and management of news' (McLuhan 1987: 203). A high turnover of news stories, made possible by novel communications technologies, makes it both possible and obligatory for politicians to 'manage' their public images through 'spin'.

As we have noted, McLuhan's conception of 'media' is extended well beyond print and broadcast to include anything that relates a person to anything else. McLuhan, then, is telling us that we should think about technological devices (and any other extensions of ourselves) in terms of relationships of mediation. Thus, speech – relating person to person – is considered alongside clothing – relating person to the elements – and alongside roads – relating persons to geographical space. In each case, McLuhan examines the impact of the medium, or mode of extension, on what people can do. Focusing enquiry on modes of extension means finding out about how things are related, how they are held apart or kept together, and how changes in these relationships can change what it is to be a social actor. This sense of intimacy between persons and extensions is perhaps best exhibited in some of the figures of speech McLuhan uses. Clothing is 'extended skin' (McLuhan 1987: 119); housing an 'extension of our bodily heat control mechanisms' (1987: 123). He does not seem to be writing metaphorically. If we turn McLuhan's insights into the importance of modes of extension to the question of dependency and independence, we might wonder to what extent examples of apparently independent action are enabled, even constituted, through our dependency on extensions.

More recently, a similar concern with relationship and mediation has emerged amongst students of science and technology (Serres and Latour 1995; Latour 1993) and of material culture. The influential social anthropologist Strathern (1992), for example, uses a concept of extension that bears comparison to McLuhan's. McLuhan's focus on, and evident excitement about, novel technologies leads him to depict 'extension' as if it were an optional feature of human existence. Strathern takes the argument further, to suggest that human beings are always living in and through extension and that extension is a mundane and ubiquitous feature of human life. In a discussion of an ethnography of Papua New Guinean Highlands societies she observes that, 'Trees and flutes appear to the Western eye as things intrinsically separate from persons.' She then adds that within the Highlands societies concerned,

> It is not just that they are extensions integral to the relationships a person makes, and 'instruments' in that sense, but that the physical body is apprehended as composed of those instruments as it is composed of relationships. The relations (the instruments) appear intrinsic to the body. They are its features.
>
> (Strathern 1992: 76)

Like McLuhan, Strathern is sensitive to the extent that Western cultures are accustomed to 'splitting and dividing all things' (McLuhan 1987: 7). Like McLuhan, and against this tendency of Western thought, she thinks of human beings' powers and characteristics as composed within and through relationships of extension. But Strathern also makes the point rather more clearly than McLuhan that extension is a mundane and ubiquitous feature of human life.

Now that we have clarified our concept of 'extension' we can ask how it might help us to approach the issue of children's dependency or independence. The following section draws on our earlier account of the emergence of childhood's independence from within the cocoon of adult protection, focusing on the modes of extension that have been at work in children's lives in different social arrangements. This should show how extension can be used to describe instances of children's dependency and independence in the same terms.

Childhoods and modes of extension

We have seen how flexible the concept of extension is. It is a way of talking about relationship in general, one that has, in the past, proven particularly useful in discussing technologies. For our present purposes, those of allowing comparison between historical and contemporary childhoods, the concept's flexibility is its principal virtue. If we restrict ourselves to an 'instrumental' (Strathern 1992: 76) view of extension, we will count only those things that are obviously technological amongst extensions. Personal computers giving persons access to web-based information sources would then be paradigmatic of a mode of extension, and our consideration of the extensions of childhood would be limited to contemporary events. We would then risk producing a 'before' and 'after' scenario restricting our ability to make comparisons between social arrangements. So let us now use the flexibility of the notion of extension to illuminate the figure of the dependent child of the post-war years.

We have noted how, in the strengthening and formalization of the welfare state in the post-war years, children became surrounded by concentric layers of adults. Many of these adults carried out their responsibilities towards children by acting in what passed for children's best interests. We described this social distribution of action, responsibility and dependency as 'cocooning'. The 'cocoon' metaphor suggests that children who found themselves cocooned were entirely sealed off from the adult world. But let us re-examine this social arrangement through our notion of extension.

In terms of extension, 'cocooning' was composed of a range of relationships between children and the adult world. These were in the main relationships of mediation in which children's principal extensions were adult humans – parents and child-care and welfare specialists. By acting on children's behalf, by mediating between the adult worlds of production and consumption, such extensions of children connected them to the adult world at the same time as they distanced children from that world. As I argued above, parents, as human extensions of children, relayed finances and goods to children and strove to limit the degree to which information about the adult world was relayed to them. It was through this mode of extension that it became appropriate to view childhood as a state of dependency. As long as the field of production was more significant than the field of consumption, this mode of extension of childhood was practically tenable. The way was clear for the professional extension of childhood, undertaken by child-care and welfare specialists, to be oriented toward the preparation of children for their future as productive participants in the economy.

These circumstances, with their specific mode of extending children, ensured the temporary dominance of the 'dominant paradigm' of childhood research that consistently figured children as 'becomings' (Qvortrup 1994). Given that certain modes of extension were firmly in place, the agenda for the study of childhood was clear – knowledge of the state of childhood was required on which to build towards children's healthy development and appropriate socialization. Social knowledge of childhood was oriented towards what each child might one day become.

Along with the rise of consumer society, however, new modes of extension appeared, such as television and other sources of advertisement. If children today participate actively in the economy as consumers this is partly through the presence of modes of extension that are an alternative to adult humans. The contemporary co-existence of modes of extension of childhood underlies today's mixed economy of children's dependence and independence. This makes today's agenda for the study of childhood rather difficult to formulate. There is no single basic definition, theory or set of assumptions concerning children that can credibly unite academic researchers, caregivers, policy-makers and practitioners. It is in this context that ambiguity and ambivalence concerning the fundamental nature of childhood,[3] though rightly depicted by Jenks (1982) as a very old problem, comes to prominence as a direct concern of child-welfare practitioners and policy-makers. I would suggest that the concept of extension, as applied to the study of childhood, not only allows us to make historical comparisons that the polarized terms of the 'being/ becoming' debate would overshadow, but could also offer a key to the study of distributions of dependence and independence that emerge from contemporary relations between children and the care-givers, practitioners and policy-makers who surround them.

In sum, I would suggest that childhood is defined in its dependency and its independence principally by the modes of extension that are available to children. To argue that children in general are fundamentally capable or incapable of sustaining independence is to mistake the nature of childhood for something that is open to settlement in general theoretical terms. I would emphasize that this is the case no matter which general image of children, dependent or independent, becoming or being, is preferred. This is not to say that general statements concerning children's ability to sustain relative independence are irrelevant, or that they can have no influence on the future conditions of children's lives. But I would suggest that an over-emphasis on cognitive or ideological matters or on attempts to define childhood once and for all can lead us to forget to identify the practical circumstances that delimit children's social activity, study those that assist children's performances of independence, and develop recommendations for policies and practices that bear children's minds in mind.

The future of childhood's extensions

Television, of course, is not the end of the story. Since the early 1990s, in an increasing number of households, the telephone has been supplemented in its role as domestic telecommunications interface by personal computers. As well as providing a platform for computer games, personal computers that are equipped with a 'modem' allow users to communicate through electronic mail (e-mail) and to access the world wide web. The increasing scope this offers children to participate in what passes for the adult world has awoken traditional fears of children's exposure to age-inappropriate communications (see Valentine and Holloway, this volume). However, some have argued that marginal social groups of all kinds stand to benefit from the development of a society of 'generalized communication' (Vattimo 1992). The argument runs that the easier it is for individuals to communicate, the easier it is for them to have a 'voice of their own', to speak for their interests on their own behalf. On this view, new communications technologies are almost inherently democratizing, lending an independent voice to the disenfranchised. Given the past complicity between household secrecy and children's infantilization, generalized communication does indeed seem to offer new avenues for children's independence (though see Facer *et al.* this volume).

Castells (1997) forges a strong connection between the development of new communications technologies in the twentieth century and the rise of 'identity politics' – the self-advocacy of marginalized groups organized around narratives of common oppression – which is a crucial feature of the conditions of enfranchisement in late twentieth-century polities. In our highly mediated and media-focused societies, we have become used to equating people's ability to speak for and to represent themselves, unmediated by other persons, with their liberation. So it is tempting to envision the world wide web as offering fertile soil in which children's self-advocacy, collective organization and subsequent liberation may take root.

It is at this point, however, that we should recall that no matter how revolutionary computer-based communication may be, it is entering children's lives as only one aspect of the mixed economy of extensions of children. The notion that children may 'speak for themselves', unmediated by adult humans, may well provide a good model of children's liberation through contemporary technologies. However, in their dealings with state agencies such as courts of law, social services and education, children, like adults, are likely to continue to require mediation by 'expert' humans. Expert adults will continue to mediate, speak about and speak for (Lee 1994) children. Our ability to live up to the UN Declaration's requirement that children be enabled to take part in decision-making concerning their own lives (Article 12 of the Declaration on the Rights of the Child, see Goonsekere 1998), will remain for many children, it seems, dependent on the precise manner in which children's human mediators extend them. For there to be constructive criticism of existing inter-generational relations of authority and responsibility and creative solutions to the problems of children's representation, we must be sure not to equate all cases of adult mediation of children with the 'theft' of their voices.

CONCLUSION

In this chapter I have argued that technologies have played a significant role in the production of children's independence. Children's social position within families was altered as the family home became a key relay in the economy. As the sphere of consumption rose in visibility and significance, so children gained independence of mind as consumers. At different times, different technologies acted so as to strengthen or weaken the complex of secrecy within the protective, private family home. Today's apparent sea-change in social scientific approaches to childhood needs to be seen in this social, economic and technological context.

Alongside this, however, I have also made a suggestion about how to study childhood and technology. Technologies should not be seen as a special kind of influence on children's lives, different in kind from adult care-givers, adult professionals or, indeed, other children. Technological devices were able to play a part in altering our understandings of childhood because they were extensions of children, which acted alongside children's other extensions both human and institutional – sometimes in concert, sometimes in tension – to bring about subtle and unpredictable change in children's opportunities for action through quite mundane processes.

Overall, then, I have cautioned against the metaphor of revolution both as a description of change in children's independence and as a source of prescription for change in children's independence. If, as I have argued, children become what they are through the patterns and styles of extension and mediation that are available to them, then neither political conviction as to their independence nor theoretical decision as to their character as 'beings' or 'becomings' can properly grasp the specifics of the various conditions that might constitute them as autonomous social participants or as independent speakers. Theoretical and political controversies on the nature of childhood and children in general, and the polarized positions that make them up, hang on the world like baggy clothes. This is partly because the mixed economy of children's extensions that commerce and state institutions together comprise puts the limitations of any overly general bid to define or regulate childhood into sharp relief. But this is also because, as I have tried to demonstrate with my technological examples, change in childhood from dependence to independence stems from changes in mundane practices, changes that have unpredictable outcomes. I hope that the notion of 'modes of extension' may be of value as a sensitizing concept in detecting and developing ways of extending children that can make for better childhoods.

NOTES

1 Pedersen's (1993) comparative study of UK and French social policy from 1914–1945 develops the notion of the 'parental welfare state' to express the increasing focus throughout the early twentieth century on the family home as an element of the State. Social policies for the 'cocooning' children were not limited to the UK.
2 Finch and Summerfield (1999) provide a very useful account of the relations between social policy debates, intra-familial division of labour and the wider labour market. Of particular significance here, they note that there was a degree of encouragement for married women, even mothers, to participate in the labour market. Part-time work was widely seen as the most appropriate means of participation, balancing the need to fill gaps in the workforce with the requirement not to disturb men's place as primary 'breadwinners'. The parental welfare state remained a patriarchal arrangement.
3 For a full discussion of the contemporary significance of childhood's ambiguity in policy and practice, see Lee (1999).

REFERENCES

Castells, M. (1997) *The Power of Identity*, Oxford: Blackwell.
Easlea, B. (1973) *Liberation and the Aims of Science: An Essay on Obstacles to the Building of a Beautiful World*, London: Chatto and Windus.

Elias, N. (1987) 'The retreat of the sociologist into the present', *Theory Culture and Society* 4: 223–247.

Finch, J. and Summerfield, P. (1999) 'Social reconstruction and the emergence of companionate marriage', 1945–1959, in G. Allen (ed.) *The Sociology of the Family: A Reader*, Oxford: Blackwell.

Friedan, B. (1963) *The Feminine Mystique*, London: Gollancz.

Goonesekere, S. (1998) *Children, Law and Justice: A South Asian Perspective*, New Delhi: Sage.

Greer, G. (1971) *The Female Eunuch*, London: Paladin.

James, A. and Prout, A. (eds) (1990) *Constructing and Reconstructing Childhood: Contemporary Issues in the Sociological Study of Childhood*, London: Falmer.

Jenks, C. (ed.) (1982) *The Sociology of Childhood: Essential Readings*, London: Batsford Academic and Educational.

Latour, B. (1993) *We Have Never Been Modern*, Hemel Hempstead: Harvester Wheatsheaf.

Lee, N. M. (1994) 'Child Protection Investigations: Discourse analysis and the management of incommensurability', *Journal of Community and Applied Social Psychology* 4: 275–86.

Lee, N. M. (1998) 'Towards an Immature Sociology', *The Sociological Review* 46: 458–482.

McLuhan, M. (1987) *Understanding Media*, Massachusetts: MIT Press.

Miller, S. (1999) 'The development of social policy', in J. Baldock, N. Manning, S. Miller and S. Vickerstaff (eds) *Social Policy*, Oxford: Oxford University Press.

Parsons, T. (1951) *The Social System*, London: Routledge and Kegan Paul.

Pedersen, S. (1993) *Family, Dependence and the Origins of the Welfare State: Britain and France 1914–1945*, Cambridge: Cambridge University Press.

Piaget, J. (1929) *The Child's Conception of the World*, London: Routledge and Kegan Paul.

Pickvance, C. (1999) 'Housing and housing policy', in J. Baldock, N. Manning, S. Miller and S. Vickerstaff (eds) *Social Policy*, Oxford: Oxford University Press.

Postman, N. (1983) *The Disappearance of Childhood*, London: W. H. Allen.

Qvortrup, J. (1994) 'Childhood matters: An introduction', in J. Qvortrup, M. Bardy, G. Sgritta and H. Wintersberger (eds) *Childhood Matters: Social Theory, Practice and Politics*, Aldershot: Avebury.

Serres, M. and Latour, B. (1995) *Conversations on Science, Culture and Time*, Ann Arbour: Michigan University Press.

Strathern, M. (1992) *Partial Connections*, Maryland: Rowman and Littlefield.

Vattimo, G. (1992) *The Transparent Society*, Cambridge: Polity.

10 Ethics and techno-childhood

David Oswell

INTRODUCTION

For some the break from childhood is easily healed. It signifies nothing more than the smooth transition to adulthood. For others it marks a terrible chasm; not merely a break, but a tremendous wound: a wound unhealable. For these others, adulthood is a form of exile. We have been outlawed and thrown out of our homeland, our social order. An unhappy consciousness. Our unhappiness is not due to our being prohibited from returning to childhood, but in our understanding that there can never, never be a return to such a land. There is no telos, no tree-rooted bed, only partial resting places; homes that are good enough; places in which adulthood is provisionally settled. The accomplishment of such settlings cannot be accounted for in the heroic and epic tales of foundational social theory nor can they be recounted in a post-modern anti-foundationalism.[1] These stories of provisional settlings are altogether more 'down-to-earth', more ordinary.

Alongside this story of the relation between adulthood and childhood, there is another story. In conditions of modernity, childhood is never permitted to surface in its purity. Childhood is never disclosed in isolation; it is always accompanied by technology. Technology makes childhood visible as a problem. In doing so both technology and childhood, like leaky vessels, leak into each other. I refer to this as *techno-childhood*: the interrelation between, and the mutual constitution of, technology and childhood. In particular, modernity reveals childhood within the compass of cultural technologies (print, radio, television, video, the internet, but also the discursive technologies of governance). It is the relation between these cultural technologies and childhood that concerns much contemporary thinking and concerns me in this chapter.

There has been much work within social history, governmentality studies, social studies of childhood, and media, communications and cultural studies concerning the effect of communications technology on children, on children's uses of the media and on the role of social and cultural technologies in the constitution and governance of childhood. These different disciplinary formations converge on study that of techno-childhood. There are four dominant approaches. First, it has been argued that representational technologies (such as painting and writing) play a central role in the historical and social invention of childhood as a distinct realm of being. The work of the Annales historian Philippe Aries is notable in this respect (Aries 1962). Second, research in media, communications and cultural studies has looked at the formation of specific media cultures addressed to and consumed by children. Print, film, television and new networked technologies (such as the internet) shape the contours of this research (*cf* Kinder 1999). Third, a number of writers influenced by Michel Foucault's work on technologies of government have shown how the 'child' figures as both an instrument and objective of government (*cf* Rose 1989). In media and communication studies such an approach has been fruitful in showing how, for example, television as a medium is shaped within a 'paedo-cratic regime' (*cf* Hartley 1987). Finally, research on children's reception of media technologies has increasingly focused on the child as a speaking subject. In this research, initially developed within social and developmental psychology but latterly within cultural studies, the agency of the child is articulated through a technology of the voice. Children's agency is made visible inasmuch as their cognitive understanding of the media is represented through their talk (cf Buckingham 1993).

In this chapter I take a reflexive approach to the study of techno-childhood. Instead of considering the organization of knowledge of techno-childhood or the reality to which such a knowledge refers, I consider an ethical relation to the child that precedes questions of epistemology or ontology. In doing so, I argue that existing research can be made intelligible through three tropes which constitute a particular ethics. These tropes – concerning a positioning of the child in relation to the ordering of the subject and the social, a critical ontology of the child and a modest attitude with regard to one's knowledge of the child – can be typified in terms of the binary tensions: centre/supplement, nature/society and humility/arrogance.

Our relation to the field of knowledge of techno-childhood can be understood in terms of whether childhood is analytically centred within mainstream social thought or whether it is a particular instance within a wider set of social processes (such as structure/agency). In the former case, childhood becomes, to borrow Latour's phrase, an 'obligatory passage point' (Latour 1990) through which thinking about the social must pass. In the latter, the child is simply an addendum to an already existing list of social collectivities (for example concerning race, gender, sexuality, etc.). Furthermore, within the field of knowledge of techno-childhood, there are various attempts to deconstruct the child as a natural phenomenon and to place the child, and childhood, fully within the domain of the social. Such attempts, in their different ways, present the child, and childhood, as a social phenomenon through a method of inscribing the being of the child as text. In doing so, the binary divide between society/nature is kept intact and the discourse of childhood remains a discourse about the ontology of the child, and childhood. My discussion of these approaches, then, is not to repeat this problematic of the ontology of the child but to show how, within this discourse of the child, there is another surface of concerns about our (adult) ethical relation to the child. I argue that the question of ethics is analytically prior to the problem of ontology. Moreover, in turning to ethics the binary society/nature itself becomes problematic. The certainty with which social constructivists proclaim the child as a social phenomenon is not to be counterposed by an equally foundational scientific claim concerning the natural child. Instead, a third dimension, the ethical, tempers such claims and becomes the measure and limitation of our knowledge of childhood and of ourselves.

In what follows I discuss the different approaches to the study of techno-childhood in relation to the tropes of centre/supplement, society/nature and arrogance/humility. I provide some theoretical ground for understanding these tropes in terms of our ethical relation to the child. I argue that these tropes constitute the basis of an ethics of childhood, but are not – in and of themselves – ethical.

CENTRE/SUPPLEMENT

Across the different approaches to the study of techno-childhood, there is a tension between, on the one hand, research which is oriented towards making the child a central matrix through which the social is analysed and, on the other, research which analyses techno-childhood as an instance of existing social processes. In the latter, childhood is another variable alongside race, gender and so on. I refer to the first orientation as 'centrist' and to the second as 'supplementary'.

The supplementary orientation, implicitly or explicitly, conceives of childhood as an ontologically distinct domain. Childhood is constituted as a particular cultural domain: forms of living – education, family, media and so on – are lived by children. Childhood houses a world of children. This form of thinking is clearly visible in Aries' (1962) history of the mentalities of childhood, but is also evident in the growing literature on children's media culture. Children's books, magazines, television programmes, films, computer games and so on are analysed in terms of their cultural form, generic conventions, modes of address and discursive repertoires (for example, Bazalgette and Buckingham 1995; Dorfman and Mattelart 1971; Drotner 1989; Hendershot 1998; Kinder 1999; Kline 1993; Oswell 1998; Seiter 1995). But also, increasingly, there is research on children's reception, use and understanding of these cultural forms (for example, Buckingham 2000; Davies 1997; Kinder 1991; Seiter 1999; Walkerdine 1997). In a recent edited collection, *Kids' Media Culture*, Kinder (1999: 1) widens the discussion to include 'the debates that have circulated around forms of cultural production – debates involving parents, teachers, children's advocates, policymakers, media producers, broadcasters, journalists, social critics, cultural theorists, researchers, and to a lesser extent, children themselves'.

Despite the investment these researchers place in studying children's media culture, and notwithstanding the importance of such work, there are others who are blind to this labour. Children's media culture is precisely another world and hence a world to be at best noted, at worst ignored. Thus to construe techno-childhood as a distinct cultural domain (or even, in Aries' terms, a distinct set of mentalities) is to risk marginalizing the study of techno-childhood and to place such study next on the list of a whole series of studies of social collectivities. Childhood becomes just another social variable.

In contrast, the centrist orientation takes the 'child' as constituting more than itself. It understands the figuring of the child as constituting more than a world of childhood. As with much research on children's media culture, this second line of thinking is interested in the way in which the child and childhood are constructed as textual phenomena. Two notable lines of thinking in this respect are the psychoanalytic and the Foucauldian. For example, in the Foucauldian work of Donzelot (1979) and the psychoanalytic work of Rose (1984) the child is constructed as the central matrix through which the subject and the social are made intelligible and regulated. In both accounts a critique of the supplementary orientation is pursued.

Donzelot, in his analysis of *The Policing of Families* (1979), has been concerned not to write a history of mentalities of childhood, a history of children's separate worlds and experiences, a history that repeats the separation that is its object of study. Donzelot argues that a history of the 'separating-out of mentalities' is unclear in its relation to economic and political transformations and that, as a consequence, the study of such mentalities can be easily incorporated into other 'theoretical machineries' or simply ignored. We can see how easily 'childhood studies' become an addendum to the 'serious work' of mainstream history, sociology and media and communication studies. As a means of avoiding such pitfalls, Donzelot suggests that we analyse the family, but more importantly for us, childhood:

> not as a point of departure, as a manifest reality, but as a moving resultant, an uncertain form whose intelligibility can only come from studying the system of relations it maintains with the sociopolitical levels.
>
> (Donzelot 1979: xxv)

The 'social' is constructed as a domain inasmuch as the family becomes the object of power/knowledge. For Donzelot, as for Foucault and others, the focus on children and childhood brings into play a set of questions and issues concerning governance (*cf* Foucault 1979a).

In Donzelot's genealogy, the emergence of the modern family is linked to the emergence of liberal governance. Whereas under the *ancien régime*, the family represents a system of alliances and a model of government (that is, the social and economic order was conceived in terms of the management of the family), in the eighteenth and nineteenth centuries the family begins to take on its contemporary meaning: namely, a realm distinct from the political and economic, but also an instrument through which populations could be governed (*cf* Foucault 1979a, 1979b). For Donzelot the emergence of the modern family is linked to the redefinitions of 'public' and 'private' and the emergence of liberalism. Minson, in his analysis of Donzelot's account, states that:

> The relations thereby set up between the political–governmental, the social and the economic turn centrally upon concomitant redefinitions of 'public' and 'private' crucial to the foundation of the nineteenth-century liberal constitutional or democratic state.
>
> (Minson 1985: 181)

The 'child' is a central means through which individuals and populations can be governed. While domestic privacies are protected through legal practices, families are normalized and regulated through public concerns about delinquency, child abuse, neglect, family disharmony and so on. Families are construed through the lens not only of the moral binaries of good and bad, but also the disciplinary binaries of normal and pathological. Donzelot talks of the establishment of 'psy' experts whose knowledge maps out the mental spaces and times of the domestic. But others, such as Rose (1989) and Walkerdine (1984), have analysed the role of the social sciences (with particular reference to psychology) in the governance of the child, family and home. The point here is that although the child is constructed as the object of disciplinary knowledge and power and is divided from the 'adult', the 'rational' and so on, such knowledge is also deployed in relation to those who are not children.

In Donzelot (1979) the child is defined through scientific language and the adult experts who deploy it. The figuring of the child is historical, contingent and strategic. In the psychoanalytic work of Rose (1984), the child is constituted within the psychical dynamics of the oedipal family. But despite such universalism, Rose, as with Donzelot, is centrally concerned with the relation between adulthood and the child as image. In contrast to the supplementary orientation, which has been concerned with the production and reception of children's media culture, the centrist orientation is not, and has not been, necessarily concerned with actual children at all. For example, in her work on *Peter Pan* and the 'impossibility of children's fiction', Rose (1984) has argued that children's fiction is a fantasy more caught up with adult unconscious desire than with real children. Children's fiction is a means through which the relations of knowledge and innocence are fixed and the child is held in its place. For Rose, the child is an impossible object of desire constructed to hold the unconscious at bay. The telling of children's stories holds the child and the unconscious in its place. In this version of children's media culture, there is no place for children's lived experience as readers or consumers. The 'child' is purely a textually inscribed phenomenon. Rose (1984: 9) bluntly asserts: 'I am not, of course, talking here of the child's own experience of the book which, despite all attempts which have been made, I consider more or less impossible to gauge.'

Although Rose's work provides a major resource for those working on children's media culture (inasmuch as it demonstrates one of the major dynamics shaping cultural production for children), her analysis extends beyond 'childhood':

> The importance of *Peter Pan* ... is not whether or not it belongs to the world of children's literature ... Rather it lies in what *Peter Pan* demonstrates about a fantasy of childhood, with children's literature as just one of the arenas in which this fantasy is played out. Nor is the fantasy which I have described here restricted to the domain of childhood itself.
>
> (Rose 1984: 138)

Rose stresses that her analysis is not concerned with 'images of childhood', but with how 'we regulate our relationship to language and images as such':

> what is at stake in an image of the child is not the child first and then the image, but the child as the most fitting representative for the gratifying plenitude of the image itself.
>
> (Rose 1984: 138–9)

Rose refers to this in terms of an 'ethos of representation'. For Rose, then, the study of children's fiction instances a set of processes whereby forms of culture are classified as 'for children' and through which psychical and social regulation is made possible. This ethos of representation can be found not simply in children's literature, but across a whole terrain of concerns about social existence.

In Rose's analysis, ethics constitutes a 'basic demand for identity in language, that is, for language as a means to identity and self-recognition' (Rose 1984: 139). In this formulation, ethics comes before language and identity, and hence also ontology. It is ethics which seeks to recognize self in the Other through language. The child becomes the central matrix for such ethics. As she says, the question of 'the internalization of rules, precepts and laws which individual books may or may not then require of the child reader ... is ... secondary, and finally marginal' (Rose 1984: 139).[2]

Whereas Donzelot (1979) considers how the image of the child constitutes a point of disjunction between language and reality (that is as a problem and as a provocation for intervention), Rose (1984) shows how the construction of the innocent child figures in the fixing of subjectivity and an imagined transparency between language and reality. Nevertheless, although both writers help to reposition the child within social thought as a central matrix of concern, they both do so at the cost of losing the child to the text (whether strategically or psychically mobilized). The child is reduced to an image: it is merely projection. In the supplementary orientation there is a substance to the child; in this centrist orientation the child so easily becomes a figure with no distinct ontological status. The centring of the child in social thought is formed to the exclusion of an ethical and strategic relation to actual children. Children, in the eyes of both Rose and Donzelot, need only ever be encountered as representation. The Other is always figural, never substantial. It has no voice of its own.

NATURE/SOCIETY

The second trope concerns our understanding of childhood as either a natural or a social phenomenon. Aries' (1962) groundbreaking work on the historical invention of childhood has become the standard reference for all work on the sociology of childhood. Aries' work has set a clear precedent, not simply for research that argues that childhood is a social construction, but also, as I will argue shortly, for more recent work which seeks to make visible the child as an active social agent. Aries' research lifts the child from the natural world and locates it firmly in a world of diaries, written documentation and images. For Aries, the emergence of modern childhood is made visible through its inscription and its representation in written and pictorial texts:

> It was in the seventeenth century that portraits of children on their own became numerous and commonplace. It was in the seventeenth century, too, that the family portrait, a much older genre, tended to plan itself around the child ... In the seventeenth century too, subject painting gave the child a place of honour, with countless childhood scenes of a conventional character ... No doubt the discovery of childhood began in the thirteenth century, and its progress can be traced in the history of art in the fifteenth and sixteenth centuries. But the evidence of its development became more plentiful and significant from the end of the sixteenth century and throughout the seventeenth.
>
> (Aries 1962: 44–5)

Notwithstanding the methodological exigency of historiography to treat its subject matter as text and image, Aries makes the claim that childhood is reducible to its representation as text and image. A proliferation of pictures discloses childhood as a social invention. Interestingly, these ontological claims concerning childhood are based not on knowledge, but on (dis)belief:

> Medieval art until about the twelfth century did not know childhood or did not attempt to portray it. It is *hard to believe* that this neglect was due to incompetence or incapacity; it *seems more probable* that there was no place for childhood in the medieval world.
>
> (Aries 1962: 31, emphasis added)

What is at stake in Aries' account is not simply that he has revealed a novelty in the representations of the child, but that he is hesitant in his claims regarding the representational evidence for childhood as a social invention. There is uncertainty in the relation between what Aries sees and what he says. The great leap from epistemology to ontology is tempered by belief. Aries' humility is quickly hidden in his own writings and in the commentaries of many others.

In the mainstream of social history and sociology, Aries is taken as a major precursor of, and innovator with regard to, more recent debates concerning the social construction of childhood. Social constructionism constitutes a dominant paradigm for thinking about childhood and technology. In the social study of techno-childhood it finds its place centrally in providing the basis for a critique of developmentalism and the notion that the child (and childhood) is a natural phenomenon (*cf* Burman 1994; James and Prout 1990; Walkerdine 1984). A normative discourse of child development is seen to shape a range of institutional arrangements concerning the child (such as schooling, parenting and the media) so that actual children are disciplined according to the normal and the pathological. The critiques of developmentalism are largely directed at Piagetian accounts of child psychology and the division of childhood into linear stages of cognitive development. Although these critiques take on different forms with regard to problems concerning developmentalism's implied normative masculine model of rationality, its function within normalizing apparatuses and its presumption of a universal childhood, they are to a large extent focused on a critique of the 'natural child'. As James and Prout (1990: 10) argue: 'The concept of "development" inextricably links the biological facts of immaturity, such as dependence, to the social aspects of childhood.' The social study of techno-childhood has sought to make visible particular forms of the 'biological facts of immaturity' (for example, those visible within developmental psychology) as social phenomena. There has been a constant attempt to lift the child from biology into society, from the natural (or quasi-natural) to the social sciences.

The notion of the natural child is used to encapsulate a number of different conceptions of the child and childhood from different intellectual traditions. Rousseau's writings on education and the natural child are easily folded into Piagetian accounts of genetic epistemology. In a series of moves that mirror debates about gender, nature is only able to be constructed within this discourse as a form of determinism. In contrast to the necessity of nature, the social is figured as a realm of freedom: '[Social constructionism] is well situated to prise the child free of biological determinism and thus to claim the phenomenon, epistemologically, in the realm of the social' (James *et al.* 1998: 28). Forms of explanation based on nature are replaced by those based on society. The child becomes a figure upon which nature is projected, but also through which society is accomplished.

Such a move makes possible two dominant research agendas within the social study of childhood. On the one hand, once divorced from the natural and made figural – a tentative, fleeting and yet versatile simulacrum – the child becomes constitutive of the social and a veritable regulative technology (as with Donzelot). On the other, the deconstruction of the natural child allows us to see children's agency as a particularly social form of purposive action. Children's agency is visible only inasmuch as it is a social endeavour. Moreover, in constructing the child as a social actor, it is argued that childhood can be seen as 'constructed and reconstructed both for children and by children' (James and Prout 1990: 7).

Although there is a claim to free the child from the constraints of nature, it is not clear how the social study of childhood might take account of the child's agency without also construing such agency within disciplinary parameters. To what extent is the child an agent outside of the disciplinary apparatuses (such as sociology and ethnography) which make such agency visible? In maintaining the dichotomy between nature and society and in favouring the latter over the former, the social study of childhood has failed to fully take on board its own instituting of childhood while continuing to institute childhood as a question of ontology. Or rather, in failing to see that the problem is not nature as such, but the organization of ontology, the sociology of techno-childhood continues to remain stuck in a problematic of the ontology of techno-childhood. As James and Prout declare on the opening page of their book *Constructing and Reconstructing Childhood*: 'At the heart of current debates lies the question: what is a child?' (James and Prout 1990: 1). The being of the child is no longer disclosed in the field of nature, but is made visible in discourse (whether enunciated by adult or child). The turn to discourse does not remove the problem of ontology, it merely reproduces it within a new dimension: one which is visibly non-unitary and complex. In this sense, the critique of the natural child in the current social study of techno-childhood is misplaced. The problem is not nature as such, but the ontology of the child. In a move resonant of Foucault's critical ontology of the self, the ethics of techno-childhood takes the form of a critical ontology of the child: namely a critical engagement with how the being of the child is made visible to thought.[3] We understand how our (adult) sense of ontological difference from the child is secondary to our sense of our relationship to the child (as Other). It is a relationship defined by our being 'for' the child, such that our sense of the freedom of the Other is ethically, not ontologically, founded.

HUMILITY/ARROGANCE

In my discussion of this final trope, I show how an ethical relation to techno-childhood takes the form of a particular attitude toward the child: namely humility. It is an attitude that is found in both natural and social sciences. Its binary opposite, arrogance, is said by those working on the social study of techno-childhood to dominate research that takes as its object of study the natural child and its development. The programmatic statements of the social study of techno-childhood assume an arrogance for psychology and the other sciences of the natural child. It is an arrogance enshrined in an image of the scientist conducting experimental research in a laboratory: a world supposedly expunged of social relations. For example, this image of the arrogance of science is present in research that is critical of what is often referred to as 'media effects research'. It is now common for those researching techno-childhood to refer to a litany of symptoms of the arrogance of effects research. For example, Kinder declares that:

> Those who see kids primarily as passive victims tend to focus on a single element of media culture (such as violence or pornography), which can readily be isolated for study or censorship, and whose representations and dangers are *presumed* to affect all children in the same way. Thus it is hardly surprising that this camp tends to rely on *monolithic depictions* not only of the texts, but also of children they affect, the media through which they are transmitted and the eras in which they are produced and consumed ... Such writers frequently rely on statistical rating surveys of violent representations, which are *rarely attentive to nuances* of context even when it is one of the announced goals of a study. To validate their arguments and support *their common sense judgements*, they also turn to empirical 'effects' studies in the social sciences, sometimes *exaggerating the findings* to make the causal links appear more conclusive than they actually are.
>
> (Kinder 1999: 3–4, emphasis added)

Kinder, as with many other critics of media effects research, mixes social scientific research with popular opinion to produce an amalgamated construction of scientific arrogance. Hers is a critique of the arrogance of normative science. Effects research is problematic, in this account, on the basis of its inability to account for the social. Equally though, Kinder, as with others, fails to account for the sociality of scientific practice (as Latour might say, 'science in action') and instead presents science as a rationalist project.

Work within science and technology studies has questioned such a rationalist conception of science and instead sought to understand the complex relations between scientific knowledge, ethical humility and the natural object. In this account of the natural sciences, the witnessing of 'truth' is an act of modesty (*cf* Haraway 1997; Shapin and Schaffer 1985). Osborne, in his analysis of science, ethics and enlightenment argues that:

> Instead of the 'spirit of system', science embodied a 'systematic spirit'. This meant not a universal rationalization of everything but rather an epistemological modesty of approach – observing, calculating, remaining sensitive to the necessary limits of human knowledge – for 'man succeeds best in discovering truths of nature when he first recognizes the limits of his own knowledge'.
>
> (Osborne 1998: 43)

The humility of the scientific approach is found not in a history of rationalism, but in the ethics of 'sensitivity', a recognition of the 'limits of understanding' but also a suspicion with regard to those limits. There is a sense then that ethics precedes one's encounter with the Other and questions the parameters through which one knows and sees the Other. This form of scientific attitude is found in both natural and social sciences and cannot be reduced to a question of method (that is, quantitative or qualitative, ethnography or social survey, etc.).

This question of scientific attitude helps us to pose the issue of children's agency in a new light. In their founding statement of the 'new paradigm for the sociology of childhood', James and Prout stated that: 'Children are and must be seen as active in the construction and determination of their own social lives, the lives of those around them and of the societies in which they live' (James and Prout 1990: 8). However, whereas James and Prout understand agency in terms of the ontology of the child, I argue that what is important in this statement is the willingness to submit to the Other on its own terms (hence the moral imperative 'must be'): namely not to prescribe and define the child as an ontology, but to recognize its freedom in shaping our world. In this sense, our analytical language for understanding children's agency and childhood is not grounded in ontology, but in an ethical relation to the child. We first have to see the child's freedom and then only secondarily can we construct a knowledge *with* them.

The ethos, or attitude, of humility is found in research which seeks to let the child speak. In cognitive developmental discourse the child is articulated through a mental machinery and to a technology of the voice. Developmental research in the 1970s and 1980s began to show how children's activity was demonstrated through their cognitive understanding and ability to make meaning (*cf* Dorr 1986). In more recent research children's active production of meaning is understood in terms of semiotics and discourse analysis. Hodge and Tripp's (1986) seminal research was firmly located in a cognitivist framework, but set in place a research agenda which sought to understand meaning-making as both a social and psychological process. Buckingham's work (1993, 1996) attempts to lift the child further out of the natural and the normative to show how both children's meaning production and their sense of self is constructed through discursive interaction. According to Buckingham, but also to the 'new' sociology of childhood, children's agency is intelligible only inasmuch as it is made visible as a social phenomenon. For Buckingham and others this involves deconstructing the primacy of the child's internal cognitive machinery in semiotic production and showing how the interaction and dialogue of children's voices is constitutive of children's sense of identity. As with Aries (1962), these researchers demonstrate a hesitancy in relation not to the child as such, but to its voice. These researchers make space for the child to speak (despite whatever normative frameworks they may employ).

For example, in Buckingham's (1996) focus group research with groups of eight to eleven year olds from East London, he clearly demonstrates his sensitivity to these groups of children as speaking subjects. What is important is not so much his discourse analytic method, but his taking into account the child before his attempt to understand it. This taking into account of the child is not reducible to a particular method or ontology. The relation of language to an ethics of techno-childhood is not fixed in a particular reason for one's relations to the child, but in a fundamental interlocution: by the very fact that one speaks to the child in order to be spoken to. Buckingham is critical of both cognitive developmental research, which understands children's talk in terms of cognitive processes in the brain, and also sociological accounts which understand talk as determined by variables such as class, race or gender. Instead he argues that: 'Identity, then, is not something that is simply fixed or given: on the contrary, it is largely constructed through dialogue' (Buckingham 1996: 58). However, in an earlier work, Buckingham issues a word of caution. He argues that there is a 'danger of exaggerating the degree of power or freedom audiences possess' (Buckingham 1993: 59). The problem, though, lies not in orienting oneself toward the 'freedom' of the Other, but in the way in which the 'exaggeration' is formed through an ontology of the child.

CONCLUSION

These different tropes, which I refer to in terms of the binary tensions centre/ supplement, nature/society and humility/arrogance, designate an orientation and attitude to the study of techno-childhood. Rose (1984) and Donzelot (1979), in their different ways, centre the child in social thought at the expense of reducing the child to image. Thus in either the fixing or the prob-lematizing of the child, the Other is always silent and never speaks from that central space of social thought. What I refer to as supplementary orientations seek to give the child a voice and to construe it as having agency, but at the expense of assuming that the critical problem lies in the 'naturalness' of the child and not with ontology *per se*. Similarly a particular epistemological and methodological perspective (namely social constructionism) cannot be used in order to understand and facilitate the freedom of the child. And yet research on the agency of the child, as found in the work of Buckingham (1993) and others, provides evidence for a humility towards the child in terms of a radical hesitancy toward our categories of knowledge.

These tropes refer to particular ethical and strategic problems through which our relation to the child might be settled. In our ethical recognition of the child as Other, the child is extricated from the technological and made human. But this is both a recognition of the 'always already' of the mutual interrelation between technology and childhood (such that we cannot simply take the one without the other) and a future orientation to the child as human.

NOTES

1 See John Rajchman's brilliant analysis of the 'ethical' in Lacan and Foucault for an understanding of such a moderate turn (Rajchman 1991).
2 In this paper I need to put to one side a full analysis of how to extricate the 'ethical' from Rose's psychoanalytic framework.
3 Foucault in his later work on the ethics of enlightenment thought argues that: 'The critical ontology of ourselves has to be considered not, certainly, as a theory, a doctrine, nor even a permanent body of knowledge that is accumulating; it has to be conceived as an attitude, an ethos, a philosophical life in which the critique of what we are is at once and the same time the historical analysis of the limits that are imposed on us and an experiment with the possibility of going beyond them.' (Foucault 1986).

REFERENCES

Aries, P. (1962) *Centuries of Childhood*, London: Jonathan Cape.
Bazalgette, C. and Buckingham, D. (eds) (1995) *In Front of the Children: Screen Entertainment and Young Audiences*, London: BFI.
Buckingham, D. (1993) *Children Talking Television: The Making of Television Literacy*, London: Falmer Press.
Buckingham, D. (1996) *Moving Images: Understanding Children's Emotional Responses to Television*, Manchester: Manchester University Press.
Buckingham, D. (2000) *The Making of Citizens: Young people, news and politics*, London: Routledge.
Burman, E. (1994) *Deconstructing Developmental Psychology*, London: Routledge.
Davies, M. Messenger (1997) *Fake, Fact and Fantasy: Children's Interpretations of Television Reality*, Mahwah, N.J.: Lawrence Ehrlbaum.
Donzelot, J. (1979) *The Policing of Families*, London: Hutchinson.
Dorfman, A. and Mattelhart, A. (1971) *How to Read Donald Duck: Imperialist Ideology in the Disney Comic*, New York: International General.
Dorr, A. (1986) *Television and Children: A Special Medium for a Special Audience*, Beverly Hills: Sage.
Drotner, K. (1989) *English Children and their Magazines*, London: Yale University Press.
Foucault, M. (1979a) 'On governmentality', *I&C* 6.
Foucault, M. (1979b) *The History of Sexuality, Vol. 1*, London: Allen Lane.
Foucault, M. (1986) 'What is Enlightenment?' in P. Rabinow (ed.) *The Foucault Reader*, Peregrine.
Haraway, D. (1997) *Modest_Witness@Second_Millennium.FemaleMan©_Meets_OncoMouse™*, New York: Routledge.
Hartley, J. (1987) 'Television audiences, paedocracy and pleasure', *Textual Practice*, 1(2).
Hendershot, H. (1998) *Saturday Morning Censors: Television Regulation before the V-Chip*, London: Duke University Press.

Hodge, B. and Tripp, D. (1986) *Children and Television: A Semiotic Approach*, Cambridge: Polity Press.

James, A. and Prout, A. (eds) (1990) *Constructing and Reconstructing Childhood: Contemporary Issues in the Sociological Study of Childhood*, London: Falmer Press.

James, A., Jenks, C. and Prout, A. (1998) *Theorizing Childhood*, Cambridge: Polity Press.

Kinder, M. (1991) *Playing with Power in Movies, Television, and Video Games: From Muppet Babies to Teenage Mutant Ninja Turtles*, Berkeley: University of California Press.

Kinder, M. (ed.) (1999) *Kids' Media Culture*, London: Duke University Press.

Kline, S. (1993) *Out of the Garden: Toys, TV and Children's Culture in the Age of Marketing*, London: Verso.

Latour, B. (1990) 'Drawing things together' in M. Lynch and S. Woolgar (eds) *Representation in Scientific Practice*, Cambridge, Massachusetts: MIT Press.

Minson, J. (1985) *Genealogy of Morals: Nietzsche, Foucault, Donzelot and the Eccentricity of Ethics*, London: Macmillan.

Osborne, T. (1998) *Aspects of Enlightenment: Social Theory and the Ethics of Truth*, London: UCL Press.

Oswell, D. (1998) 'Early children's broadcasting in Britain, 1922–1964: programming for a liberal democracy', *Historical Journal of Film, Radio and Television* 18(3).

Rajchmann, J. (1991) *Truth and Eros: Foucault, Lacan and the Question of Ethics*, London: Routledge.

Rose, J. (1984) *The Case of Peter Pan: Or the Impossibility of Children's Fiction*, London: Macmillan.

Rose, N. (1989) *Governing the Soul: The Shaping of the Private Self*, London: Routledge.

Seiter, E. (1995) *Sold Separately: Parents and Children in Consumer Culture*, New Brunswick, New Jersey: Rutgers University Press.

Seiter, E. (1999) *Television and New Media Audiences*, Oxford: Oxford University Press.

Shapin, S. and Schaffer, S. (1985) *Leviathan and the Air-Pump: Hobbes, Boyle and the Experimental Life*, New Jersey: Princeton University Press.

Walkerdine, V. (1984) 'Developmental psychology and the child-centred pedagogy: the insertion of Piaget into early education' in J. Henriques, W. Holloway, Urwin, C. Venn and V. Walkerdine (eds) *Changing the Subject: Psychology, Social Regulation and Subjectivity*, London: Cambridge University Press.

Walkerdine, V. (1997) *Daddy's Girl: Young Girls and Popular Culture*, London: Macmillan.

Index